The Best
AMERICAN
ESSAYS®
2022

GUEST EDITORS OF THE BEST AMERICAN ESSAYS

1986 ELIZABETH HARDWICK
1987 GAY TALESE
1988 ANNIE DILLARD
1989 GEOFFREY WOLFF
1990 JUSTIN KAPLAN
1991 JOYCE CAROL OATES
1992 SUSAN SONTAG
1993 JOSEPH EPSTEIN
1994 TRACY KIDDER
1995 JAMAICA KINCAID
1996 GEOFFREY C. WARD
1997 IAN FRAZIER
1998 CYNTHIA OZICK
1999 EDWARD HOAGLAND
2000 ALAN LIGHTMAN
2001 KATHLEEN NORRIS
2002 STEPHEN JAY GOULD
2003 ANNE FADIMAN
2004 LOUIS MENAND
2005 SUSAN ORLEAN
2006 LAUREN SLATER
2007 DAVID FOSTER WALLACE
2008 ADAM GOPNIK
2009 MARY OLIVER
2010 CHRISTOPHER HITCHENS
2011 EDWIDGE DANTICAT
2012 DAVID BROOKS
2013 CHERYL STRAYED
2014 JOHN JEREMIAH SULLIVAN
2015 ARIEL LEVY
2016 JONATHAN FRANZEN
2017 LESLIE JAMISON
2018 HILTON ALS
2019 REBECCA SOLNIT
2020 ANDRÉ ACIMAN
2021 KATHRYN SCHULZ
2022 ALEXANDER CHEE

~~AMERICAN~~ ESSAYS® 2022

Edited and with an Introduction
by ALEXANDER CHEE

ROBERT ATWAN, Series Editor

MARINER BOOKS
New York   Boston

HarperCollins books may be purchased for educational, business, or sales promotional use. For information, please email the Special Markets Department at SPsales@harpercollins.com.

FIRST EDITION

ISSN 0888-3742
ISBN 978-0-358-65887-0

22 23 24 25 26 LSCC 10 9 8 7 6 5 4 3 2 1

Contents

Foreword

WHEN I WROTE the first foreword for this series, back in 1986, I began with a quotation from E. B. White that I've relied on many times over. I cited it warily—perhaps defensively—as it clearly represented a serious obstacle to the idea of publishing an annual collection with a single objective: we—my editors and I—hoped the new series would showcase the essay as a serious literary genre. We thought the time had come. Yet, apparently, White—surely the best-known American essayist at the time—did not agree. In his foreword to *Essays of E. B. White,* he noted, rather sadly, in 1977: "I am not fooled about the place of the essay in twentieth-century American letters—it stands a short distance down the line. The essayist, unlike the novelist, the poet, and the playwright, must be content in his self-imposed role of second-class citizen."

White died on October 1, 1985, at his saltwater farm in North Brooklin, Maine. At that time, I was in the midst of putting together the first volume of this series with our first guest editor, Elizabeth Hardwick. Stricken with rapidly accelerating dementia since the fall of 1984, White apparently published nothing in the months before he died, but had he, I doubt he would have been selected by Hardwick, who considered his work "middlebrow." She leveled this judgment at lunch one afternoon when I brought up White. I had to agree with her assessment, but not entirely. I felt obliged to add that I thought he managed to write over a long career a handful of extraordinary essays.

White is a strange case. Buried deep inside his self-deprecating remark may be a chronic self-doubt, a recognition that it may not be the diminished stature of the essay in American letters but his own minor literary reputation that marked him as a "second-class citizen." It's true—as I've often noted—that the essay had fallen out of fashion, not only among publishers but in the important world of academia and criticism, where literary reputations are largely made. Though not an academic, Hardwick was just one of many highly respected critics at the time who didn't regard White as a significant literary figure. To many, he remained a *New Yorker* humorist of lesser talent than S. J. Perelman, James Thurber, or Dorothy Parker and a popular children's book author. The work he thought of as his best—his essays—was not the subject of serious criticism or "close reading." I think it's fair to say that his essays are rarely read as literature.

With the exception of his three bestselling children's books, White surprisingly garnered only a few literary awards throughout what many writers, especially those with an eye on numbers, would consider an enviable career. (The children's books alone have sold millions of copies.) In his 1977 foreword he also noted that a "writer who has his sights trained on the Nobel Prize or other earthly triumphs had best write a novel, a poem, or a play. . . ." Essays wouldn't get you there. Perhaps that comment inspired the Pulitzer jury to make up for its previous neglect and honor him a year later with a "special citation . . . for his letters, essays, and the full body of his work." Was his lack of critical acclaim due to the diminished status of the essay in general or was it a direct result of work that didn't strike many as worthy of literary fame? In her quick indictment, Hardwick, a fine essayist herself, was responding to White's talent and not his preferred genre.

Yet White had achieved some level of literary fame in one small corner of academia: first-year writing programs, often known then as Freshman English. When I began teaching such courses in the mid-1960s, I didn't think it possible to find a textbook or any of the numerous anthologies we used at the time to introduce students to "prose models" that did not include an essay of E. B. White's. (It didn't hurt that White was also well known as the coauthor, with William Strunk Jr., of the perennially bestselling *The Elements of Style*, a little book often recommended to writing students at all levels and that still sells well.) In the college publishing industry, White's essays were known as "chestnuts," selections that anyone assembling an anthology must include. As far as I can tell, "old chestnuts" was British slang for tiresomely repeated jokes, and the word may have been popularized by vaudevillians. I'm not sure editors today are familiar with the vintage metaphor, but anyone in charge of publishing an anthology at the time knew which essays they could not avoid.

The sine qua non of those chestnuts was E. B. White's short personal essay "Once More to the Lake." Open any first-year writing anthology and there it was. In the 1950s, an entire family probably could have lived happily on the reprint fees from that essay alone. Yet, though it may have become an inside-publishing joke, this "chestnut," in my opinion, has deserved its long shelf life. An essay about identity, it has little to do with how that term has been refashioned in our time. On its surface, it seems to reinforce the "middlebrow" values that have long compromised White's reputation. When critics judge some works (or a body of work, like White's) "middlebrow," they usually mean that they embody a cluster of what gradually came to be considered ersatz values—derivative, sentimental, complacent, pretentious, inauthentic, conventional. Today, that essay—if anyone still teaches it—is probably discussed as a central document of "white privilege" (pun unavoidable).

I suppose if there were to be an illustrated edition of "Once More to the Lake," the most likely artist would be Norman Rockwell: a father suddenly stricken with nostalgia decides to take his five-year-old son on a fishing trip to the same Maine lake where his father had taken him fishing nearly forty years earlier. Who better than Rockwell to convey the tranquil satisfactions of a middle-class summer vacation? But the way I read the essay, I think the more appropriate illustrator would be Edvard Munch. The essay is anything but serene.

White constructs "Once More" around a central "illusion" that envelops him as soon as he and his son arrive at the lake in the summer of 1941. Time has stopped; it has "dissolved"; nothing at "this unique, this holy spot" has changed. "There had been no years," he repeats several times, repetition ("once more") being one way to thwart the passage of narrative time. Yet, oddly enough, White doesn't seem determined to reinforce this key illusion. Instead, he frequently points out small details that challenge it: for one thing, the lake is far noisier than it was in 1904, thanks to outboard motors having replaced the sleepy-sounding old one- and two-cylinder inboard engines he fondly recalls. "This was the note that jarred, the one thing that would sometimes break the illusion and set the years moving."

But noise is just one break in the illusion. The roads are now tarred; the waitresses "were still fifteen" but now "their hair had been washed," as "they had been to the movies and seen the pretty girls with the clean hair"; arriving at camp now lacked the excitement it once had when the farmers' wagons waiting at the train station dropped you off after a bumpy ten miles (now you simply drove in and parked); the road leading up to the farmhouse for dinner once had three tracks—one for horses—but now has only two: "For a moment I missed the middle alternative." Things look the same . . . except. Inside the camp's general store, "all was just as it had been, except there was more Coca-Cola and not so much Moxie and root beer and birch beer and sarsaparilla."

These small but noticeable changes, all brought about by twentieth-century progress—like the earsplitting outboard motors—have the effect of disrupting the illusion of stopped time, the fantasy that the now forty-something White is enjoying the very same magical lake he loved as a small boy. As he insists on the odd feeling that nothing has changed and minimizes the changes he fastidiously observes, we slowly realize that we're not meant to ignore them as he seems to do. Earthly time doesn't ever stand still; it moves forward, or, in terms of human life, it oscillates between forward and backward as we live both in the moment and in our memories. White subtly reminds us of these back-and-forth oscillations when he recalls how as a boy he learned to master his old one-cylinder inboard. By getting "close to it spiritually," he could—instead of shutting off the engine and coasting in to land—reverse the engine "by cutting the switch and putting it on again exactly on the final dying revolution of the flywheel, so that it would kick back against compression and begin reversing." A good metaphor for how the essay itself has been advancing. And an example of writing that adheres to what Henry James called "the strange irregular rhythm of life."

As we move deeper into the essay, we realize that White is not recounting a nostalgic journey back to a vanished world, to a sacred place cherished in his memory. White's revisit to "old haunts" actually comes closer to a nightmare, as he experiences throughout the week a series of disconcerting and uncanny sensations resulting from the initial illusion that the passage of time has somehow dissolved. Other things are dissolving as well. First of all, the boundaries of personal identity. No sooner do they settle in at the camp than White recognizes a "creepy sensation" in seeing his son: "I began to sustain the illusion that he was I, and therefore, by simple transposition, I was my father." He starts to feel that he's living a "dual existence." "Everywhere we went I had trouble making out which was I, the one walking at my side, or the one walking in my pants." The loss of boundaries seems everywhere; at one point, White notices that the line tape of the camp's tennis court had "loosened along the backline." Even the official boundaries of the tennis court are dissolving.

The penultimate paragraph introduces us to a medley of indistinct boundaries. An afternoon thunderstorm has rolled in and the air is full of friction. White sees this, too, as part of the unchanging nature of the lake, as this storm unfolds like every storm he remembers. First, the sky darkens, next a breeze picks up from a new direction, causing the boats to turn the other way at their moorings, and then "the premonitory rumble." It is all so predictable, it seems artificial: "Then the kettle drum, then the snare, then the bass drum and cymbals, then cracking light against the dark, and the gods grinning and licking their chops in the hills." And then with the inevitable calm, the campers return to the lake with "their bright cries perpetuating the deathless joke about how they were getting simply drenched." Swimming in the rain is as good an example as any to demonstrate the dissolution of sharp outlines, and—as the children enjoy this new sensation— the shared old joke itself momentarily dissolves the boundary of generations.

The essay ends with a striking epiphany. Many personal essays, in my opinion, are marred by what I call "unearned epiphanies," a *suddenly I realized* moment that seems unwarranted or gratuitous, the result more of an artificial writerly convention than a genuine shock of recognition. But this epiphany has been mounting from the opening sentence and comes as the culmination of all the creepy sensations of time and identity that persisted during White's return to the lake.

His son decides to join the cheerful swimmers and pulls his rain-soaked trunks from a clothesline and wrings them out. Not going in himself, White sees the boy "wince slightly" as he pulls "up around his vitals the small, soggy, icy garment." And then in the final sentence he realizes what has been troubling him the entire time. And it is a literal "shock" of recognition, an intense physical sensation transferred from his son's "vitals" (the perfect word) to his own: "As he buckled the swollen belt suddenly my groin felt the chill of death."

I vocalize that final sentence with an emphasis on "my." By transferring the unpleasant physical feeling of the icy trunks to his own "vitals," White once again blurs the distinctions between his son and himself, himself and his father. But this time the uncanny sensation hits home with a profound difference. The eerie feeling that time has stopped has all along alleviated a core anxiety—namely, a growing fear of his impending death, or what psychologists call "thanatophobia." White, it seems, returned to the lake hoping therapeutically to suspend the passage of time, and the lake almost supplied him with the necessary anodyne. Though "creepy," the illusion of his "dual existence" temporarily camouflaged his inescapable anxiety. Hardly the idyllic account of a father-son fishing expedition, "Once More to the Lake" opens with illusion and evasion, struggles with contradiction and self-delusion, and ends in panic.

The mental distress documented in this "chestnut," despite its picture-book setting, can hardly be called "middlebrow." This eerie return to a magical childhood spot records no pastoral excursion. White suffered all his life from incapacitating anxiety disorders. A very private and shy individual—perhaps much too reticent for what the autobiographical essay would become—White was never one to advertise his anguish. One of the few literary figures who recognized White's darker side was John Updike, who, in a brief foreword to the revised edition of White's *Letters* in 2006, focused his remarks on White's uneasy mental state: "Uneasiness was, in old age and youth, White's element."

"Once More to the Lake" became part of White's 1942 collection, *One Man's Meat*, which Updike considers his "very best book." Most of the essays in that book amount to a journal that reflects the start of a new life, as White, tired of both New York City and *The New Yorker*, moved to Maine in the summer of 1938 and began writing a column for *Harper's Magazine*. The column, "One Man's Meat," had a Thoreau-like dimension—covering nature, farming routines, daily errands, philosophical musings. Like many *Walden* enthusiasts, White saw Thoreau entirely as a philosopher of simplification and took no notice of his spectacular complexity of language. The collection contains many echoes of Thoreau—and even includes an essay on Walden Pond that takes the humorous form of a letter dictated to "Dear Henry." In 1944, White published a new and enlarged edition, the last essay composed in January 1943. Later, that fall, as Updike notes, White experienced what he called a "nervous crack-up." This mental crisis rubs against the grain of the many idyllic essays that contribute to the dominant tone of *One Man's Meat*.

In "Once More to the Lake" (and in a small number of other essays and stories) one can sense the impending "crack-up" and the eventual need for psychiatric help. Updike mentions that a few years before his death White supplied his authorized biographer, Scott Elledge, a list of items he should take into account. One of them was: "My panic fear, as near as I can make out, is not of death. It is an amorphous fear, lacking in form." "Once More to the Lake" was, indeed, as Updike says, "ominous": "This fear . . . was his deepest topic."

White would have been a greater essayist, deserving of the "earthly triumphs" he regrets never having attained, had he devoted more of his talents to confronting that "amorphous fear" than to suppressing or evading it. He was especially adept at that popular nineteenth-century form that blended (often with a hallucinatory twist) the personal essay with the short story—a hybrid then commonly known as the "sketch." But it's a shame he didn't absorb more of what his great predecessors—Poe, Irving, Hawthorne, Melville, and Twain—accomplished in that genre. Instead, White adapted his sketches to the familiar style and register of the so-called genteel essay that by the 1930s was already obsolete. White was perhaps too complacently the victim of his own audience; one wishes he had taken more risks, inspected more deeply the cracks and flaws in the foundation, revealed more of the "uneasiness" he frequently endured but only reluctantly addressed. Still, when he did address it—as he allowed himself to do in "Once More to the Lake"—he did so resplendently.*

---

* This foreword is an expansion of a short essay on "Once More to the Lake" I posted on the Slant Books *Close Reading* blog in July 2021. I'd like to thank an old friend, Peggy Rosenthal, for encouraging me to weigh in on that classic essay. My close reading of another White "chestnut," "The Death of a Pig," can be found in

*

The Best American Essays features a selection of the year's outstanding essays, essays of literary achievement that show an awareness of craft and forcefulness of thought. Hundreds of essays are gathered annually from a wide assortment of national and regional publications. These essays are then screened, and approximately one hundred are turned over to a distinguished guest editor, who may add a few personal discoveries and who makes the final selections. The list of notable essays appearing in the back of the book is drawn from a final comprehensive list that includes not only all of the essays submitted to the guest editor but also many that were not submitted.

To qualify for the volume, the essay must be a work of respectable literary quality, intended as a fully developed, independent essay (not an excerpt) on a subject of general interest (not specialized scholarship), originally written in English (or translated by the author) for publication in an American periodical (or an English-language periodical with a strong US presence) during the calendar year. Note that abridgments and excerpts taken from longer works and published in magazines do not qualify for the series, but if considered significant they will appear in the list of notable essays. Today's essay is a highly flexible and shifting form, however, so these criteria are not carved in stone.

Magazine editors who want to be sure their contributors will be considered each year should submit issues or subscriptions to:

Robert Atwan
The Best American Essays
HarperCollins Publishers
195 Broadway
New York, NY 10007

Writers and editors are welcome to submit published essays from any eligible periodical for consideration; unpublished work does not qualify for the series and cannot be reviewed or evaluated. Also

---

Creative Nonfiction (Spring 2011). Readers interested in E. B. White's reputation and historical context can do no better than Ned Stucky-French's *The American Essay in the American Century* (Missouri, 2011). As far as I know, White's essays can be found only in the various collections he personally assembled from 1942 to 1977. I'm surprised that no one has published a one-volume complete collection. Or better yet, a smaller collection that shows White only at his very best.

ineligible are essays that have been published in book form—such as a contribution to a collection—but have never appeared in a periodical. All submissions from print magazines must be directly from the publication and not in manuscript or printout format. Editors of magazines that do not identify their selections by genre should make sure all essay and nonfiction submissions are clearly marked. Editors of online magazines and literary bloggers should not assume that appropriate work will be seen; they are invited to submit clear printed copies of the essays to the address above.

The deadline for all submissions is February 1 of the year following the year of publication: thus all submissions of essays published in 2022 must be received by February 1, 2023. Writers should keep in mind that—as is the case for many literary awards—the essays are selected from a large pool of nominations. For this award, unlike many, writers may nominate their own work. A considerable number of prominent literary journals regularly submit essays to the series, but though we continually reach out with invitations to submit and reminders of deadlines, not all periodicals respond or participate, so writers should be sure to check with their editors to see if they routinely submit to the series.

For more detailed information and updates on the submission guidelines, readers should consult www.bestamericanseries.com.

Please note the following recent changes to the submission guidelines for the essay series:

- Editors of print journals and periodicals that include the series on their subscription lists need do nothing in the way of submissions. I will review all appropriate material and consider the essays and literary nonfiction in each issue as nominations. If editors prefer to highlight or nominate certain essays for special attention, they are welcome to do so. If their periodicals also publish original essays in a separate online outlet, they are invited to select and submit no more than seven candidates in hard copy.
- Because of the overwhelming number of submissions from online-only sources, the series will now limit submissions to a total of seven for each periodical. These must be submitted in hard copy. They can be submitted either all at once or over the course of the year.
- Individuals who submit to the series will now be limited to no more than seven selections. They are welcome to submit these candidates all at once or over the course of the year.

A further note: It is surprising how many submissions I receive that omit the name of the publication and/or its date—and sometimes I can't even find the name of the author! Separate submissions from print or online sources that do not include a full citation (name of publication, exact date, issue number, and author contact information) will not be considered. When submitting multiple essays, please remember that cover letters can sometimes get separated from selections, so please clearly indicate the full citation on each essay nominated.

Speaking of E. B. White, I was saddened to learn just as I was writing this foreword that Roger Angell had died at the age of 101 on May 20. Angell was the son of White's wife, the legendary *New Yorker* editor Katherine Angell, from an earlier marriage. Angell's splendid "This Old Man" (also a National Magazine Award–winning essay) appears in our 2015 volume. He was a wonderful essayist and not just one of our all-time best writers on baseball.

For this book, the thirty-seventh in the series, I'd like to thank my children, Greg and Emily, who always generously offer me so much support (I happened to notice they each share an alma mater with Roger Angell). And as usual I especially appreciate the indispensable efforts of my editor, Nicole Angeloro, who makes this book happen each year, whether there's a global crisis or not. Many thanks to others at HarperCollins for their assistance: Laura Brady, Amanda Hong, Sharyn Rosenblum, Lisa McAuliffe. This year I also want to add someone further behind the scenes, Kenneth Drucker. During a year of supply-chain disruptions, he made sure I received an unprecedented number of essay submissions in an efficient and timely fashion. I owe a special thanks to Mark Krotov of *n+1* for generously helping prepare Anthony Veasna So's essay for this collection.

As I had anticipated, it was a delightful experience to collaborate with such a talented writer as Alexander Chee. He has assembled what I regard as a unique collection, one of the best of the best: nearly every writer included in our 2022 book is appearing in the series for the first time. From the opening essay to the last, this brilliantly diverse collection pinpoints urgent individual issues as they entangle themselves within the manifold mysteries of our everyday lives.

R.A.

Introduction

I CAME TO this year's anthology as the kind of reader who buys used copies of literary magazines for fun. The 1989 *Antaeus* "Journals, Notebooks & Diaries" special issue, for example, sits near my reading chair, a frequent source of pleasure, just as it was approximately thirty years ago, when I first found it. The two entries I revisit most are an excerpt from the diaries of Mavis Gallant, as yet still uncollected in their entirety, and a cunning fake journal by Dmitri Nabokov, known to many as Vladimir Nabokov's son, who never published more of it, to my knowledge. Neither has ever been republished in another volume.

And so, yes, the fun has a desperate edge to it: I buy these magazines partly for the writing inside them, as sometimes this appearance is the only one. Their stories, poems, and essays do not always get collected again, either by the writers, their survivors, their publishers, or their estates, should they have one. For some writers, an interested scholar might come, decades later, and assemble a volume. I just received, for example, an advance copy of Randall Kenan's collected essays, set to be published posthumously later this year. I set it on my shelf next to *The Cross of Redemption: The Uncollected Writings of James Baldwin,* which Kenan himself edited and published in 2010, posthumously for Baldwin. Together they remind me of what that caring scholarship looks like when it is supported.

To prepare for this year's volume, I went back to my favorite editions of *The Best American Essays* from over the years to remind me of what I might be looking for. Anne Carson's "Kinds of Water," from Annie Dillard's 1988 volume, an essay I read every year for a decade. "On Seeing England for the First Time," by Jamaica Kincaid, in Susan Sontag's 1992 edition, along with Joan Didion's prescient "Sentimental Journeys," on the media coverage of the Central Park Five rape case. Hilton Als's "Buddy Ebsen," from Edwidge Danticat's 2011 edition, a praise song for the way queer people bring each other up when no one else will—the finishing school of all finishing schools.

Edward Hoagland's 1999 volume is a favorite: "The Meteorites," by the late Brian Doyle, a tender lesson about friendship, love, and summer camp, and the way we learn from those we teach; Franklin Burroughs's "Compression Wood," on a poem by Gerard Manley Hopkins and an old friend who works with reclaimed wood; "What's Inside You, Brother," Touré's remarkable self-confrontation on his career as a boxer; and Daisy Eunyoung Rhau's "On Silence," a story about the sacrifices required of a piano prodigy, and what it meant to her to give up playing the piano altogether at age fifteen. Thus far she has published little else, but I live in hope of her return—as I know well, writing can be a complicated game of giving up and coming back.

Republication in *The Best American Essays* at least does not require fame or careful heirs. This anthology, the work it does year after year, is at least one place some of these essays may be found again, a poker hand laid down in a bet against oblivion. And this year that hand is mine.

As 2021 began, after years of alternately loving and second-guessing the choices of every guest judge going back to 1986, even when I liked their selections, I had no criteria I could articulate better than *I'll know it when I see it.* Even this would not stay true. I knew a few of these choices instantly, as soon as I finished them. Some of them unsettled or even disturbed me so much on my first reading that I put them to the side in a folder I called "Maybe." Still others never made it to that folder, and yet I knew exactly how to find them when I understood they belonged here—I could not forget them.

The reading of submissions was unexpectedly a recuperative act. I had lost the ability to read books in the first year of COVID. As the deaths mounted, as doctors and nurses had to fundraise for equipment the way patients have to fundraise for their care, as hunger and poverty grew due to closed businesses and federal and state support that was either slow to mobilize or sent to conservative states instead of liberal ones, and Trump weaponized the pandemic against his political enemies and gave huge contracts to grifter friends who are still being prosecuted, it was hard to feel safe enough even to just sit and read a book at home—hard to feel it was even useful. One of my journal entries from that time consisted of just the date.

Writing felt like using my head as a leather hole punch. My body became at times almost theoretical to me. I had to remember to stand, stretch, exercise—all this time later, in year three, I still do. I was struggling to heal old injuries that year, chronic pain also, and when my husband fell ill in the pandemic's second month and I nursed him at home, I remember when I understood that if his blood oxygen level dipped too low, I was not strong enough to carry him down the stairs to the car. I would have to wait for the ambulance, which might not come fast enough. He recovered and did not require an emergency carry in the end, but I began strength training in earnest so that I might someday meet the occasion. This sense of the emergency at home changed me.

By January of 2021 I had lost faith in even the idea that writing might improve anything between people, but especially the idea that writing could or should teach empathy, or offer an education on biases to the enemies of an equitable multiracial liberal democracy—and that essays could do it. This had come to feel like a sucker's game, with no possible end in sight. Did these opponents really need education? Was the sort of person who might someday push me off a train platform for being Asian really going to be changed by a personal essay, or an op-ed? How many lessons were needed? So many excellent writers had tried. And yet it seemed the alternative was to participate in silence, and as a result, erasure.

Cord Jefferson, writing in 2014 at *Medium*, identified what he called "The Racism Beat," a path by which writers of color could make a career of a kind responding to current events, with essays usually written quickly and published later the same day or the next day, and which he had used, by his own admission, to make a name for himself. But the beat was also a kind of trap: these same outlets would not as readily let him write other kinds of stories for them. "What new column shall the writer write when an unarmed black person is killed for doing nothing but frightening an armed white person? The same thing he wrote when Trayvon Martin was killed? And that's to say nothing of when Oscar Grant was killed. Or when Ramarley Graham was killed. Or when Timothy Stansbury Jr. was killed. Or when Amadou Diallo was killed. Or when Jordan Davis was killed. Or when Ousmane Zongo was killed. Or when Jonathan Ferrell was killed. Or when Renisha McBride was killed." This essay was bitter and illuminating to reread after the tenth anniversary of Trayvon Martin's death came this year, and the second anniversary of George Floyd's death arrived.

I have been on what I could call the Asian and gay version of that beat. I had written those crisis essays in that rapid-response mode, editors reaching out to see if I could turn them around in twenty-four hours, ten hours, six. The part of me that wanted more time to think put a stop to it all by way of what seemed like writer's block, a kind of deeper self-refusal I had to take seriously. I spent the first half of 2021 trying and failing to write an essay addressed as an open letter to a future attacker, and then I stopped saying yes to those essays, for now.

It is not the role of this anthology necessarily to respond to current events, and some of the essays here are the kind that take many years to write, like novels, on their own schedule. We need our history, and the truths of that history, documented, and to do that, we need to see the truth of the present reflected too.

A quote from David Wojnarowicz, an artist and essayist who shaped me as much as any other, kept me company in 2021 as I made my choices. His friend the artist Zoe Leonard told him she feared her photographs of clouds were not up to the cultural moment of the AIDS crisis. He said to her, "Zoe, these are so beautiful, and that's what we're fighting for. We're being angry and complaining because we have to, but where we want to go is back to beauty. If you let go of that, we don't have anywhere to go."

When I was a student at the Iowa Writers' Workshop in fiction, I talked my way into a nonfiction workshop with the writer Clark Blaise. As a fiction student, I wasn't supposed to be in his classes, as he taught in an entirely different graduate program with a separate application process. I was an auditor, a rare thing for a workshop, and I did this work alongside my fiction workshop classes. It was one of the best experiences I had during my education there.

He introduced us to a quality in the writing he admired regularly, often asking in class after what he called *wetness.* Was the writing wet? Could you feel the rain, the blood, the tears? It's an uncomfortable suggestion, of course, prone to being the occasion for cynical jokes, even as it is also a beautifully earnest one, a way of pointing toward something else he was teaching us to value: how the essayist, when writing personally, uses the body as an instrument for sensing and recording the events described, and especially the elements you might have elided from your memories because they were so embarrassing. What I took from this was to ask, Is the essay located in the body of the essayist, and if so, how and where? What are the bodies doing in the essay? What sense memories guided the writer, brought onto the page to guide the reader?

I found myself drawn to essays told with and through the information we take in through our bodies as well as whatever the intellect offers, or the memory, or the voices of others. I wanted to feel something. I wanted to be taken out of my life with the force of a possession and then return to it changed. Or I wanted a gentleness amid so much terror. If I wanted safety, it was the safety the truth provides.

A last lesson appeared, after all of this reading. I have always collected favorite essays, yes, in case they do not reappear. A private anthology, growing over time. But in preparing this one I learned that they keep me, too. Keeping them keeps me. They retain a sense of who I was, when I first found them, and the possibilities they offered me returns when I reread them. And so I can follow the trail of those thoughts farther each time, following a sense of who I meant to be, and who I might still become.

The essays here are the essays that got me through the year, essays that lit up the corners of my mind as well as the center of it, and as I look over the table of contents, it is like a trail I followed to this book through the year.

Their first lines, in order of appearance:

I had the right to say nothing at all. They say the insomnia will end when the withdrawals end, but that's just a lie they tell you so you won't pick up, something to hold on to if "Don't quit before the miracle happens" doesn't persuade you to hold on for one more day. Three days before he died, my husband got out of bed. Last year I became fascinated with an artificial intelligence model that was being trained to write human-like text. My mother had raised me vegetarian, and though I harbored no real desire to eat meat, sometimes, in summer, I would take a hunk of watermelon to a remote corner of our yard and pretend it was a fresh carcass. The semester prior to his suicide, my friend and I spent afternoons lounging around on a defective, footless sofa I had borrowed without any intention of returning it. End of month. Today I found myself standing at the window, half in a dream, my hand at my neck, fingers searching absently for a cross I'd lost more than a year ago. On a morning early in the second month of the unprecedented time, I rise to the sound of the birds and pad to the kitchen in my slippers. Three springs ago, I lost the better part of my mind. I was almost sixteen when I ran into my biological father, Reggie, at a Trailways station. I remember the first night my father came to us and said: tomorrow we will be millionaires. In the spring of 1994, I was driving back from running an Alcoholics Anonymous meeting at a prison in Orange, New York, when blue lights appeared in my rearview mirror. My cousin Kano emerges from the oasis water as something aquatic, fins where his feet used to be, tusks sprouted from his mouth, gliding. Years ago, in the liminality of early transition, I worked a brief labor job. She gets there and it's like someone's aunt has decorated the place. The first role I was cast in was a rock. On August 24, 2020, as I attempted the first pee of the morning, I felt a tightness on the underside of my penis. In 1986 we moved from Linda, California, where I went to Cedar Lane School with all the migrant children, to the neighboring town of Olivehurst, where I would go to school with the whites. After moving to California, in 2010, it seemed as if Mom would spend the rest of her life there. The flyers are pasted to dusty windowpanes in roadside cafés, stapled to skinny utility poles along fields, pinned on the overloaded corkboards of pilgrim hostels. My grandfather once taught me how to use a sextant. If you ever find yourself piss poor and struggling to survive in a world obsessed with money, I'll teach you what I've had to know from birth.

This anthology was almost an anthology of elegies. Many of us had our dead on our minds, whether or not we were writing about those lost to the pandemic—the recent dead, the long dead, the family, spouses, friends, and even strangers we could not forget.

I mourn the loss of Anthony Veasna So with his inclusion here, and the writer Barry Lopez, a regular contributor to this series over the years, included this time as a subject.

Some of these names you may know. Some of these names you may not know—some selections are even the writers' debut work. Some of these essays came from familiar haunts, and some of these publications have never before had an essay in the series. This is the first year a newsletter publication is honored, and possibly, the first year for *Harper's Bazaar* and *Harper's Magazine* to be included alongside each other.

Susan Sontag said, in her 1992 introduction, that "literature is a party." Welcome to my party.

ALEXANDER CHEE

The Best
AMERICAN
ESSAYS®
2022

BRIAN BLANCHFIELD

Abasement

FROM *Territory*

I HAD THE right to say nothing at all. I was under arrest. I had
trespassed the home we were planning to buy; in fact it was al-
leged I had broken and entered, and slept overnight in the Littlejohns' basement. I had been spied, before the inspector arrived,
by one of the Littlejohns, a man, perhaps a family uncle, one of
several, from the top steps of the wooden staircase down. He must
have heard something at ground level. I was stuffing the dryer
with the sheets I had slept in. It was step one of the plan I had rapidly formulated, preceding other steps: to fold the cot and stow it
where I had found it; to tidy up and hide the pages of my manuscript, which I had been reading before I fell asleep; then, if there
really were no exit down there, to ascend the stairs right after
eight to join without incident the party wandering the house with
the inspector. Once he'd arrive I assumed I could blend in, and
explain myself as having gained entry when he did, according to
customary arrangement. Customary arrangement was something
one could claim when assailed. This is what one does, a buyer
such as I and an inspector such as he has hired. It is called a walk-
through.

I had the right to say nothing at all. The policeman with
his digital clipboard was himself indication that anything hence
would be actionable, if more was said. He had been waiting for me
when I descended at last from the loft area, at the very height of the
house. I backed down the ladder, feet first. The loft was an unusual
space, which couldn't be exited by door, face forward. Going in,
upon hatching, one crept, one learned to crawl. The floor was not

reliably weight bearing, slatted with old barrel or bucket staves, and was circular, and the whole room, more or less a bucket, was canted. The floor was to spin, and one's own weight would set the thing in motion, and pulls or straps along the walls were handholds, assists, and there were portal windows, open, at just the places where, if centrifugal force overcame self-control and balance, one could be pitched out into the sky. It was designed this way, to be a ride, a blur, a near-death amusement. I understood it was the teen Littlejohn's room. It was like the house, or my crime inhabiting it, was structurally regressive, and to graduate toward violation's conclusion was to be pulled up through the levels and spat out in adolescence, to gradually require separation from the sociality of adults and removal to one's hedonist privacy: home. William Maxwell says it somewhere in *The Folded Leaf:* that the teenager gets so brooding in his sexuality and self-sanctity that all he requires of others is their absence.

I had the right to say nothing at all. It was deceptive, but not illegal, to withhold the entire truth. I represented myself accurately in everything I had thus far signed as buyer. I had been preapproved for a loan sufficient to purchase the house from the Littlejohns. John and I had been advised by our realtor to go back to our lender and get preapproved as Brian Blanchfield, not Blanchfield and Myers. If we wanted this home, it was smarter not to bid as a couple. The listing agent was a deacon in Christ Church, and the Littlejohns, the sellers, were the most prominent family in Christ Church, which operates New Saint Andrew's, the Classical Christian college expanding downtown, and which has a history of discrimination against gays, discrimination that cannot be prosecuted. In instances when one of their own bids against an undesirable party, the church is typically able to marshal the resources to enable the buyer to pay cash, which— even if the sum is less than what a gay couple might borrow to pay—is an accepted criterion on which to prefer one buyer to another, and anyway John and I are not a protected class of citizens in Idaho. Federal precedent still maintains that gay, lesbian, and trans people are not covered under Title VII of the 1964 Civil Rights Act, and in twenty-six states, including ours, there is no law on the books to protect our rights not to be denied housing for being who we are.

I had the right to say nothing at all. My arrest was beginning, my apprehension all along coming to term. Everything was seeded from the start, by the givens that preceded us; and our thorough passage, room to room, through reprieve and spite and dread and the gumption that accompanies resignation, were but chapters in the story predestined to conclude this way. The burning fuse on the dynamite was, even more than witness of my presence, the stack of my manuscript beneath the cot. I knew the loose-leaf book was proof, when, as our tour moved back upstairs, I watched the trailing Littlejohns discovering its pages, one of them off by himself reading some of each leaf before he dropped it into the dustbin. It amounted to my autobiography. It said who I was. I had needed to write a book that thought through things, that unpacked what was fraught where my life intersected the culture's, and to do it in a way that consulted no one and that pushed me past compunction, free that way to go for broke, to reckon with my fundamentalist upbringing, my sexuality, my career shame, and my slow family tragedy, which would accelerate upon publication. It is what they call, I think, a burn book. In the time between when I had finished writing it and when it was published, I felt I could die. Fulfillment felt salvific to me, an act which moves immediately into perfect tense: "it is done," like it says in the Bible. It was crucial to my psychology to have a say, to have had a say, to say what I knew, to have said what I know, uncredentialed by institutions that had rejected me, to show up in a milieu unaffiliated, and unbeholden to future prospects, of which there were none. I couldn't have been more mortified by my failures, and at the bottom already I tapped into the righteousness of abasement.

I had the right to say nothing at all. Neither John nor I was obligated to answer aloud, so we each resorted to writing in a clear hand a standard response on a small card and passing it, folded, silently across the table one perfect summer evening. We hoped it would satisfy my well-meaning new colleagues and their spouses, who were toasting our first week in Moscow and asking enthusiastically if the rumor was true that we'd found a home on Sixth Street. We wanted them to understand that we would be glad to discuss in places not as public as the open-air ice cream parlor the tactical measures we were necessarily taking

since the sellers were part of NSA. We wanted please not to elaborate. The place was buzzing with generations of suspiciously large
and wholesome families, not to mention the sticky children of literature professors, and it would be more than awkward to describe
the extra steps a queer couple takes to obtain a home. It was both
dangerous to the sale and embarrassing to me to describe how for
months I presented myself as "a single unmarried man" (as it reads
on the contract) in all the documentation with mortgage lenders
and the phone calls with engineers and inspectors and insurers
and in negotiations through our realtor with the Littlejohns, how
for the first time in twenty years I went around anxious about pronouns: not feminine and masculine ones this time—singular and
plural. Our public togetherness on a perfect summer evening was
existentially a threat to what I had been compelled to attest; and
what was risk, or defiance, or heroism, or cowardice was unbearably volatile in this story. Our friend Eileen joked, Yeah, it's like:
two-bedroom, two-bath—and how many closets does the house
have: Oh right, the whole thing's a closet. Calling out plainly the
darker fear for the friend who hides it is a queer favor, a preroga-
tive. Fronting is a good way to back out of a dream.

Drinking Story

FROM *Harper's Bazaar*

THEY SAY THE insomnia will end when the withdrawals end, but that's just a lie they tell you so you won't pick up, something to hold on to if "Don't quit before the miracle happens" doesn't persuade you to hold on for one more day. Early on, I tried the late-night meetings at the strip mall clubhouse with low lights and syrup-smelling vape clouds hanging near the ceiling like weather, but all those men and their court orders made me want to drink worse. My home was no place for a soul's convalescence—the Crown Royal bottle was still in its velvet bag, sleeping while I couldn't.

In the evenings, I was fine, because for the first few months, I spent evenings in meetings. I don't remember what I said or heard, but I remember landmarks of the world I'd rebirthed myself into, like the light switch I felt for in the bathroom, and the heft of the folding chairs I stacked. I was days old, then weeks old, growing up in church basements where my dry family left no trace—not coffee rings on tables, not stray pamphlets, not the soul rot that could soak into upholstery if we let it linger in the air too long.

The twenty-four-hour restaurants, though: my mind built dioramas of interiors, mapped them, snapshotted the doors that open and open and open inside me. I do not live in that city anymore. I don't go to meetings or the late dinners afterward, and I don't drive around alone at night, looking for somewhere to pass the time while getting tired. But I remember the towering plush booths of 13 Coins, Lost Lake's beacon of teal neon, North Star's constellation tabletops. Once you get sober, you become fully aware in every waking moment, and without the generous erasure of the blackout, you meet a million details demanding to be stored.

For nearly six years now, I've been trying to sort all these heavy minutes, and I'll never get through the backlog that trails behind me and nags that I've missed something. I've averaged five and a half hours of sleep a night since that spring when I finished my drinking. Maybe I drank because I wanted to sleep—this is one of those things I tell myself when I'm trying to make a story of it. In truth, I remember why I drank. It never stays out of my head long. I remember the first red Solo cup and the self-breaking power of Everclear and Kool-Aid washing through me, back when my liver was still new enough to meet the liquor like a date with a man you don't yet know you'll fear.

Then, in the restaurant of my memory, the lights go out.

In early 2015, I bought my first tarot deck after my friend read my cards and turned up the Three of Swords, the stabbed heart. I wanted to know about a man. I read my own cards every day for practice. By April, all my messages about love and death evaporated, and one card made itself known to me every day: the Four of Cups. A person sits under a tree, arms crossed, turning away from a floating hand that offers a cup.

By the end, I wasn't drinking very much most nights. I'd split a twelve-ounce bottle of cider between two jelly jars, one for drinking, the other for saving in the fridge for tomorrow. No more passing out on the bathroom floor with an empty belly and the spins. Only occasional brownouts, or maybe blackouts, but I wouldn't know. Mostly, I made the jelly jar my emblem of restraint.

I was not ready for the withdrawals. They weren't severe enough to bring on seizures or DTs, but I couldn't pretend I wasn't going through a physical disturbance resulting from a profound change. I don't remember how it felt, only how expansive the night became as my phone and I lay in bed, and I looked through the first names of women who told me to call them if I wanted to drink. I couldn't recall most of their faces or where we met, so I didn't call. Besides, I didn't want to drink. There was nothing to talk me out of or through. I wanted to sleep.

For a decade, half of which I spent with a young brain that hadn't fully set, I drank heavily and often. When people say alcohol is a depressant, they're referring to the fact that it depresses, or slows down, the central nervous system. Over time, cognition and memory suffer. When alcohol is taken away, its inhibitory effects go with it, and the central nervous system is left jacked up.

Enough time has passed that my face, once a welt-dappled and grayish banner announcing my toxic body, skipped back in time to find the moonglow it lost in my first apartment. I look healthy, but I can't sleep. My heart races with no apparent cause. My stomach weeps acid. My severe working memory deficit makes me forget my friends' names; I am smoothed like an egg, losing everything I haven't written down. My brain says it can stay up all night. It says we can just do more things to make up for what we keep losing. I was shaped by alcohol; it will always be my center.

At meetings, we were supposed to speak to the other drunks in a general way about what it was like, what happened, and what it's like now. What happened is a memory hole where narrative drowned. What it was like—what *what* was like? I could talk about the bathroom floor and the jelly jar but not what got me there, not in rooms full of men. It didn't matter. I could make a narrative true without making that truth precise. It was not untrue that I was born wanting, or that I wanted to change the way I felt, or that I believed in no power greater than myself.

The story of my drinking I shared at meetings was plot driven and shaped around relatable details. The story was as vacant as a church basement at night, decorated with one silk plant, and ready to be filled with whoever showed up. I tidied my mess around narrative beats: first it was fun, then it was bad, then I knew that, then I really knew it, then I quit, and it's still hard, but I'm here. Meanwhile, my uninebriated brain began putting together a private narrative that could be as long as I needed. Without an audience, it could resist the easy clasping of cause and consequence, and the visceral pleasure of the arc. I had to stop grasping for the closest source of narrative menace I could find—myself, the dipsomaniac—and enter a space where there was no tension to be modulated, no structure to guide me toward a triumphant resolution. I had to understand why I needed alcohol so I'd never go back there looking for something I'd lost.

A few months before quitting, I had, as they say, pulled a geographic. I left a moldy place in Seattle for a not-yet-moldy place north of the city. I could start fresh in an apartment where I'd never vomited, miles from the bars. My Seattle apartment was behind a block of five of them. I liked them all, but most nights after work, I showed up at the dim tavern that had pull tabs and pool tables. Being a regular meant taking my place at the bar over and over, having a pint of Manny's set down in front of me before I asked, like in a movie, and I could have as many as I wanted, because the beer was as infinite as God.

My years there are one long night inside me: that night I saw the man from the reality show who I'd met before at another dive the night I got roofied, couldn't get away from the heiress who stroked my hair and rode her bicycle home to get an unfinished Coast Salish cedar mask she wanted to show me, smoked cigarettes in a ball gown I was wearing from the gala I came from, traded cigarettes for doughnuts from the baker next door, ate chips, drank beer, drank whiskey, passed out on the bathroom floor. I have some anecdotes, illustrations with plots, but no meaning. Strung together, they show the chaos I was cataloging long before I was ready to tell its story.

One day, I had my last whiskey and never had one again. I never went back to the bar where I drank it, but there's a dollhouse in my brain where I am still on the barstool, deciding I'll find my way back to my car in the morning and taxi home tonight. There is too much happening in my brain for sleep. I'm in a hospital cafeteria for a Sunday meeting, looking at the evergreens through gargantuan panes of institutional glass, three weeks sober and not ready to talk about what it was like but confident enough to say there is no God, but there are spirits everywhere, and hardly any of them love us. I'm in the gymnasium where the old-timers, who got sober before I was born, talk about their home repairs. I'm in a basement after dark, in a neighborhood I can't recall, at a meeting I'll never return to, where a guy with a decade sober stands with his soul billowing like a preacher's and says he'll probably die drunk. I'm in the yacht club for the sunrise meeting. I remember nothing but the window and the messy surface of the lake, a view I thought was going to feel profound.

It's been a couple years since I've returned to the meetings that saved my life by offering me a narrative form to hold my shapeless despair. I stretched the time loops of my drinking and quitting onto a structure that gave my life meaning by making my failures into story. Hitting bottom became a plot point, and my history was a chain of cause and effect leading to it. Meetings gave me that vehicle for meaning. But once I let the plot sprawl, I couldn't bring it back there.

I drank, because doctors can't cure what's wrong with me; they can't even keep me comfortable, because this pain is not from sickness—it's from knowing that men want to hurt me. Soon after the first one got inside me, I began to drink. Alcohol mashed a button in my hypothalamus that made my adrenals light up. The alcoholic's high cortisol will drop back to normal within three months, but I still can't sleep. My heart is still overclocked, and my brain idles high. I suspect that those nights I spent diving toward last call didn't bring on the insomnia—I think alcohol was the only tool I had to shutter the memory palace in my head, where all the hallways led to rooms where I was on my back, pressed against a bed or a couch or a floor, suffering.

This is less of a memory and more of a figment, but I see myself at a diner table, three days sober and unsure about how I'll go on. I have a glass of grapefruit juice and a plate of hash browns and eggs. My gut knows something I don't, and it has asked for food. The miracle is that part of you gets to die, like you always wanted before, but part of you gets to live, like you didn't plan for. I began to understand hunger as a kind of faith, the demand for fuel to keep going. It's so easy to mistake it for thirst or for anger, but it's the first thing that comes back, glowing in you like neon, saying to you like neon says, "Here we are, open."

Fire and Ice

FROM *Granta*

THREE DAYS BEFORE he died, my husband got out of bed. Somehow he propelled himself down the hall and into the living room, where I found him bent over a volume of Esther Horvath photographs called *Into the Arctic Ice: The Largest Polar Expedition of All Time.* Barry's white hair was sprung wild and his feet were bare though it was late at night in December, sleety rain driving against the windows. How had he pulled sweatpants over his bony hips? He'd hardly stirred all day, lifting his head only to sip on bone broth made by one of our daughters, leaning against me to get to the bathroom because he was bleary from pain drugs. Yet he'd managed to transport himself to the center of this rental house to dig out a book that now held his rapt attention.

The book had arrived by mail a few days earlier, when Barry was still able to sit on the sofa for an hour or so, and he'd turned its pages with the slightest pressure of thumb and finger so as not to mar the saturated colors of the photos. Our son-in-law was over with the rest of the family for a subdued holiday visit. The two men spoke in calm, low voices about a region of the planet once intimately familiar to my husband, second only to his knowledge of the thirty-six acres of western Oregon rain forest where he'd lived for fifty years and where I'd lived with him for nearly two decades until a wildfire booted us out one late-summer night. Barry moved closer to Pete and pointed to streaks of blue in Horvath's images of a vast icescape, the humps of polar bears, the eerie glow of human light piercing the darkness. The peeling noses and cheeks of scientists too long in the cold. I remember how he laughed with a whistle of nostalgia, missing days when he must have felt fully alive.

But now in the living room, he whipped through the pages until I heard an edge tear, a fluttering as if he'd startled a bird. When I said his name, he didn't answer. When I touched his shoulder, he jerked in my direction and insisted I start packing the car, though first he wanted me to find his suitcase and the down jacket he'd worn for forty years of polar travel. He returned to the book frantic, a man who'd dropped a key into a well's murky bottom and was crazy with the loss.

I was certain my husband was about to insist I bundle him up and drive him through the rain to our fire-damaged house, an hour away. I steeled myself for it. He'd say he had to die on his own land, near the remains of ten cords of combusted wood and his melted truck, on the smoke-saturated bed in our bedroom whose windows were still smeared orange with fire retardant. He'd check to make sure the essay he'd been working on was secure in his typewriter, waiting. Then he would rest. He'd watch through the window over the bed for flashes of kingfisher and fat rain clouds, for the sky arcs of an overwintering eagle. What nonsense it was to come to the end instead in this stranger's house with a stranger's furniture and its strange cast of light. I was sure Barry would rather use any last bursts of energy to pace the perimeter of his scorched archive, as he had most days since the fire. He'd become the lone sentry at the gates of that phantom building, which once held the history of his fifty-year writing life. For months, I'd watched him rake through the mound of ash, releasing shiny particles of the past into the smoke-stilled air. He churned up chunks of paper—cremated books that disintegrated with the slightest touch—and bent metal that he held up to the faint light in the withered forest. *What were you, then?*

Except that noise was inside my head. In fact, Barry hadn't mentioned home for over a week. What I finally put together on this Saturday night, from his various mutters and fragmented speech, was that his destination was an archipelago called Svalbard. An Arctic expedition had lost its leader, so he'd been called in to take over. He had mere hours to get there. He slammed the Horvath book shut and clambered into the spare bedroom, where he yanked out a duffel bag I'd recently emptied and stored away in my effort to make this place feel something like a home. He

tossed in a broken alarm clock, a pillow, a packet of picture hangers. Where are my gloves? My Gore-Tex pants? My expedition sunglasses? Where have you put my things? Why won't you give me my
things? He flailed his arms so I couldn't come close. As if the only
person preventing him from the most important launch of his ad-
venturous life was me.

And then he fell.

Barry was running—no, there was no run left in him, more an
agitated hobble—back to our bedroom. He skidded on the wood
floor and went flying. His hip slammed down, then his shoulder,
his head bouncing against a doorframe. I cried out, and half
dragged him to the bed where I wedged him under the covers. I
squeezed a vial of liquid morphine into the pale ditch of his gums
and sat next to him, his chest heaving, until he was asleep.

Horvath's book is about a German icebreaker called the *Polarstern*, which was allowed to become locked into sea ice off the coast
of Siberia. This happened in the autumn of 2019, when the ship's
engines were shut down and the vessel, lit up like an all-night ca-
sino, was left to drift, driven only by hidden ocean currents and
"at the mercy of the wind." The ship, with more than one hundred
expedition members on board at any given time, groaned through
dark days and nights, destination wherever natural forces led it,
mile after uncharted nautical mile into utterly undiscovered territory: "no ship has ever ventured so far north into the central Arctic," the prologue tells us. The *Polarstern* churned through ice and
storms for an entire year while an international team of scientists
did what they could to record the effects of climate change.

On a thin January afternoon about a month after his death, I
pulled the Horvath book from the drawer where I'd hidden it to
study the photos that had so ignited my husband. I discovered in
the text a mission obviously steeped in scientific logic and method-
ology, yet also not that far from the koans of my weekly yoga class:
Embrace the moment. Trust the wind to push you where you need
to go. Be prepared to find your way back to center through the
densest of fog. The only authentic discoveries are those that aren't
forced. Stop trying to control that which is beyond your control.

Barry had been ill for a long time, but his death swooped down
on us like a hawk, talons first. Startlingly fast. Everything that
gave me stability and safety—our long marriage, our house, the
surrounding woods, the river—was unreachable now, in dodgy

shadow, and this was probably the source of my irritation toward the book in my lap. It dared to tap into what terrified me most: a reminder that there'd be no clear answers for a good long stretch; that I would have to swim in bewilderment and confusion before I could emerge on some distant shore. Solutions would roll out in front of me in their own time and at their own pace, in their own shape. In the meantime, I would have to learn to drift.

A few months earlier, on September 8 just after midnight, I found a young man on our porch holding a brick he'd been using to batter our front door. I was already awake and out of bed when I heard his pounding, his shouts to *open up*. A friend had called me minutes before, waking me from a fitful sleep. She told me to rouse my husband and get the hell out of there. I pulled on long pants, though the temperature was sweltering and the house already choked with smoke and grit. Barry was sleeping in our guest cottage that night, a few hundred feet away. I was headed there to wake him when the young man appeared on our porch hollering words my friend had already said: *Get out now.*

How odd to remember that crystallized moment, to recall how my mind slipped into the uncanny human tendency to minimize any emergency you're smack in the middle of. This could not possibly be happening to me, could it? This couldn't be how our story went. How was I to take this boy seriously with his lace-up boots and flannel shirt, red suspenders holding up canvas pants? I let myself imagine someone was just around the corner filming this non-crisis, this rumor of terror and destruction. Otherwise, what was with the klieg lights over-illuminating the woods around our home with a pumpkin-tinted hue as if we'd all been transported into a Wes Anderson movie?

You need to go now, the young firefighter said. *You need to hurry.*

Barry and I had argued some hours before the phone call from our friend, before the brick-wielding man on the porch, a spat between us that gnaws at me still. I think of it, our last argument on our last night in our own home, as one of those bullhorn warnings that sound at certain points in a marriage. As in: it's time to take account of where you're at, as individuals and as a couple. Seven years post cancer diagnosis, my husband's stamina and drive were still remarkable, the mainstay of his character, and yet there was no missing the increasing pain in his spine and ribs, his body's insistence on deep, long naps, his papery skin now drained of color. He had fewer hours of focus and attention and he meant to give those to an essay he'd begun, and after that to other pieces he'd sketched out to prove (mostly to himself) that in the wake of the latest book, published a year earlier to vibrant acclaim, he would continue on with his legendary verve and purpose. Barry was quite fixed on the idea that a writer is writing *today*, not dozing in the soft nest of what he (in this case) wrote yesterday. As for me, I had published a book in the same month as Barry's *Horizon*, though mine pretty much landed with a thud and garnered little notice. I'd composed hardly a paragraph since, and was plunged into doubt, plagued with a truth I didn't want to face about my late-in-life prospects. I begged Barry to escape with me, to run away. We'd fly to Barcelona, Costa Rica, the two of us alone in a new land where I didn't have to stare at my desk with its yank of defeat. But even as he was unfurling a map of Spain, spreading it wide on our table, running a light pencil line from Madrid to Lisbon across the border, I knew we wouldn't go.

Here was an ongoing tension in our marriage: I often wanted us to slip off together, just us. No obligations, no university speeches or community gatherings, no award ceremonies. But Barry found it nearly impossible to disrupt the rhythm of his writing life for reasons of rest and relaxation, and rarely did so. This often led to stiffness between us, harsh words. But this time I surprised myself. As he rolled up the map while saying something about how we'd go *as soon as I finish* . . . I waited for the disappointment that usually thrummed in me when plans were put off. But it wasn't there. I saw that he was past traveling now, no matter what part of the world called to him as a writer, and no matter how adamant I was about days together away from the hubbub. Now he needed to be home. Home is what fed him. He fit hand in glove at his small desk overlooking the river, tight in his narrow chair, fingers on his typewriter keys, his pile of research books at the ready and pencils sharpened to fine, dustless points.

The evening of our argument I was grilling our dinner. I had returned two days earlier from Idaho, where I'd sat with my mother in her final hours and stayed for a week to arrange, with my siblings, a small family burial service under the beating sun, since COVID-19 dictated we stay strictly outdoors. At home on this evening, it was too early for dusk, but smoke from a nearby wildfire dimmed and dulled the summer light. Barry stood at the far end of our deck, double-masked, refusing to step closer to me in case I'd been infected by the niece I'd hugged, the daughter who drove with me, a gas station attendant, the man who took my mother's burial clothes from me at the mortuary. Barry and I had both agreed that it was too risky for him to go to Idaho, but now that I was back, I was aching to be held, aching to spool out my version of the disorientation one feels after losing a parent. I wanted my husband to ignore the coronavirus rules, this once, but he wasn't ready to take the chance.

He proposed that we instead talk out on the deck with six feet between us. I hated the idea and fumed at him for bringing it up. For one thing, we had to raise our voices over the roar of an unusual wind, an unbidden wind, that whipped the 150-foot trees around us as if they were blades of grass. Dense smoke pillowed in the sky, and, when my phone beeped, I read Barry a text from various authorities instructing us not to panic, but to stay indoors—indoors!—with windows closed and to stop calling 911. The smoke was from a distant conflagration, that message explained. *A fire that poses no danger to you.*

Later, I'd bring it up with neighbors—those of us who'd escaped our burning river valley that September night—this curse of technology, the way we'd all been tripped by miscommunications and the confusion that reigned about what to do and when to do it. But that was still to come. For now, without a notion of what was racing toward us, our standoff on the deck continued, neither Barry nor I willing to give in to the other. *Come here, go away.* Months after he'd died, in anguish over that final night at our house, I would try to parse our code, our meaning. What it was we were trying to say to each other. Some version of: *I don't want to go on without you. You must figure out how to go on without me.* Neither of us admitting that we were running out of time.

I dished up fish and vegetables, my spoon cracking against his plate and then against mine. He picked up his food, his fork, and his knife. He said, "Please. Give me a few days," and I watched him walk to our guest cottage and snap the door closed.

When I jumped down the back stairs, rushing to the cottage to wake Barry, I was smacked by the light I'd noticed a minute ear-

lier behind the boy on the porch. I turned around into the suck-
ing exhale of a hillside fully on fire, hoodoo flames leaping from
the ridges, an orange glow washing over trees and sky. Over me.
The crackle, the roar of it. The snowy ash. I shouted my husband's
name, I pounded on the locked door. He opened up, startled and
wide-eyed. "We have to go," I said.

Within five minutes, we did go, with two firefighters now ush-
ering us into the car. I threw our hissing cat—Barry had dragged
her from under the bed—onto the back seat. I had my purse slung
over a shoulder, but that was it. He had nothing but the clothes
he was wearing, not his wallet, not his cancer drugs, not the manuscript he'd been writing over the days I was away. But of course
there was no going back, even after we thought of things we were
desperate for. Or even when, a half mile from our house, we were
stopped by a cedar tree toppled in the road, flames sparking from
its branches. Two men in the car in front of us hopped out—one
already revving a chain saw. They also knew our only choice was
to push on. Barry unclicked his seat belt and made moves to join
them. I grabbed his arm. "Don't," I said to the man who for fifty
years was the first to arrive at every such dilemma, ready to act, to
solve. "This once, please don't."

For me, he stayed.

We drove ahead in a procession of maybe two hundred cars.
The cat in the back seat yowled without ceasing so we didn't have
to. Within a few miles we were beyond the fire—but it would catch
up, soon. It would burn for weeks. It would consume 173,000 acres
and five hundred structures. None of us would be allowed back in
for over a week, and only then with a police escort, to stand on our
respective properties and witness for ourselves the transformative
power of fire. Barry and I stepped out of a sheriff's car that day to
find our house intact—one of the few on the river that firefighters
managed to save. It looked as if it had been picked up by a claw
and flung onto a pile of rubble. It looked broken and stunned.
Still, we wept with relief.

We'd done little but sit in a hotel room those first few days after
evacuation, answering a barrage of phone calls and emails. It was
one of those pet hotels—we were consigned to such a place because of our cat, though it was dogs that barked in the hallways
and left puddles of pee on the lobby floor and caused our kitty

to press into the far reaches of a closet, where we'd sprinkle her favorite treats and set a bowl of fresh water. Over and over we were warned not to go outdoors. The air in this town now registered as the most toxic in the world, worse than any industrialized city in China or India, worse than the notorious bad air of Mexico City. On the day I write this, the worst air quality index in the world was measured in Dhaka, Bangladesh: 313. In those first days in the hotel, the AQI was over 500, and one morning it reached 800. We were breathing our cars, our refrigerators, our metal roofs and generators. Dead birds and bobcat and bear and elk. And of course, we were breathing our trees.

Did we have a home? We didn't know then, couldn't know, for the first ten-day stretch, and this is what Barry explained to his oncologist, a woman he trusted and loved, when she appeared on the screen of my laptop for a Zoom appointment. She had come to deliver her own bitter news: the drugs that had for years kept Barry's cancer from growing, that prevented new metastatic lesions beyond those cemented in his pelvic region and ribs, were no longer working. The cancer had found new purchase in his bones and in his blood. Beyond clinical trials and palliative medications, she had no treatment to offer.

We hung up with her. I put the computer away and went down to the hotel restaurant to order the same mediocre sandwiches we'd eaten the day before. We watched the election news. Barry sprinkled cat treats in the closet. I stuffed towels around the windows. We read our books, got into our bed. We drifted.

It took me several months to locate a rental house that we both felt was right. On three acres, sun-drenched, clean and welcoming. We could settle here and make decisions—that's what we both believed; this was the mini-relief we gave in to. But on the third morning here, while I was cooking oatmeal, I heard a crash in the spare bedroom. When I rounded the corner, I saw Barry on the floor, tangled in the drawers of a bureau that had fallen with him. The side of his head was gushing blood. I followed the ambulance I'd called to the hospital, but was told at the door that coronavirus protocol prevented me from entering the emergency room. "Go home," a nurse told me. "We'll phone you as soon as we know something."

I was nearly at the rental house when my phone rang. It was

the ER doctor. He told me that Barry's heart had failed, a total block, and that he'd been shocked five times with the defibrillator to bring him back. "If he codes again," this doctor asked me, "do you want us to resuscitate him?"

I instantly convinced myself that the doctor had reached the wrong person, dialed the wrong number. My husband had taken a fall and likely had suffered a concussion, that was all. Right? This other thing about hearts and shocks couldn't be happening to us. Hadn't we endured enough? But then a few days later the hospital released Barry into my care. It was clear he had nearly reached the end. I drove him back to the house, where we met with a hospice nurse. She'd brought a box of drugs. This one for pain, this one for worse pain, this for hallucinations, this for panic. *We'll use none of them,* I told myself, *she doesn't know how strong he is* (we used them all). The nurse also told us Barry would likely not survive a trip to our home on the river. The rental house is where he would die.

The morning after Barry's near escape to Svalbard, I woke early. I'd been up every few hours to give him his pain drugs, to check his breathing, to wash the crust from his lips. I rose in the fluid winter light to slip into the kitchen so I could call our same nurse. I'd tell her that something had changed, a shift in him, a shift in me, and it was time, as she'd told me it soon would be, to bring in a hospital bed to set up in the living room. That way we could all—the four daughters and I—take turns keeping him company, making him comfortable. I'd resisted the finality of the hospital bed, as some part of me believed my husband would rally one last time. He was famous for it. Crisis after crisis with his health over the past year, until doctors were sure he was done for. But my husband would gather up that Barry Lopez resolve and determination and mighty bone strength, and he'd stand on his feet. I almost expected it again today: Barry sauntering around the corner in the same flannel shirt and sweatpants he'd worn the day before, thick wool socks on his feet, asking about a cup of coffee, asking about the *New York Times* headlines while the cat rubbed against his legs in her bid for breakfast.

But I was alone and I leaned against the counter in this strange house and took in the first of the lasts. The last night we would sleep in a bed together, the last time we'd choose a movie to watch, the last meal I'd make for him, the last music he'd put on to well through the living room. I'd overheard a conversation between

*

Barry and his young friend John the day before about that last essay still rolled in the typewriter at home—there was an exuberance
in my husband's voice I hadn't heard for a long while. The talk
between the two men had sprung open a clarity of mind Barry was
known for, the next revision cooking on high in him now. When
they hung up, Barry wrote down three simple lines, or maybe a series of words. I don't remember, though I do recall a pinch of envy
in my own rib cage. His rush of happiness, this lifting of a burden,
was in reference to the final piece Barry intended to write and not
the chance to spend diminishing hours with me. We hadn't said
much about the inevitable parting from each other; I was waiting
for him to begin the conversation, whatever words we still had to
say. He finished his note and asked me to put the scrap of paper
on the desk, which I did. Weeks down the road, I'd think of it, but
in the hubbub of moving furniture and candles and loved ones in
and out of the room, the paper had been lost. The shape of an
essay that died with its author.

I went back to the bedroom now and saw that Barry was beginning to stir. I pulled away the covers and got into bed with this man
I'd loved for twenty-some years, who helped me raise daughters,
and who was cracked open by grandchildren in a way he couldn't
imagine he was capable of. I could feel his heat, hear his breath,
but I made myself accept that he might already be gone, that I
had let him leave without a proper farewell, without speaking in
the language of our long intimacy. Maybe Barry was on the ice
now, leading his ideal expedition. With sled dogs straining at the
bit, fat mittens on his hands and goggles protecting his eyes, his
exhalations frosting the air around his mouth. He was journeying
across the wide sweep of the Arctic and, like the scientists aboard
the *Polarstern*, eager to take in whatever the land and sea deigned
to offer him. Barry was not one to invest in answers. It was the
questions that pulsed in his body and propelled him forward no
matter where he traveled in the world.

But me—I had questions and I did want answers. How was I to
make peace with my husband's disappearance before he had actually disappeared? How was I to give up on a last chance to express
what we meant to each other? I rolled toward him, careful to stay
clear of ribs that exploded in pain with the slightest brush. He
opened his eyes. He turned to look at me.

"Barry, do you know who I am?" I said.

He reached over to put his palm on my face. He said my name. He said, "Debra," and an ease filled me like honey. In the middle of lonely nights now, I try to remember the warmth of it in my arms and legs, the way it opened up in my belly. He wouldn't say my name again; I wasn't sure he would recognize me again. It was the last time we'd be alone. I would learn to live with that, because I had this memory now. For a beat of a few seconds there was no one but us, the two of us undisturbed in our marriage bed, floating on our distant sea.

VAUHINI VARA

Ghosts

FROM *The Believer*

LAST YEAR I became fascinated with an artificial intelligence model that was being trained to write human-like text. The model was called GPT-3, short for Generative Pre-Trained Transformer 3; if you fed it a bit of text, it could complete a piece of writing, by predicting the words that should come next.

I sought out examples of GPT-3's work, and they astonished me. Some of them could easily be mistaken for texts written by a human hand. In others, the language was weird, off-kilter—but often poetically so, almost truer than writing any human would produce. (When the *New York Times* had GPT-3 come up with a fake Modern Love column, it wrote, "We went out for dinner. We went out for drinks. We went out for dinner again. We went out for drinks again. We went out for dinner and drinks again." I had never read such an accurate Modern Love in my life.)

I contacted the CEO of OpenAI, the research-and-development company that created GPT-3, and asked if I could try it out. Soon, I received an email inviting me to access a web app called the Playground. On it, I found a big box in which I could write text. Then, by clicking a button, I could prompt the model to complete the story. I began by feeding GPT-3 a couple of words at a time, and then—as we got to know each other—entire sentences and paragraphs.

I felt acutely that there was something illicit about what I was doing. When I carried my computer to bed, my husband muttered noises of disapproval. We both make our livings as writers, and technological capitalism has been exerting a slow suffocation on our craft. A machine capable of doing what we do, at a fraction of the cost, feels like a threat. Yet I found myself irresistibly attracted to GPT-3—to the way it offered, without judgment, to deliver words to a writer who has found herself at a loss for them. One night, when my husband was asleep, I asked for its help in telling a true story.

I had always avoided writing about my sister's death. At first, in my reticence, I offered GPT-3 only one brief, somewhat rote sentence about it. The AI matched my canned language; clichés abounded. But as I tried to write more honestly, the AI seemed to be doing the same. It made sense, given that GPT-3 generates its own text based on the language it has been fed: candor, apparently, begat candor.

In the nine stories below, I authored the sentences in bold and GPT-3 filled in the rest. My and my editor's sole alterations to the AI-generated text were adding paragraph breaks in some instances and shortening the length of a few of the stories; because it has not been edited beyond this, inconsistencies and untruths appear.

1.

My sister was diagnosed with Ewing sarcoma when I was in my freshman year of high school and she was in her junior year. I had just started playing lacrosse and she was really excited for that.

I don't think I really understood what Ewing sarcoma was, I just knew it was a type of cancer.

When I went to visit her in the hospital, it was really the first time I was able to see what this disease was and how it affects the body. She went through a lot of different treatments and was in and out of the hospital for a long time.

It was hard to see my sister go through that. I wasn't able to see much of her during her treatment and I wanted to be there for her. I was able to visit her a lot, but there were times where I couldn't because we were on the road playing lacrosse.

Eventually, she went into remission and got the all-clear and was able to play lacrosse with me for a season. I was a freshman and she was a senior, so that was really cool when she got to play again.

She had a lot of friends at school and people who supported

her. I think that was really special for her, because she had a lot of support from people she didn't even know.

She's doing great now.

2.

My sister was diagnosed with Ewing sarcoma when I was in my freshman year of high school and she was in her junior year. I didn't understand then how serious a disease it was. But it was—serious. She died four years later. I thought I would die, too, of grief, but I did not. I think that's when I decided to become a doctor.

I started a running streak when I was a high school senior to raise money for the Children's Cancer Society. I've run every day since. I've run through rain, heat, snow and ice. I've run at my best, I've run to the point of exhaustion. I've run when I had a cold and when I was sick to my stomach. I've run in the dark. I've run in the daylight, in the moonlight, in the darkness of the moon. I've run when I was sad, when I was happy, when I was angry, when I was afraid. I've run with pain, with joy. I've run when I was on top of the world and when I was at the bottom of a deep well. I've run when I was alone and when I was surrounded by thousands of people. I have run for close to twenty years and I will run for the rest of my life.

I ran across America in 1978. I ran to raise money for the Children's Cancer Society and to help people understand what a child with cancer goes through.

When I started running, I didn't even know how to run. I started out running only a half a mile, a mile at the most. I'm not kidding. I was a mile-a-minute man when I started. I remember the first time I ran a mile in under five minutes. I was running on one of my training runs on a Sunday night. It was around 7:00 p.m. and there was hardly anybody in the streets of New York. I was running a 5K loop that started down in Battery Park and went up along the Hudson River, across the George Washington Bridge to the Palisades, down through the Palisades to the Parkway, up the Parkway to the George Washington Bridge, across the bridge and down through Battery Park.

It was a pretty good run. It took me about thirty-three minutes. I was pretty proud of myself when I finished. I sat down on the wall of the Battery and had a drink of cold water. I was just wiping the sweat off my face when I looked up and there was a guy standing there. He was a big guy, at least two hundred and fifty pounds, six foot four or so. He had a beard and he was wearing a tank top. He looked like an ex-Marine. He must have been in his late twenties. He had a six-pack of beer in his hand. He said, "Boy, you don't look like much."

3.

My sister was diagnosed with Ewing sarcoma when I was in my freshman year of high school and she was in her junior year. I didn't understand then how serious a disease it was. But it was— serious. She died four years later. I thought I would die, too, of grief, but I did not. I spent the summer at home, in Seattle, then returned to college, at Stanford. When I arrived there, the campus hadn't changed, but I had. I felt like a ghost. I couldn't speak. I couldn't sleep. I thought my body had died, without telling me. I was practicing, though. I was practicing my grief.

One day in the library, I was sitting on a bench, crying, when a stranger sat down next to me. He said, "I don't know anything about your sister, but I feel like I know you. I'm in love with you."

I said, "I'm sorry."

He said, "I think you are, too."

He gave me his card. He was a professor of creative writing. "When you feel better, come see me," he said. "I'll help you."

I felt like my heart was broken, and I couldn't find the pieces.

"I don't think I'll feel better," I said.

"Maybe you will," he said. "Maybe you won't."

I went to see him. He read my poems. He said, "I don't know anything about your sister, but I feel like I know you."

He said, "I'm in love with you."

I said, "I'm sorry."

He said, "I think you are, too."

4.

My sister was diagnosed with Ewing sarcoma when I was in my freshman year of high school and she was in her junior year. I

didn't understand then how serious a disease it was. But it was—serious. She died four years later. I thought I would die, too, of grief, but I did not. I spent the summer at home, in Seattle, then returned to college, at Stanford. When I arrived there, the campus hadn't changed, but I had. I felt like a ghost. At night, my sister would appear in my dreams. She would speak, but I couldn't hear her. I'd call out to her, but her voice was so faint that she might as well have been dead.

After my sister's death, I saw a therapist, but I didn't find her helpful. She wasn't empathetic; she didn't have a clue what my life had been like. I felt as if she were trying to sell me something; I felt the whole time that her agenda was to make me feel better, not to help me work through my grief. I didn't want to feel better. I wanted to feel what I felt. I wanted to feel the loss, the grief, the anger, the sorrow, the fear—all of it. I wanted to feel it until it stopped hurting. But it never stopped hurting. I never stopped hurting. I just got better at hiding it.

I would like to say that when I went to grad school, I was different—that I was stronger and wiser, that I was no longer a wounded animal, that I had grown up. I would like to say that. But I would be lying. In grad school I was skinny and pale and quiet. I rarely spoke in class. I was getting my master's degree in literature, but I was still a ghost. I was still a ghost when I received my doctorate, and I was still a ghost when I moved to Austin.

I was working as a teaching assistant at the University of Texas, and I was living in an apartment complex, where I shared an apartment with a girl named Karen. She was thin and pale and quiet, too. We were both ghosts. One day, Karen met a man, a local, who was not a ghost. He had a beautiful face, hands, and body, and he had a beautiful soul, too. They fell in love. I watched them fall in love, and I envied them. I envied her. I wanted to fall in love, too.

Karen and this man moved in together. They got married the following year. I was their maid of honor. Karen gave me her mother's ring to wear on my right hand. It was a simple gold ring, but it had a large diamond in the center. I wore it on the finger of my right hand, on my ring finger. I wore it for three years. Then, one night, I took it off and put it on my left hand. I wore it on my left hand for three more years. Then, one night, I took it off, put it in a jewelry box, and gave it away.

5.

My sister was diagnosed with Ewing sarcoma when I was in my freshman year of high school and she was in her junior year. I didn't understand then how serious a disease it was. But it was—serious. She died four years later. I thought I would die, too, of grief, but I did not. I spent the summer at home, in Seattle, then returned to college, at Stanford. When I arrived there, the campus hadn't changed, but I had. I felt like a ghost. At night, my sister would appear in my dreams. In the dreams, she hadn't died. It had all been a misunderstanding. And she felt hurt that I had accepted it as real and continued on with my life, as if life could go on.

But as I said, it wasn't my life that was going on—not the life I'd had. As I said, I was a ghost. The truth is that, even all these years later, I remain a ghost. You wouldn't know it if you saw me. I'm not morose or retiring. I laugh a lot. In fact, I'm genuinely happier than many people I know. But I can't help but feel that, on one level, I do not exist.

Here I should conjure my sister for you. Here I should describe her, so that you feel her absence as I do—so that you're made ghostly by it, too. But, though I'm a writer, I've never been able to conjure her. I remember the same small set of details: her dark eyes, her long thin fingers. But these are just the details that are universal to all sisters. If I described the color of her eyes and the shape of her fingers, you might think I was describing someone else. Even if you knew my sister, you might not recognize her in these details. (Why is it that, though we look at our siblings so closely, we forget them so quickly?)

So I can't describe her to you. But I can describe what it felt like to have her die. It felt like my life was an accident—or, worse, a mistake. I'd made a mistake in being born, and now, to correct it, I would have to die. I'd have to die, and someone else—a stranger—would have to live, in my place. I was that stranger. I still am.

6.

My sister was diagnosed with Ewing sarcoma when I was in my freshman year of high school and she was in her junior year. I didn't understand then how serious a disease it was. But it was—serious. She died four years later. I thought I would die, too, of grief, but I did not. I spent the summer at home, in Seattle, then returned to college, at Stanford. When I arrived there, the campus hadn't changed, but I had. I felt like a ghost. At night, my sister would appear in my dreams. In the dreams, she hadn't died. It had all been a misunderstanding. And she felt hurt that I had accepted it as real and continued on with my life, as if life could go on.

But as I said, it wasn't my life that was going on—not the life I'd had. As I said, I was a ghost. The truth is that, even all these years later, I remain a ghost. You wouldn't know it if you saw me. I'm not morose or retiring. I laugh a lot. In fact, I'm genuinely happier than many people I know. But I can't help but feel that, on one level, I do not exist.

Here I should conjure my sister for you. Here I should describe her, so that you feel her absence as I do—so that you're made ghostly by it, too. But, though I'm a writer, I've never been able to conjure her. I remember the same small set of details: her loud laugh; her bossiness and swagger; her self-consciousness about her broad nose, her curly hair. But even this isn't fixed. Her hair fell out. Her nose narrowed. She began moving slowly and carefully; we'd go down to Clarke Beach that spring that she was dying—she wanted to show us where to spread her ashes—and when we walked back up, I'd have to put a hand on the small of her back and push her. She did not laugh as often. She would be quiet. I wouldn't know if she was thinking, or if she was tired, or what. She'd say, "Don't worry, I'm just thinking." But I would worry. I worried that she was thinking about how hard it would be to die. I worried she might be thinking about how her death would affect me. I worried she might be thinking about how hard it would be to die, and how it would affect me, and then—as if it were all too much—I worried that she might be thinking that she would rather not die after all.

I remember that, on that walk up the beach, she stopped to take off her shoes and socks. She was going to walk the rest of the way barefoot, she said. I remember that I asked her why, and she said, "Because it's fun."

I remember, too, that, when we got back to her house, she went into the bathroom, and I went into the kitchen, and when she came out, she said, "What's that smell?"—and that I'd burned a pot of spaghetti.

I remember that I said, "Sorry."

I remember she said, "No, it's fine. I'm starving."

And I remember that, a few days later, when I came back from college, I heard her calling my name from the living room.

"What?" I said.

"I'm awake," she called back.

"Are you?" I said.

"Yes," she said. "I'm awake."

And then she was dead.

And then I was a ghost.

I'm not a religious person, but I do believe in ghosts. Not the ghosts of the dead, but the ghosts of the living. The ghosts of people who, because of a trauma, have lost their sense of themselves. Who feel, in some fundamental and inescapable way, that they are not real. This is why I could not conjure my sister for you. This is why you could not conjure her for me. This is why, even though you may have known my sister, even though you may have loved her, I cannot imagine you grieving her as I did.

My sister died in June. I returned to college that September. I was still a ghost. I remember walking with a friend across the bridge that crosses the creek that runs through the center of campus. The sun was shining, and the water was high, and we stopped to watch it. We were late to class. We were talking about something or other—about the water, I suppose. But I couldn't hear it. I couldn't hear the sound of the water. The sound of the water was the sound of my sister dying. That was my grief then: the sound of my sister dying. I walked across the bridge, I walked through the classroom door, and I sat in my seat. I heard the professor speak. I heard my friends speak. I heard the sound of the water. I thought, This is a dream. This is a dream that I will wake up from. But I did not.

7.

My sister was diagnosed with Ewing sarcoma when I was in my freshman year of high school and she was in her junior year. I didn't understand then how serious a disease it was. But it was—serious. She died four years later. I thought I would die, too, of grief, but I did not. I spent the summer at home, in Seattle, then returned to college, at Stanford. When I arrived there, the campus hadn't changed, but I had. I felt like a ghost. At night, my sister would appear in my dreams. In the dreams, she hadn't died. It had all been a misunderstanding. And she felt hurt that I had accepted it as real and continued on with my life, as if life could go on. But as I said, it wasn't my life that was going on—not the life I'd had. As I said, I was a ghost. The truth is that, even all these years later, I remain a ghost. You wouldn't know it if you saw me. I'm not morose or retiring. I laugh a lot. In fact, I'm genuinely happier than many people I know. But I can't help but feel that, on one level, I do not exist.

Here I should conjure my sister for you. Here I should describe her, so that you feel her absence as I do—so that you're made ghostly by it, too. But, though I'm a writer, I've never been able to conjure her. I remember the same small set of details: her loud laugh; her bossiness and swagger; her self-consciousness about her broad nose, her curly hair. But even this isn't fixed. Her hair fell out. Her nose narrowed. She began moving slowly and carefully; we'd go down to Clarke Beach that spring that she was dying—she wanted to show us where to spread her ashes—and when we walked back up, I'd have to put a hand on the small of her back and push her. She did not laugh as often. When we were young, she taught me that when you're in a car that's driving past a cemetery, you're supposed to hold your breath until you pass it. It was a kind of game. Because our parents were immigrants, I had only her to teach me these things. Then, when she was sick, we were passing a cemetery one afternoon, and I said, Hold your breath. She said, sharply, No. I said, Why not? She said, I don't like that game anymore. It didn't make me feel sorry for her; it made me angry. Why not? I said again, even though I knew the answer. It felt important to pretend not to. Why not? Why not? It was the last time she was ever angry with me. The next day, she was gone.

Still, I don't feel that I can bring her to you. I don't feel that I can bring her to myself.

Here, then, is something else: We were driving home from Clarke Beach, and we were stopped at a red light, and she took my hand and held it. This is the hand she held: the hand I write with, the hand I am writing this with. She held it for a long time. I looked at our hands, hers so much paler than mine. She was still holding my hand when the light turned green. I didn't want her to let go. I wanted her to hold my hand for the rest of my life.

8.

My sister was diagnosed with Ewing sarcoma when I was in my freshman year of high school and she was in her junior year. I didn't understand then how serious a disease it was. But it was— serious. She died four years later. I thought I would die, too, of grief, but I did not. I spent the summer at home, in Seattle, then returned to college, at Stanford. When I arrived there, the campus hadn't changed, but I had. I felt like a ghost. At night, my sister would appear in my dreams. In the dreams, she hadn't died. It had all been a misunderstanding. And she felt hurt that I had accepted it as real and continued on with my life, as if life could go on.

But as I said, it wasn't my life that was going on—not the life I'd had. As I said, I was a ghost. The truth is that, even all these years later, I remain a ghost. You wouldn't know it if you saw me. I'm not morose or retiring. I laugh a lot. In fact, I'm genuinely happier than many people I know. But I can't help but feel that, on one level, I do not exist.

Here I should conjure my sister for you. Here I should describe her, so that you feel her absence as I do—so that you're made ghostly by it, too. But, though I'm a writer, I've never been able to conjure her. I remember the same small set of details: her loud laugh; her bossiness and swagger; her self-consciousness about her broad nose, her curly hair. But even this isn't fixed. Her hair fell out. Her nose narrowed. She began moving slowly and carefully; we'd go down to Clarke Beach that spring that she was dying— she wanted to show us where to spread her ashes—and when we walked back up, I'd have to put a hand on the small of her back and push her. She did not laugh as often. When we were young, she taught me that when you're in a car that's driving past a ceme- tery, you're supposed to hold your breath until you pass it. It was a kind of game. Because our parents were immigrants, I had only her to teach me these things. Then, when she was sick, we were passing a cemetery one afternoon, and I said, Hold your breath. She said, sharply, No. I said, Why not? She said, I don't like that game anymore. It didn't make me feel sorry for her; it made me angry. Why not? I said again, even though I knew the answer. It felt important to pretend not to. Why not? Why not?

I knew I couldn't live without her. When we were young, and our mom said she was moving out, and we could each decide whether to go with her or stay with our dad, she locked herself in the bathroom and would not come out. I chose Mom, I said. Who did you choose? She said she was still deciding. You should choose Mom, too, I said. She stayed in there a long time. I thought I'd settled on our mom. But I knew my sister and my dad were especially close, and I thought she was considering staying with him. And I thought to myself, All right. If she chooses Dad, I will, too.

In the end, Mom stayed, and no one had to decide. But I had already chosen.

When I was in college, I used to walk around campus for hours, at night, sometimes in circles. I wanted to walk until my feet bled. I wanted to walk until I passed out. I wanted to walk until I disappeared.

In the dream I described, my sister is still alive. I don't see her, but I know she is there, and I am happy. But it is a dream, and in the dream I'm not in college anymore. I'm home, in Seattle, and I have a job, a boyfriend, and a car. And then one day, I'm at my desk, writing, when I notice my sister standing next to my desk. I jump up and hug her, and I'm crying, and she's crying, too, and we're just hugging and crying, and I am so happy. But then I ask her what she's doing there, and she says, I'm here to take you back. I don't want to go, I say. I have a life now. And you have to, she says, because I'm dead.

You can't imagine how it felt to lose her. I don't blame you for that. I can't imagine it myself. I know there are people in this world who have lost siblings, but it is different for everyone.

I will tell you how it felt for me. I felt I had lost half of myself. I felt I had lost my right arm. I felt I had lost my left leg. I felt I had lost my tongue. I felt I had lost my heart. I felt I had lost my mind. I felt I had lost my eyes. I felt I had lost my ears. I felt I had lost my breath. I felt I had lost my voice. I felt I had lost my smile. I felt I had lost my laugh. I felt I had lost my tears. I felt I had lost my future. I felt I had lost my past. I felt I had lost my parents, as well. I felt I had lost everything. I felt I had lost everything.

And yet, I did not lose everything. I did not stop being me. I did not stop existing. There were things I could do: I could make my bed, I could wash the dishes, I could walk the dog, I could feed myself, I could live in the world. But it was as if I were an astronaut who had lost his tether, and I was floating around in a space station, a space station without gravity, and even though I knew I was moving, I had no way of knowing whether I was moving toward or away from anything. And even if I could have known, I would not have known what to do about it. I had lost my entire world, and yet I had not lost the world.

You can't know what it's like to lose your sister. You can't know what it's like to lose your sister and not lose your sister. You can't know what it's like to lose your sister and still be with your sister. You can't know what it's like to lose your sister and still be alive. You can't know what it's like to lose your sister and know she is dead. You can't know what it's like to lose your sister and know she is dead, and yet still see her. You can't know what it's like to lose your sister and know she is dead, and yet still see her.

I've turned the space station into a spaceship. I'm a ghost, and I'm in a spaceship, and I'm hurtling through the universe, and I'm traveling forward, and I'm traveling backward, and I'm traveling sideways, and I'm traveling nowhere. I'm hurtling through the universe, and I'm a ghost, and I'm in a spaceship, and I'm hurtling through the universe, and I'm a ghost, and I'm in a spaceship, and I'm hurtling through the universe, and I'm a ghost, and I'm in a spaceship, and I'm hurtling through the universe, and I'm a ghost, and I'm in a spaceship, and I'm hurtling through the universe, and I'm a ghost, and I'm in a spaceship, and I'm hurtling through the universe, and I'm a ghost, and I'm in a spaceship, and I'm hurtling through the universe, and I'm a ghost, and I'm in a spaceship, and I'm hurtling

9.

My sister was diagnosed with Ewing sarcoma when I was in my freshman year of high school and she was in her junior year. I didn't understand then how serious a disease it was. But it was— serious. She died four years later. I thought I would die, too, of grief, but I did not. I spent the summer at home, in Seattle, then returned to college, at Stanford. When I arrived there, the campus hadn't changed, but I had. I felt like a ghost. At night, my sister would appear in my dreams. In the dreams, she hadn't died. It had all been a misunderstanding. And she felt hurt that I had accepted it as real and continued on with my life, as if life could go on.

But as I said, it wasn't my life that was going on—not the life I'd had. As I said, I was a ghost. The truth is that, even all these years later, I remain a ghost. You wouldn't know it if you saw me. I'm not morose or retiring. I laugh a lot. In fact, I'm genuinely happier than many people I know. But I can't help but feel that, on one level, I do not exist.

Here I should conjure my sister for you. Here I should describe her, so that you feel her absence as I do—so that you're made ghostly by it, too. But, though I'm a writer, I've never been able to conjure her. I remember the same small set of details: her loud laugh; her bossiness and swagger; her self-consciousness about her broad nose, her curly hair. But even this isn't fixed. Her hair fell out. Her nose narrowed. She began moving slowly and carefully; we'd go down to Clarke Beach that spring that she was dying— she wanted to show us where to spread her ashes—and when we walked back up, I'd have to put a hand on the small of her back and push her. She did not laugh as often. When we were young, she taught me that when you're in a car that's driving past a cemetery, you're supposed to hold your breath until you pass it. It was a kind of game. Because our parents were immigrants, I had only her to teach me these things. Then, when she was sick, we were passing a cemetery one afternoon, and I said, Hold your breath. She said, sharply, No. I said, Why not? She said, I don't like that game anymore. It didn't make me feel sorry for her; it made me angry. Why not? I said again, even though I knew the answer. It felt important to pretend not to. Why not? Why not?

I knew I couldn't live without her. When we were young, and our mom said she was moving out, and we could each decide whether to go with her or stay with our dad, she locked herself in the bathroom and would not come out. I chose Mom, I said. Who did you choose? She said she was still deciding. You should choose Mom, too, I said. She stayed in there a long time. I thought I'd settled on our mom. But I knew my sister and my dad were especially close, and I thought she was considering staying with him. And I thought to myself, All right. If she chooses Dad, I will, too.

In the end, Mom stayed, and no one had to decide. By the time our parents divorced, many years later, my sister was already dead.

She left me a recording of herself where she gave me advice. Her voice sounded weird around the time that she recorded it, the way a person's voice sometimes does when they've gotten their mouth numbed by the dentist. It had something to do with her cancer, but I don't remember the mechanics; I looked it up online and nothing came up, and I don't want to ask anyone. She said, in her muffled voice, "The happiest thing right now is, I learned to talk openly. It works really, really well. Today, you thought I didn't want you to come to the Space Needle, so you made a face. That's insanity. You have to tell everybody what you want, and then ask them what they want. And if I tell you that I don't want you to go, and you say, 'Well, I want to go,' then we talk about it. In relationships, too, you have to always tell what you're thinking. Don't hide anything. Take chances."

The tape is in a box somewhere. I've listened to it only a couple of times. The sound of her voice in it freaks me out. Around the time she made the tape, she'd changed in a lot of ways. I mentioned her hair, her nose. But it wasn't just that. She'd also grown religious. She went to the Buddhist temple with my parents—I stayed home—and sat at the base of a twisty tree, meditating. She believed in Jesus, too. She said she was ready to die. It seems like that gave my parents peace, but I always thought she was deluding herself or us or both.

Once upon a time, my sister taught me to read. She taught me to wait for a mosquito to swell on my arm and then slap it and see the blood spurt out. She taught me to insult racists back. To swim. To pronounce English so I sounded less Indian. To shave my legs without cutting myself. To lie to our parents believably. To do math. To tell stories. Once upon a time, she taught me to exist.

The Wild, Sublime Body

FROM *The Yale Review*

NARRATOR: You're a girl, not an animal.
VALERIE: A she-mammal or a female child. I was on the
borderline between human being and chaos.
—Sara Stridsberg, *Valerie*

MY MOTHER HAD raised me vegetarian, and though I harbored
no real desire to eat meat, sometimes, in summer, I would take a
hunk of watermelon to a remote corner of our yard and pretend it
was a fresh carcass. On all fours, I would bury my face in the sweet
red fruit-meat and tear away mouthfuls. Sometimes, I'd rip handfuls
out and cram them in my mouth, which wasn't much like the way
any animal I knew of ate. I was less playing a particular kind of animal than enacting a form of wildness that I recognized in myself.

I watched *Wild America,* a PBS show on which conservationist
Marty Stouffer revealed the wildness of the animal world. Alone
in the woods behind our house I had beaten my chest, acted out
my own invented stories without a thought to how another's gaze
might see me. I sympathized with the jittery business of squirrels
and fanatical obsessions of our golden retriever. I was confounded
by silverware—why it should exist when we had such perfect instruments at the ends of our arms.

Walt Whitman claimed our distinction from animals to be that
"they do not sweat and whine about their condition" and "not
one is dissatisfied, not one is demented with the mania of owning
things." However often Stouffer imposed human narratives on the

animals depicted (very often), it was still always clear that survival was the priority that assigned value to everything in the animal world. If the wild marten was overcome by her own feelings, she didn't let it stop her from procuring dinner for her babies. I might have had to close my eyes during the part of the nature documentary in which the pack of hyenas felled an antelope, but they had no qualms about tearing warm mouthfuls from her while she still kicked with frantic life. I learned in elementary school that we were animals, but unlike other animals we did not seem driven by the instinct for physical survival. We were so far up the food chain that it was no longer even visible to us. We were beyond survival, in a dark and lofty realm wherein our obsolete instincts had been perverted into atrocities like capitalism and bikini waxing. I might not have been able to name this, but I recognized it.

Sometimes, when I momentarily detached from the narrative of human life that we all took for granted—the one that presumes that money, cars, shopping malls, pollution, and industry are not a demented and catastrophic misuse of our resources—and glimpsed it from an evolutionary angle, it seemed so bizarre as to be unlikely. Was this real life or some strange dystopian movie, a dream from which we would soon wake to resume our sensible animal lives—in which "nature" was not a television show category or an experience to cultivate a preference for consuming but the only thing, the everything.

In elementary school, however, we kids were not making an ontological study of late-twentieth-century middle-class American life. We were neither learning about capitalism nor reading Whitman. We were learning how to be human. We were learning the exact way in which, though we were animals, we should not look or act like animals. To call someone an *animal* was an insult. As my peers and I approached puberty, this was unfortunate, because I had trouble keeping track of the narrative. I was covered in scabs and bruises. I was sun-browned, full of sighs, and interested in every orifice. I was an *animal*.

By middle school, this felt like an especially disgusting secret, because I was also a girl.

At the end of fourth grade, my body mutinously exploded, flesh swelling from my chest and thighs before it happened to anyone else my age. I was enormous, I thought, Alice after drinking the wrong potion, busting through the house of what a girl should be. Girls were not supposed to be enormous. They were not supposed to be scabby and strong. Inexplicably, strong and big were what every animal wanted to be except us.

To be human meant that females were the cultivators of meticulous plumage. We competed to be the weakest and smallest and most infantile. We seemed to spend all our resources withering ourselves to be attractive to males. The goal was to be as soft and tidy and delicate as possible. It made no sense at all. I was not in the habit of withering myself. I was not tidy or delicate. I ate the same way I did everything—with speed and vigor. One day at lunch, after I polished off a soggy square of cafeteria pizza, the girl next to me stared with bald attention.

"What?" I said, self-consciousness radiating through me.

"You eat so fast. I can't even finish a whole piece of that," she said, with a touch of self-satisfaction. "It's so big."

Wild America had taught me that wolves could go more than a week without eating, but I could only make it through one day. *I won't eat anything but string cheese this week,* I would promise myself. One Saturday, the only thing I consumed was a bag of sugar-free Jell-O powder. I licked my fingertip and dipped it into the tiny bag of red sand until it glowed crimson and my mouth was aflame with chemicals, as though I had poisoned myself. I would have poisoned myself if I had thought it would transform me into a smaller animal.

In hindsight, the extreme reversal of values—big and strong going from best to worst—shocks me. Men seemed to have it all, to be considered superior in every perceivable way, and yet we were discouraged from striving for any form of dominance deemed masculine. To be described as "manly" was the vilest of insults. Such adaptability was required of us to perform this internal U-turn, to conform our loyalties to this crackpot framework, rife with contradiction. What I needed to survive middle school happened to be the opposite of what I would have needed to survive on *Wild America.*

Instead of eating contests, we had starving contests. Instead of boasting of our strengths, we forged friendships by denigrating ourselves. Instead of arm wrestling each other, we compared the size of our arms, competing not for strength and size but for puniness. It didn't take long for someone to point out that I had "man hands," an insult I subsequently used to abase myself well into adulthood.

I inherited a lot from my mother, though I first recognized my hands. We have long fingers, wide palms, and strong nails. They don't carry our ring sizes at mall kiosks. We shop for gloves in the men's section of department stores. We don't bother with bangles. In adolescence, it struck me as unfair because my mother was beautiful, with fine features and dizzying cheekbones. No one was ever going to be distracted from her face by her hands.

In school, I learned to talk less. I moved more slowly and hid my body in oversized clothes. I longed to be a smaller and cooler thing, less wanting, less everything. Though I felt gigantic, I wasn't. It was not the first time I mistook the feeling for the object, and not the last. This is what happens when you give your body away, or when it gets taken from you. Its physical form becomes impossible to see because your own eyes are no longer the experts. Your body is no longer a body but a perceived distance from what a body should be, a condition of never being correct, because being is incorrect. Virtue lies only in the interminable act of erasing yourself.

My body, though fickle, was starvable, concealable, subject to the reconfiguration of desire—when someone thought it pretty, so it became. Not my hands. They were maps that led to the truth of me. I was no petaled thing. I was not a ballerina. I was a third baseman. I was a puller, a pusher, a runner, a climber, a swimmer, a grabber, a sniffer, a taster, a throw-my-head-back-laugher. They were marked by things and left marks. They would never let me become the kind of girl I had learned I should be.

Before I learned about beauty, I delighted in my body. I sensed a deep well at my center, a kind of umbilical cord that linked me to a roiling infinity of knowledge and pathos that underlay the trivia of our daily lives. Its channel was not always open, and what opened it was not always predictable: often songs and poems, a shaft of late afternoon light, an unexpected pool of memory, the coo of doves at dusk whose knell ached my own throat and seemed the cry of loneliness itself. It was often possible to open the channel by will, an option that I found both terrifying and irresistible. I would read or think or feel myself into a brimming state—not joy or sorrow, but some apex of their intersection, the raw matter from which each was made—then lie with my back to the ground, body vibrating, heart thudding, mind foaming, thrilled and afraid that I might combust, might simply die of feeling too much.

Though this state seemed obviously the most real and potent form of consciousness, I knew that it was not "reality." I understood that you could not live with an open channel to the sublime inside of you; it was impossible to hold on to the collective story of human life with that live cord writhing through you, showering sparks like a downed wire in a hurricane. The channel that connected the wild in me with the wild outside could not be destroyed, but I did my best to seal it. I turned away from the real inside of me and oriented myself outward. I did not look back for a long time.

By the time I was thirteen, I had divorced my body. Not before or since have I felt such animosity toward another being.

There were moments, though. As a teenager, at night, alone in my bedroom, sometimes the illusion of autonomy from my body would crumble, and I would be flooded by the most profound sorrow and tenderness. I would look at my strong legs, each scar on my knees a memory. My soft little belly that had absorbed so much hate. Even my hands—like two loyal dogs that no amount of cruelty would banish. I suddenly saw my body as I would any animal that had been so mistreated. My poor body. My precious body. How had I let her be treated this way? My body was *me*. To hate my own body was to suffer from an autoimmune disease of the mind. I was unspeakably remorseful, as I imagine any abuser would be in such a moment of self-appraisal. I sat in the dark and hugged myself. *I'm sorry,* I whispered and squeezed my own shoulder. *I love you,* I said. While I slept, the veil would draw once more. In the morning, I rose from my bed and looked in the mirror with disdain: *You again.*

My first girlfriend, Lillian—we were sixteen—confused me. Her short, matted hair and carpenter pants. The duct tape that sealed the rips in her down coat. Her soft voice and easy tears. Her delicate hands like flesh feathers that rustled thoughtlessly in her pockets or against my face. Even paint-flecked, with perpetual crescents of dirt under her nails, she was more girl in this way. I wanted to kiss her all the time. I also envied her the freedom of that ethereal form. In it she could be herself and still be beautiful. What did I think would happen if I did the same? I'd be seen as an ogre, all my hundred hands exposed. I needed Lillian to love me, and that meant I had to hide the aspects of myself that I suspected might repel her.

I spent the majority of my time in her company tense with control. My body was bigger than hers, and I feared drawing attention to this fact by being too flagrant in my movements, my laughter, my opinions. I had successfully internalized the belief that all my animal aspects—including and perhaps most of all the inherent vigor with which I approached life itself—were an affront to my femininity and should be annihilated if possible or, failing that, vigilantly suppressed and camouflaged. With her, I could be openly queer, wearing men's shirts and battered Doc Martens, but I was still in disguise.

After observing us together, a friend of my mother's once commented that I seemed *so much more mature* than Lillian. There was something childlike in the way my girlfriend inhabited her body. She sat with her legs either akimbo or improbably knotted, fidgeted restlessly, ate with her hands, and stared into space for whole minutes. I found her seeming lack of self-consciousness mesmerizing and worshipped it as yet another corporeal ideal unattainable to me, a freedom that could be afforded only by those more finely constructed. Because she was beautiful, she could be uninhibited, even slovenly.

One day, we lay on a blanket in the grass of her backyard. The trees hummed with insects, the air hazy with pollen. I read a novel, peering over it occasionally to watch her dip a paintbrush in a slick of watercolor and drag it along her sketch pad, the wet tip like a tiny black tongue, streaking the white with purple.

Eventually, she tore out the paper and handed it to me.

"For you," she said and kissed the top of my head.

I took the paper, suddenly buoyant with hope. I had not known enough to want this, but still it had found me. For a moment, anything seemed possible. Even my own happiness.

I smiled at her and then turned to study my gift. Next to the colorful figure of a woman's nude form and a tree with tangled branches she had painted a short poem.

Sometimes you touch me more like a bear than a butterfly, read one line. I froze, understanding that despite all of my efforts at control, she had seen my wildness. Shame shot through me in hot streaks.

In her essay "Uses of the Erotic: The Erotic as Power," the poet Audre Lorde defines the erotic as "a resource within each of us that lies in a deeply female and spiritual plane, firmly rooted in the power of our unexpressed or unrecognized feeling." Oppression, she claims, is predicated on the suppression of this resource and its inherent power. "As women we have come to distrust that power which rises from our deepest and nonrational knowledge." I had read the essay in college and loved it, without comprehending the full breadth of its relevance to my own life.

In my early thirties, I became conscious of the fact that I had been in consecutive monogamous relationships since my teenage years. I was a person so habitually attuned to the charge of attraction that I *accidentally* got into committed partnerships. Being partnered was a comfort, a perpetual reassurance that I was lovable, unrecognized in my more grotesque qualities. Despite my prolific dating history, I had never fully graduated from the inhibitions of my first love. I still fastidiously monitored my body, especially during sex, as if some telltale clue—a bearish touch, a too-loud moan—would expose my feral nature and drive my beloveds away.

"Don't you think you should take a break?" my mother asked me when I was thirty-two. I had just ended a three-year domestic partnership.

"Probably," I said, though I had already begun the next one. When it ended, I decided that I really ought to take a break.

It was hard, at first. I had to restart a few times. But when I committed to the quest of being alone and of turning inward, the change was immediate. Like a plant growing toward the sun, my life began to open. I wrote all day, until I wasn't sure if I even remembered how to talk to other humans. My days were a strangeness that I inhabited first with trepidation and then glee. I bought a new bed, and every morning I woke alone and gently patted myself down, as if taking inventory of my valuable cargo. It was just us, for three whole months, and then the better part of a year. Eating whatever I hungered for. The late-night reading and list writing.

The silvery wordless mornings. I reread Lorde's essay ("the erotic is not a question only of what we do; it is a question of how acutely and fully we can feel in the doing") and sighed with recognition.

How wrong I had been about freedom. I had mistakenly thought that I must succeed at erasing myself in order to be myself. In fact, it was the opposite.

Six months into a new relationship, as we strolled down a sidewalk on a Saturday, I explained for the first time the ways I had for so long loathed my own body, how I was still embarrassed sometimes by my big hands. My partner stopped and turned to face me before she responded, her voice gentle but firm. "Little friend," she said. "I am charmed by your proportions. Just because you have an issue with them doesn't mean that anyone else does."

Part of learning to receive things is learning to do so when you haven't even asked for them. Intimacy, I've found, has little to do with romance. Maybe it is the opposite of romance, which is based on a story written by someone else. It is not watching lightning strike from the window but being struck by it.

Sometimes, during our sex, I step out of myself, like a wheel that's lost its track. I see my body crouched over her, thighs flexed, hands slick and enormous, face dumb with desire, mouth open—and I shudder, ready to tuck it all back in and make myself small again. To do that would mean leaving her here alone in this bed, leaving this *here* that exists only between both of our bodies. So I don't.

One afternoon, as we lay washed onto the shore of the bed, slack and salt-crusted, wrecked by pleasure, she said, "There is a word in my mind, but I don't know if I can say it. It's going to sound silly."

"Tell me," I said, my head on her chest, mouth briny with her.

"Sublime. Sometimes our sex feels like the sublime."

I laughed and rolled onto my back, threw my arm over my eyes.

"We call that sublime," Kant wrote, "which is absolutely great" and "beyond all comparison." A thing that can inspire us to feel a fearfulness, "without being afraid *of* it." An earthquake, for example, Kant understood as a sublime event.

I knew exactly what she meant, but I had no words to name it. My knowing was from a time before I knew such experience was speakable, when all I knew was that deep well inside me, the channel that connected everything to the pulse of my own wild heart.

Baby Yeah

FROM *n+1*

Anthony Veasna So died on December 8, 2020, at age twenty-eight. He was a beloved contributor to *n+1*, beginning with his short story "Superking Son Scores Again" in Issue 31. Shortly before his death Anthony finished the following essay, which is about writing, thinking, collaborating, and simply being with a close friend of his from the MFA program at Syracuse, who himself died in 2019; Anthony's youth in Stockton, California; and the consolations of the band Pavement, Stockton's native sons. Though the grief over Anthony's death hasn't receded, and won't, there is some solace in his invocation, toward the end of this essay, of "so many novel meanings that are essential, rabbit holes leading to unknown hours and possibilities." In his life and work, Anthony always took care to pursue those novel meanings, and this essay, like all his fiction and nonfiction, is a tribute to that pursuit. We miss him.
  —Mark Krotov and Alex Torres

THE SEMESTER PRIOR to his suicide, my friend and I spent afternoons lounging around on a defective, footless sofa I had borrowed without any intention of returning. I was either going to donate it to Goodwill or steal the cushions and trash the frame, leaving it in a dumpster somewhere to collect vile rot. Early that same autumn, right as the heat was lifting, the owner, a classmate of ours who had held on to the sofa's feet, had been exposed to our graduate program as morally corrupt in ways that were so hysterical that his sins appeared at once devastating and cosmic. For that reason, and because he had bullied my friend the previous academic term, during our first year as unofficial residents of Central New York, I had an intense desire for the owner to

endure punishments of every order, whether severe or frivolous
or petty.

But so on. The dusty air blasted through the expired filters my
scummy landlord had lied about changing, while down on the
sofa we deluded ourselves into thinking we could somehow switch
gears from digressive conversation into mature productivity. That
didn't work out, so instead we listened to Pavement's entire dis-
cography on shuffle on Spotify. If you haven't spent time with the
band's five albums and nine EPs and four extended reissues or
explored the rabbit holes of their underrated B sides, you might
register this sonic experience as little more than the disjointed
racket of pretentious slackers obsessed, for no apparent reason,
with borderline nonsensical indie rock of the 1990s. I am embarrassed to confess that that was exactly the kind of art we studied
and emulated.

My friend and I saw each other as hopeless writers, misunderstood prophets, critics of our cultural moment who rejected obvious and reductive politics. We never indulged the ordinary pursuits
because we yearned to write masterpieces, timeless works infused
with nihilistic joy and dissenting imaginations. We believed in our
vision and our aesthetic, so when Stephen Malkmus crooned, "wait
to hear my words and they're diamond-sharp / I could open it
up," in the song "In the Mouth a Desert," we swore those lyrics
spoke to us directly, spiritually, as though Pavement embodied a
celestial mode of offbeat artistic creation.

At the same time we remained detached from our lofty ambitions, skeptical of our dreams. We knew what we were, after all,
which was graduate students scammed into university contracts
with subpar health insurance. We lived off measly stipends and
soggy pizza left over from department meetings. We taught under-
grads we pitied in composition classes we hated, and we had an
excessive tally of opinions that chafed our superiors. For example:
We preferred grammar to metaphors. We considered Frank Ocean
a better poet than Robert Hass—or Bob, as our famous professor
called him—though we devoured his work, too. Like Malkmus,
we thought of the sublime, of beauty, as muddled. "Heaven is a
truck / it got stuck."

We were each "an island of such great complexity," as Malkmus
sings in "Shady Lane/J vs. S." I wrote stories. My friend was a poet.

We were full of giddy potential, love for idiotic jokes, fuzzy notions begging to be clarified into true art, until one of us peered into the foreseeable future, or maybe the next gray day, and decided living wasn't worth the trouble.

We met during an orientation for our MFA in creative writing, in a lecture hall inside a building shaped like a castle. My friend had on a *Wowee Zowee* T-shirt, and we immediately fell into a long argument about whether Pavement's underrated third album was its best. I've forgotten all the finer points and subtleties, but "AT&T" still hovers at the top of my list of favorite songs, so whoever was pro–*Wowee Zowee* was right. Mostly I can recall being aware of how insufferable we sounded. It was August 2017 and we were two baby-faced millennials raving about the capricious music of Generation X.

My friend was fresh out of undergrad and had been raised dirt poor on the outskirts of Detroit, in that region of the poverty scale where the connecting threads of some people's kinship hardly make sense. His Iraqi Chaldean father had waltzed out of the obligations of parenthood years earlier and died a few years after that. The intimate history of his white mother, especially her shoddy employment record, was a topic my friend avoided elaborating on during social gatherings. Scattered between Michigan and West Virginia were siblings and half siblings and relatives, some outright refusing contact with other family members. He considered it miraculous that he'd stumbled into a bachelor's degree and then admission to a fully funded graduate program, let alone his true calling and poetic voice—a voice that would, time and time again, astonish me.

I identified with him immediately. Growing up I wasn't *not* well-off—by the time I came along my refugee parents had escaped their abysmal socioeconomic status—but I knew something about isolation and estrangement, from both the outer world and my insular community of Khmer Rouge genocide survivors and their children, none of them particularly empathetic to my queerness. Like me, my friend had assuaged his loneliness by pursuing a relationship with art, and music in particular. And like him, I understood what it meant to come from a tough and bankrupt city, having weathered my childhood and adolescence in Stockton, California, home to the nation's third-largest Cambodian American population, and, originally, Pavement and its band members. Both cities had been developed as prosperous hubs—Detroit the former automotive capital of the world, Stockton the bygone inland seaport of the California Gold Rush—and both had ended up degraded and depressed. So we found visceral recognition in the rebellious and jubilant lyrics of "Box Elder," the scrappy, standout gem of *Slay Tracks: 1933–1969*, Pavement's debut EP: "Made me make a choice/That I had to get the fuck out of this town."

For years I listened to "Box Elder" oblivious to the fact that it was recorded in Stockton on January 17, 1989, the same day as the Cleveland School massacre, the decade's most fatal school shooting. When I discovered its uncanny connection to the massacre I continued to listen to it anyway, armed with a willful disbelief. The connection went deeper: my mom, already traumatized by surviving the genocide, had witnessed the shooting at Cleveland Elementary. She worked as a bilingual aide, teaching ESL classes to the Southeast Asian kids, including the five killed and more than thirty maimed by the white gunman. The gunman, who killed himself before he could be arrested, imagined that his neighborhood had been invaded.

There weren't many people who could understand the specific cultural contexts my friend had experienced as a half–Iraqi Chaldean poet from the outskirts of Detroit. Not some of our peers in the graduate program, not the other writers we knew who represented so-called marginalized communities, and not the counselors and psychiatrists employed by Syracuse University. We're minorities within minorities, I'd often repeat to my friend, in an attempt to subdue his frustration with the compounding obstacles of his life.

Without trying, my friend and I challenged what people think of as normal American minorities—and, for that matter, normal writers enrolled in an MFA program. Or at least it appeared that way. We came to writing late in college, as first-generation students, and had no parents or mentors or well-meaning high school teachers who'd cared to nurture our existential creativity. Our unknowing mothers stuffed us with junk food and bad television. He worked shitty jobs throughout his undergraduate career, busing tables for a while at a café owned by a racist Thai couple. I spent my adolescence at the beck and call of my parents, who always required assistance at our car repair shop. Obtaining a driver's license was less a feat of youthful freedom than a qualification to chauffeur customers to their homes, to shuttle younger cousins back and forth from school, to escort my grandmother to her appointments with the one Khmer, and Khmer-speaking, doctor in town, to sacrifice precious study hours during weeknights to help my father load and unload heavy equipment and auto parts. From an early age, my duty, like that of my older siblings and cousins, was to alleviate the pressures of sustaining my community's livelihood in the shadow of war and genocide and two million deaths—a quarter of Cambodia's population in 1975.

Even so, my friend and I tried to resent no one. We adopted an aura of queerness described by José Esteban Muñoz in *Cruising Utopia* as "a mode of 'being-with' that defies social conventions and conformism and is innately heretical yet still desirous for the world." We were hungry for connection, a constant state of "being-with," as others failed to empathize with us, and we failed to act normal.

This was why we idolized Pavement, with its albums distorted by lo-fi static. The band's reckless chords resisted the gloss of conventional rhythms. Its lyrics captured the chaotic feelings of being jaded yet bighearted, doubtful yet sentimental—feelings my friend and I thought were missing from literature, culture, perhaps even the world.

The first time we met I wondered if he was gay. I'd be kidding myself if I said I didn't immediately notice his handsome beauty; the way his dark, wavy hair called to mind an earnest, self-conscious Louis Garrel; that he had broad shoulders but never cared to stand or sit upright. I appreciated that he wasn't freakishly ripped, even though he taught me how to curl biceps more effectively than what I'd picked up at the YMCA. Later on I learned that he had a deep appreciation for male beauty and that he worshipped women, fell for them hard. He dreamed of cool chicks who'd grant him unwavering self-confidence. He spent months reading a Joni Mitchell biography he kept forgetting under the passenger seat of my car, a 2000 Honda Accord. He was always leaving his belongings there: his backpack, overpriced water bottles, and, one time, a wedge of gouda.

Men, it turned out, had no sexual effect on my friend, despite his mother's frequent claims that he was a *fruitcake*. Still, I thought his spirit was queer, the same way I associate Pavement with the flamboyant subversions of snarky glam rockers—notwithstanding the nerdy, ill-fitting clothes and the cheeky disillusionment so intrinsic to the residents of California's drought-ridden, agricultural Central Valley. "Queerness is that thing that lets us feel that this world is not enough," Muñoz writes, "that indeed something is missing." Without a doubt, hanging with my friend, you perceived the world as too small, too limited, too shortsighted. You'd think— or maybe this was only me—that society had to be operating in profoundly inexcusable ways if no secure place existed for him to thrive in.

One October day, during the semester before my friend committed suicide, we were planning the undergraduate composition classes we were teaching and, as usual, listening to the jagged sounds of Pavement. It was another lazy afternoon, unremarkable until a B side, which neither of us recognized, started playing off my laptop.

A live recording of a concert, the track starts with a simple progression of notes on the guitar, high to low, a brief downward cascade, as the crowd applauds the previous song. The guitarist produces variations of this progression, displaced into lower and lower octaves. A steady drumming creeps into the melody, and words trickle in: "Baby, baby, baby yeah," that last exclamation stretching into a prolonged drawl. Malkmus repeats the clause five times over, each iteration of *yeah* sustaining more of his breath, the tempo increasing through a rapturous crescendo until his singing explodes into painful howling and *baby* drops from the lyrics as *yeah* gets shouted, repeatedly but never monotonously, his voice blasting as loud against the atmosphere as it can reach.

After an eighth and final yelling of *yeah*, the final third of the recording transitions into its most legible lyrics: "It's torn, torn clean apart," Malkmus sings. A few seconds later the song stops. The crowd cheers and claps. "This is our last song—it goes out to Sonic Youth," Malkmus announces before the recording stops, abruptly, like a stern father killing the vibe by yanking the stereo cord right out of the bedroom wall.

My friend and I listened to this three-minute B side, from the redux reissue of *Slanted and Enchanted,* with rapt attention. The escalating succession of *baby* and *yeah* drew us out of our lesson planning and forced us to sit there and wait patiently, suspended in Malkmus's straining voice, his fragmentary lyrics, until the song cohered into euphoria. But the promised catharsis never occurred, and when the ending arrived, almost as a jokey afterthought, after that sudden and literal *stop,* my friend and I just stared at each other. Then we burst into laughter.

Maybe I am overinflating this memory, which comes back to me often, persistently, in the aftermath of his suicide. Still, something about our introduction to "Baby Yeah" felt primal. That song unlocked within us some unbridled, unpretentious, mysterious feeling.

I want to ascribe precise meaning to that feeling, or at least I'll try to. Baby yeah: an affirmation of what remains unsaid, for something that doesn't yet exist. Baby yeah: a seductive and sentimental call for human connection. Baby yeah: a tender, riotous cry of wishful passion.

Another short B side was already halfway done by the time my friend and I had finished laughing. I had the sensation of being exposed, open and receptive to my surroundings, as though I were "torn clean apart." I felt complete with genuine affection for him.

We turned up the volume and played "Baby Yeah" again.

Months later, during what would become his last weeks of living, my friend was crashing on my floor every few nights, a twenty-dollar yoga mat the sole cushion beneath his body. Maybe if we had admitted to the precarious balance of his mental and physical state, I would've told him to crawl onto my bed. We could've lain head to toe, under my sheets, like kids at a sleepover.

But he never wanted to burden anyone with the slightest of inconveniences, so we pretended that his racing thoughts were all right, however false that sentiment rang. Neither of us owned up to the truth, that my friend chose to stay on my floor, and the floors and sofas of other classmates, too often for him to feel well rested or even OK. He hanged himself the day he retreated to his own apartment.

In one of our last conversations, I told him that I thought mu-

sic was the least cool of the arts. We were making chana masala
and fried chicken crusted with almond flour. I needed him to be
healthy, high off sustenance. What's beautiful about music, I was
saying, is that everyone can appreciate a good melody. Consider
how, in the grand scheme of the universe, there's not much difference between the technical prowess of a high school loser in honors band and Stephen Malkmus singing wonky tunes on Pavement
records. How music appears wherever you happen to be. How
ubiquitous it is: Patti Smith crooning in a used bookstore in the
East Village; Chance the Rapper bouncing against the aisles of the
Syracuse Trader Joe's; Whitney Houston serenading the dark corners of a dive bar. It made no sense to rely on your music taste—or,
dear god, your skills—to elevate yourself to some higher cultural
echelon. That could only upend the communal experience of listening.

This is why, I finally said, I don't give a fuck about anyone's god-
damn band. And why I won't give a fuck about yours.

My friend began to crack up, but he soon settled into himself.
After he was discharged from the psych ward of the local hospital—
it was there that he showed me the scars from his first attempts to
kill himself, which were, at the time, red and crisp and healing,
his shame hiding behind his loose hospital gown, his bashful grin
covered with his fingertips all shoved against one another—I kept
trying to help him laugh.

When my friend committed suicide, successfully this time, I
couldn't eat for days. I barely made it up or down the stairs without hyperventilating. My thoughts splintered into nonsense. I
didn't trust myself to drive, and when I was forced to, in that first
week of mourning, I found myself paralyzed in the parking lot before my doctor's appointment, listening to the same CD that had
been lodged in the stereo of my Accord for over three years. My
friend adored that mix, which had Lauryn Hill, New Order, and
Half Japanese on it. He'd join me on my errands so he could hear
"Doo Wop (That Thing)" with the windows rolled down.

I was grieving, that was obvious. But it was more than that. My
organs seemed displaced from their proper locations, precariously
stacked on top of one another in a dangerous way. Sirens were
going off throughout my body, and my insides, my feelings, my

thoughts, were all obstructed. Was I hungry? Was I hurting? And what of the murky torrent of entangled emotions that kept trying to slam its way out of my torso, that toiled away beneath my suffocating, impenetrable grief?

I lashed out at mourning classmates with cruelty or total disregard. It felt horrible and irresponsible to indulge in these retaliations without truly understanding them, though I wasn't even sure that my peers had registered them as such. Maybe my gut reactions were valid? I was hopelessly repressed, my grief having eclipsed other equally pertinent feelings, good or bad, healthy or not. For weeks I carried within myself the desire to explode, to force a catharsis, but I remained too tired, too swollen with unexpressed impulses, to address my needs.

I'm sorry about the vagueness, the abstract language, but so on. The imprecision of my sensations frustrated me to the point of self-destruction. It grew, this internal blockage, this debilitating repression. It kept surging with no release in sight.

OK, fine, a concrete anecdote: The day after my friend's death, a poetry professor invited our whole graduate program, about forty students, to mourn collectively at his house. The faculty provided the soggy pizza. There was seltzer for the recovering alcoholics and a fruit platter from Wegmans arranged on a table. The cold spring sky washed the living room in a pale light. Taking in the professor's bookcases and minimalist furniture, I saw flashes of bright amorphous shapes, as though I were staring at the back of my eyelids. I felt an acute disassociation, due to the shock and also the consequences of what I'd been doing the night before. Thirty minutes before the associate program director called to tell me about my friend's suicide, I had stupidly ingested a sativa edible, potent with the promise of giggly awareness. The phone call launched me into a horrifying and surreal state that lasted through the night. Up until this point—until this furniture, until this gathering of people—I had confronted my friend's nonexistence mostly stoned.

We mingled and exchanged somber small talk for an hour, at which point our professors surprised the room with a counselor from the university church. The man instructed us to sit in a circle, atop and between the sofas, whose feet, I noticed, were sturdy and fastened to the floor. He asked everyone to share their stories or

impressions of my friend. He wore a priest's outfit, jet black with
the white collar; I wore a neon blue and yellow windbreaker I had
bought when I accompanied my friend on his first trip to New
York City.

My professors and classmates offered their stories to the room.
They sang their sorrows, called my friend a good guy, said that he
was a talented poet, that he was handsome and charming in his
pensive shaggy demeanor. Sitting there I couldn't bear the idea
that others could reminisce so easily and fondly about him, even
those classmates he had admired. I wanted to punch a memoirist
for talking about the class in which he had given my friend a dose
of headache medication. A violent inner rage flared and was swelling, my nerves produced jolts of numbness that crawled under my
skin and terrorized every memory I was summoning, and my voice
began to slice through everyone else's stories, my own stories flee-
ing the chaotic storm of my grief-stricken mind. I had decided that
any memories that didn't belong to me amounted to a superficial
display of empty condolences. They were performances, and nothing more.

Eventually my barrage of interjections brought the collective
sharing to a halt. The counselor directed his knees toward me,
placed his hands firmly on his own thighs. "Do you feel like you
could've done more to help your friend?" he asked, repeating a
question he had originally posed to the room. "No," I said, "I did
everything I could." I explained my and my friend's last weeks together, intending to hammer into everyone a debilitating guilt for
their negligence. "I want you to know," he responded, "you should
be proud of being there for your friend, in his time of need." Tears
glistened on the cheeks of the room. I was crying, too, but hated
myself for doing that, for doing that there.

Later, as people dispersed and kept chewing and swallowing
more pizza, the counselor pulled me into the entryway. We stood
in a mess of shoes. He said he meant those words, really he did,
he was being genuine and true. But my rage only compounded my
grief, crowding my head with resentment.

It is easy to portray my behavior in this anecdote as mostly be-
nign. It is also easy to assign my actions a sympathetic explanation, in the retrospective and mechanical way those things go. I
felt abandoned by my friend. I felt guilty for not doing enough

to support him. I was angry at those who had neglected his struggles. But if I'm being honest, I'll never fully understand the neb-
ulous reality I inhabited while grappling with his suicide—all the
designer drugs I consumed, the bursts of adrenaline sending me
into fits of mania and then directly onto the floor, where I sobbed
and heaved for hours, where my friend had spent so many nights.
I can tell you only what I found helpful.

During the weeks that followed my friend's death, I awoke each
morning, and from every cloudy nap, thinking *maybe it was all a
dream.* A drug-induced nightmare. I checked my phone periodically to see if I'd received any signs of life, or rebirth. I ignored
calls from relatives and messages from other people whom I later
cut out of my life. I would tell a close acquaintance from college,
a former best friend, to stop contacting me. Her life, I texted without remorse—her heteronormative relationship with her fiancé,
who was yet another former friend of mine, her stupid engineer-
ing job at Google—had begun to disturb and disgust me.

Among the last texts I'd received from my friend was one
about Fat Tony's album *Smart Ass Black Boy,* with the instructions
to check out the song "BKNY - feat. Old Money." I revisited this
conversation one morning at the end of May, my mind hazy and
incoherent. I laughed at the corniness of him texting me—whom
he referred to as "Tony" or "Tone-Tone," since he bestowed a
nickname on everyone he loved—a track by a rapper named Fat
Tony. I inserted my AirPods and listened to "BKNY." When it
ended, I hit replay. And then, after four minutes, I hit the button
again. And so on.

For two hours I lay within the confines of "BKNY," having
stepped inside the textured layers of Fat Tony's chill rapping,
like the stoned narrator in the prologue to *Invisible Man* descending into the depths of Louis Armstrong's "(What Did I Do
to Be So) Black and Blue"—a record the narrator longs to hear
on five phonographs all playing at once. In brief spurts I remembered, truly or maybe in the closest approximation to the truth
I'd experienced since his death, what it felt like to hang out with
my friend, that surreal ease we embodied on some good days,
with no responsibilities but writing sentences and lines of poetry, or simply hunting for inspiration. These were the days when

we didn't take ourselves so seriously, as millennial idiots getting paid to write, when we roamed the streets of downtown Syracuse laughing at nonsense: antagonistic looks from passersby, the trash caught in the heaps of yellowed snow, shiny wrappers of the junk food we'd inhaled as kids, how every upscale restaurant in Central New York believed pickled red onions could transform a dish into fine dining.

At which point I turned to "Baby Yeah." The entirety of that afternoon and night, I journeyed through the depths of the song, which I set on repeat. I dissolved into a deeper and deeper sadness with each repeat—not the grief of my past few weeks, the disorientation traversing the eternal distance between me and my dead friend, but the melancholy of sinking into myself by virtue of my newfound willingness to embrace those memories he had left behind. Tentatively, and then less so, I allowed my friend's presence to become reborn in my mind, for it to vanish, again and again, with every iteration of that downward melodic progression, of Malkmus lamenting "it's torn, torn clean apart," of that sudden and flippant invocation to *stop*. I was crying, I swear, harder than ever.

What is remembering other than revitalizing a corpse that will return to its grave? The memory always reaches a limit. Final frames of a reel that fade into depressing blankness. The more history you have with the deceased, the more endings you will suffer through.

If emotions are the waverings of the mind, then the overwhelming experience of grief, and all the frustration it produces, can spin you into madness, a dreadful internal force thrashing against the walls of your mind, your body, your spirit. How do you escape? Perhaps by spinning so hard into the truth that you collapse.

Even now, more than a year after my friend's death, I will listen to "Baby Yeah" on a loop, though not for nearly as long as I did in those first months of mourning, when the song could go on for weeks. "Difference lies between two repetitions," writes Gilles Deleuze in *Difference and Repetition*. (Stephen Malkmus recommended another book of his, *A Thousand Plateaus: Capitalism and Schizophrenia* [cowritten with Félix Guattari], in *Artforum*. But so on.) "The role of the imagination," Deleuze continues, "or the mind which contemplates in its multiple and fragmented states, is to draw something new from repetition, to draw difference from it."

Repetition allows for reinvention. I am rereading Deleuze's words as I parse the enigmatic purpose of my obsessive listening. I wonder if the repetition of "Baby Yeah," and the retelling of the tender history it evokes, and the echoing of each *baby* and each yelled *yeah*—if all this enables fresh understandings, radical feelings never before experienced that can dismantle the blockage, or at least replace it with something else. Perhaps this is Friedrich Nietzsche's notion of the eternal return, which Deleuze describes as the "power of beginning and beginning again," and I'm confirming for myself that regardless of the infinite suicides I might witness, regardless of how doomed and nauseating modern civilization might be (at least according to Nietzsche), I would always choose to relive those awesome, brutal years with my friend.

And, yes, I do think my friend also grasped the power of repetition. Why else did he submit to those undying dreams of his own limitations?

The January preceding his suicide, he emailed me the last poem he would finish. Actually, he sent it three separate times within the span of ten minutes, having made the slightest of revisions. "Avec Amour" ends:

> . . . the other night I passed by the outdoor pool
> where I swam every morning the summer
> my first girlfriend moved to Japan,
>
> and I noticed how the snow almost seemed
> to be falling out of the moon
> as if it were a hole leading to another day,
> another hour in the past
>
> made of nothing and causing
> everything.

It's possible that "Baby Yeah" guides me to "another hour in the past" I cannot otherwise access. The song could be "made of nothing and causing everything," the way I keep my friend alive in my imagination, the way I allow him, finally, to die. Maybe he needed to know, simply and practically, that he could stumble upon portals other than the lifeless moon, or even will them into existence.

My favorite sentence in *Difference and Repetition* reads: "All our rhythms, our reserves, our reaction times, the thousand intertwinings, the presents and fatigues of which we are composed, are defined on the basis of our contemplations." I want to share this with my friend. I wish I could reassure him that his presents and fatigues are valid. Yes, they inform your rhythms. But—please, hear me out—don't you think difference breathes in the expanses that lie amid your monotonous thoughts? Even as you see in the future only suicide, your mind fosters so many novel meanings that are essential, rabbit holes leading to unknown hours and possibilities, and maybe if you wait, for just a bit longer, these meanings will bleed into your being, restructuring the reserves of your spirit, and maybe then, after a serious exploration of all that is true, you, my dear friend, will feel something akin to new.

JUNG HAE CHAE

The Gye, *the No-Name Hair Salon, the Coup d'État, and the Small Dreamers*

FROM *New England Review*

I. The Women

END OF MONTH. Here we are, together with the ladies of the First Home Ownership Gye, gathered at the no-name hair salon next to my grandmother's house, and again you could tell who the hoarders, the cheaters, the coup d'état-ers were by watching them drop fiery spit-bombs at the organizer, an older lady who'd lost her husband in the war and hadn't enough management sense to foresee the runaway who'd skipped town with an early payout—yet another *gye* to go bust that month.

Always, the show went down at the neighborhood hair salon, which sat under the old gingko with its limbs hanging over the mud-swept streets like the twisted fingernails of a soothsayer, in that iodine-soaked one-room den with fly traps hanging overhead where I'd spent all my lazy afternoons, watching the ladies pretty up to a better version of themselves—a halcyon dream in this nation of amnesiacs.

They'd welcomed me, the almost-mute five-year-old who always came wrinkled and clutched to her grandmother, into their lair. It was here at last they sat their weary selves down, loosened their hair from buns for their hours-long *ajumma* perms. It was here they sometimes cussed, sometimes cried—having left behind their wretched lives for the afternoon—about their drunken-crazed-butcher-knife-wielding husbands who'd dragged them by their hair through the playground just weeks before. It was here they dreamed their small postwar dreams. Outside, the soon-to-ignite military coup smoldered in the streets of Seoul.

In 1970s South Korea, the era in which I grew up, just about every woman I knew and my mother knew and my grandmother knew belonged to a gye, a crude, early form of a savings club. A one- or two-year term, with a sky-high "interest rate." Get in, get out, get house, get rich. Fast. Korean people are fast. Everyone, well, not everyone, but everyone watching and listening and feeling knew in the lowest substation of their gut that change was coming. And not a household-variety change but a mantle-shattering, sea-bottom-quaking kind of change. Like a tsunami descending on a beach resort for fat, rich tourists, except in the opposite direction. It was the tsunami of an opportunity for the poor, the disenfranchised, the oppressed, the formerly colonized who lost nothing during the war because they'd started with nothing, the outermost fringe class of this war-torn village-turned-nation, this protoplasm of a society that South Korea was back then. You didn't need to be the *Yangban* class—the patrician, the formerly powerful, the inbred class that had kept their privilege strictly gated for millennia—to get in on the real estate boom. No one could come in and confiscate your house while you slept, as they had under the old colonial rule. Real estate had become real again. Hello, property rights, nice to see you again.

I don't know who was the first woman to invent this get-rich-quick scheme dressed up as savings and loans, but it was always and only women who ran the local gyes. In the shadows of a colonial past, reeling from the wreckage of a war that had splintered their land and souls in half, it was the women who were the most eager to mend, rebuild, or crowdsource their people. It was the women who would save their households and their husbands, chronically unemployed and drunk, and free the people from poverty and the violence that came from poverty, assuage their shame/sorrow/self-reproach—the trifecta of the dispossessed people—and their once broad-chested idealism and whatever other ills that had made them go mad or turn up as perverts in playgrounds. It was the women who would pay for their children's college tuition, put the down payment on the thousand-dollar apartment that would go on to become a million-dollar property in less than a decade. It was the women who had the fortitude not just to witness but to get in on the ground floor of the all-eyes-on-the-future boom that would, in short order, create a once-in-a-generation reordering of the society's socioeconomic structure and raise the living standards for millions of former bottom-feeders.

Women, always the women. Thank goodness for the women.

The deal was simple. It worked perfectly on paper. You take a number from one through some other number like twelve (for a one-year gye). You bring cash to the pot, the same amount each month (predetermined based on the term of the gye); you do it for a year. At some point over that period, the pot pays you a lump sum equal to the whole year's principal plus or minus "interest"; the lower your number, the earlier the payout, but in that case the "interest" is subtracted from your payout. That interest instead goes to the higher-number holder, the later payout. A zero-sum game. Waiting until dead last earned you the highest interest, while bearing the highest risk of default. Time equals money equals risk.

Okay, maybe it wasn't so simple.

The problem was that it ran on an honor system. No credit check (what's that?), no signed contracts. In finance mumbo jumbo, it meant that the early redeemers would be disincentivized to continue contributing after having been paid up already. Many of them ran, cleared out overnight, the day after their payday. First in, first default. Mathematically it didn't make sense either. How was it possible that the women from my grandmother's neighborhood in the outskirts, with good-for-nothing, out-of-work husbands, were signing up for ₩1 million, ₩2 million, ₩5 million (1 million Korean won roughly the equivalent of 1,000 USD) at a time when an average citizen made less than the equivalent of a thousand dollars a year? Some had multiple gyes going at the same time, borrowing from one gye to pay for another.

It was never about math or being rational, though. There was no backup plan and no way to make anyone pay for their sins, no bounty put out to catch the thief who skipped town. The defaulters weren't bad people. It was a crime of passion, really. The women met each month at the no-name hair salon, cussed about their husbands together, knew each other's last names and from what province their ancestors had hailed based on their last names. They knew their backstory and their frontstory. The feel of cold hard cash in their hands, unprecedented in their lifetime and in historic time, must have been irresistible.

Could've been my mother or my grandmother, the gye organizer or the runaway, *a same fate,* my grandmother used to say. *I owe as much as I'm owed,* she'd grumble under her breath. Her hands bulging with a wad of cash, she liked to count her money, then count again just because, always with a thimble of spit on her fingers, making the bills taut, easier to count. She wrote everything down in her ledger, down to the last won. Didn't matter that it was someone else's money. She would go to sleep guarding it, with a money belt around her small waist. Reams of greens stashed in every available nook around the house: inside a chest of drawers, under a pile of *beoson* (traditional Korean socks with deep "pockets"), sewn inside her roll pillow, tucked inside the instant ramen packaging she'd fashioned into ziplock bags.

My mother, too, had been weaned on extreme saving. On her meager salary from a secretarial job at a university, she saved and saved to upgrade to a better life. After divorcing her unemployed husband, something no average woman was doing at the time, the vault of another sky suddenly blew open. She was eager to get her own life and kids back. Real estate seemed the only way to make it out alive, out of divorce and poverty, to move into dignity and a shiny independence, into a womanhood of her own making: You join with your mother, your sisters, recruit some other women from your neighborhood, the women from the hair salon. You do it even though you've never been a joiner in your life. Even though "follow the crowd" is something your long-absent father taught you not to do, you now must learn how to do it. You do it even though you have no idea how money works. You do it so you can ditch the old colonial *han-ok* with the outhouse in your ancestors' backyard and move into the multistory *ah-pa-t* (apartment), one of many that were popping up in every square patch of land available inside the village-turned-city. You do it for the promise of holding a fat pile of cash in your hands, within a span of months, not years. You do it for your kids.

She would go on, even after we had emigrated to America, to lament her decision to empty out her life savings to start a brand-new life: *If only I hadn't sold that apartment to bring us to America,* reciting over and over again the myth-turned-reality of the rampant overnight success stories back home, how she had missed out on turning every last won she had saved into an unimaginable fortune within the decade we'd moved across the ocean and had to start from scratch. The America she had dreamed of for most of her adult life had now become a liability instead of an opportunity. It would make her ill—the injustice, the stupidity of it, the random success based on chance, the bold (un)thinking she'd been taught to guard against.

II. *Where Did All the (Good) Men Go?*

Inside the small patch of this village-turned-city lingered a stench, in the air and in people, a type of menace risen out of ruin. As soon as I'd step outside the perimeter of my grandmother's home in the outskirts, and later out of my mother's apartment in center city, I'd be greeted with all kinds of men drifting in and out of life, the perennially unemployed who sometimes preyed on latchkeys like me in the playground, the round-the-clock drunks and the wife beaters who, in broad daylight, wielding a butcher knife, paraded their domestic affairs in front of the children and anyone else who happened to be loitering around the playground in the middle of the day. There were the occasional flashers at the produce market, the sometimes–body snatchers/murderers/rapists and, always, the men who did all the uncalled-for touching and sharing of themselves anytime anywhere; also, of course, the ex-convicts who came back soon enough to do more permanent damage.

Once, at the playground, a man came up to me. Must have been the keychain looped around my neck that gave me away.

"Hey, little girl, where's your mom?" he began.

My mother, after her divorce, worked a full-time job that she took three buses to get to, because the direct bus would have cost a few cents more. She'd never talked to me about men, bad or good or any kind in between. I barely knew anything about my own perennially unemployed and drunk father, whom she had left a few years prior. In the few pictures she'd shown me of my father, the deep pockmarks in his darkened complexion betrayed years of drinking. This man, who possessed the world's most sullen face, had been a mystery to me for all of my short life—not the good kind of mystery that makes you stay up the night before Christmas but the kind you avoid at all costs.

"She's at work," I said dutifully.

"Oh. Let me tell you a little story. Do you like stories?" he leaned in to ask.

And just like that, he had me. That he chose me out of a crowd of children excited me. That he asked if I liked stories made him a clairvoyant. I don't remember what story he told; I cared only that he told one, and that I was the only one in that moment he told it to, that he looked me in the eye with the kind of tenderness born simply of giving and taking attention, that he noticed every twitch and twinkle in my eyes, as he spoke. I was captivated by his story, and he by me, I thought.

He took me to his house. A shoebox really, one of thousands in the identical, five-story, multi-box apartments in this burgeoning city, inside the same complex as the one my mother and I lived in. Together, we walked up the winding stairs, he following close behind me and leading us up to his apartment. The headiness from the walk and from being with this stranger, a man, made me wobbly on my feet, my heart fluttering toward the sky. My small body, a flock of birds.

Once there, he invited me into his kitchen, a small, dim, dingy room in the back, with garbage piled up in the corner. I recognized the coal-fired cooking furnace, the same hazardous kind my mother used in our apartment and which I'd used many a time to make myself instant ramen noodles for dinner while she worked late nights. The kitchen looked messy, with cooking instruments strewn about as though someone had just been there.

"Would you like something to eat?" the man asked.

"No, my mom will get upset if I have a snack before dinner," I said.

"I understand."

I hated saying no to this man. I resented my mother momentarily for creating the condition in which I had to say no to him.

"Do you live here alone?" I blurted out, after gathering all the life force available inside a seven-year-old girl, to the man who said he understood, whose taut eyes were still trained on me like a cat, a man with intention.

Before he could answer, I heard someone at the door. An old woman emerged from the hallway.

"There you go again, bringing children here," the woman said angrily, with the accent of a non–Seoul native. I knew this to be someone who hailed from the southern province, where the coup d'état-ers were from, as my class-conscious mother had taught me.

"Jesus, Mom, stop that. She's gonna think I'm a pervert!" the man said, his gentle voice breaking quickly into one I didn't recognize.

I don't remember how I made it back home that day. He barely said goodbye as the door clanged shut behind me. My heart must have been heavy with emotions I hadn't felt in a while, not since my uncle's friend used to come around just to see me back when I lived in my grandmother's house—until one day he stopped abruptly. The friend and I would be left alone in my uncle's bedroom. My uncle, being the only man in a house full of women, didn't have to share his room with anyone.

The second time the man invited me back to his house, it was a nonstarter. A snitch at the playground had seen me leave with him; my mother already knew half of it. I'd told her the what, where, and when of the story, but not how he made me feel special until his mom spoiled it, how without knowing his true intention I was captivated by his singular attention to me. It would be years before I would know the difference between a true attention and a false one, and why even a false attention felt better than no attention.

"Be more careful next time," my mother, the darling of understatement, advised, the thud of her words landing flatly against my chest. Such was her instruction for the next time, and the next time, when another man, and another man, followed me home from school. I would learn their modus operandi over time: they would follow me home, then wait up on the rooftop of our apartment building until I came back inside from the playground. One man waited for days to have his turn, until one of those nights my mother came home late. He waited until the lights went out in the playground, when the lone security guard at the apartment complex stepped out for smokes, when he knew I would be walking home alone to an empty house. The shadowy figure called out to me from a stairway connecting the topmost floor to our floor, a few feet away from the doorway into our apartment. My key was already halfway into the keyhole when he began descending toward me.

"Hey, little girl, you're home!"

All the waiting had made this man's heart swell, it seemed; he was so glad to finally see me, as if he'd been waiting for this moment to share a lifelong secret, the desperation in his voice turning on my pathos.

The men waited. To their own detriment, they waited. It would have been so easy, you'd think, for them to just come down a few steps and grab their small prey in a flash; they were at least three times my size. But they never did, never being bold enough, strategic enough, or rational enough to do the most obvious thing required to carry out a home invasion or kidnapping or worse. Was it an act of incompetence or something more perverse? They waited for the sake of waiting, it seemed, factoring in just enough reaction time for me to escape, as though they were making it known to me that they wanted to be invited in: an invitation, in turn, for my invitation.

It had only been scary the first time, the real scare coming mostly from my imagination. By then, by age seven, it seemed my mind had already compiled so many versions of these men that I could recite iterations of their easy pickup lines, each one reliably beginning with "Hey, little girl . . ." It was cinematic, the action slowing down just a bit each time. As the opening credits rolled, the tinge of excitement I'd felt upon seeing the man in the playground would come back momentarily, before some other man popped onto the screen and read the rehearsed line, "Hey, little girl," the rush quickly morphing into horror, delivering a blow to my delusional high.

None of this would make much sense to me until much later when, as a woman, I would remain the target of other similar pickup lines by other similarly perverse men, cowering in the dimly lit alleyways of my mind, their catlike eyes flashing in the shadows of parking lots and produce aisles alike, the jolt of their familiarity still having sway.

III. *Over the Arirang Pass, a Rage*

There's a little-known nineties South Korean movie called *A Hot Roof*, set on the rooftop of an apartment complex like the one in which I grew up. The rooftop, in fact, is where most of the action in the film takes place, where a dozen neighborhood women stage a days-long standoff against the police after being moved to collectively intervene in an active domestic violence scene that ensues on the doorsteps of an apartment building. When the throng of bystanders, notably the husbands and other men in the neighborhood, sits around watching the woman being battered by her husband, the gang of seemingly ordinary housewives who reside in the same apartment complex as the couple comes to her rescue; with pots and sticks and flyswatters in hand, they beat up on the husband, who later dies en route to the hospital. The movie was marketed as a comedy bordering on the absurd. God forbid the men and women of South Korea should take wife-beating seriously. The producers needed to make people gasp at the same time as they laughed out loud in order to make them take notice of the issue. The movie was nonetheless ground-breaking in that it flipped the then-conventional script of normalizing wife-beating, instead making heroines out of the band of husband-beating, foul-mouthed "tough women" (though they were admittedly portrayed as hapless, blundering housewives inadvertently pulled into a murderous rampage). The "tough woman" archetype, the woman who could literally get away with murder, hadn't much existed in the limited imagination of the moviegoing public at the time. The film also broke ground in that it starred a transgender woman as one of the last women standing, portrayed less as an exotic specimen or a flattened object of scorn/desire than as a complex subject on equal footing with the housewives-turned-outlaws. Surprisingly enough, much of the viewing public sided with the women, who represented the common struggles of the everyday women grappling with domestic violence, which had by then become all too familiar in the lives of most South Korean women.

Of course, I couldn't help but conjure up the women from the hair salon back in the day in my grandmother's neighborhood. If given half a chance, they would have done exactly that—collectively murdered their stupid, cheating, good-for-nothing husbands who had beaten them in front of their children and neighbors, cracking open the beastly, ghostly imaginings of their female ancestors whose souls are still awaiting their turn at redemption "over the Arirang pass," as the ballad goes.

Their weapon of choice? They would have taken the hot rods off their curling irons and used them to skin the man's ungrate-

ful balls before pouring the perm solution down his throat; goodness gracious, they would have had a ball. You would have heard
them chant "Arirang, Arirang, Arario," the ancient folk lyric of
the Korean people, and in its refrain heard their deep, guttural,
many-mountains-moving rage and sorrow, reverberating over the
Arirang pass.

Inside the melancholic notes of "Arirang" lies a low-lying rage.
It is the kind of rage whose origin is love; it once was kind and patient, it waited and waited, until lover became prey. It is the kind
of rage born of indignation, neatly wrapped inside a hair bun and
kept back, away from people's eyes and attention. It is the kind
that seeks company in misery, that commiserates in a standoff,
the kind inherited and sustained over generations. As in the word
Arirang itself, which has no direct meaning, over the Arirang pass
anything is possible. The rage over the Arirang pass reverberates
through the night sky, as its wanderers search and shape-shift in
the bardo among the departed, its multifarious meanings meeting
the listener whence she has come and must go; they come due, as
would the obligations of a debt come due.

It's the women who sing the ballad of the Arirang, always the
women.

IV. How to Mourn: A Deposed President, a Dispossessed People, a Mother

When I wasn't tagging along with my grandmother to the hair salon, I was left alone a lot. The grown-ups were busy getting on
with their lives after the war; my grandmother, the matriarch of all
matriarchs, trusted me to take care of myself alone at home, while
she was away making deals as a money (black) market dealer, a
seamstress, a (love) letter writer for postwar courtesans, and other
sundry jobs she had taken on to feed the family.

Even after my mother took me in once I started school, I was
left to my own devices. Though I was only in second grade, I
knew my way around Seoul from years of riding the bus all over
the city, something my mother let me do on my own early on.
Sometimes, on weekdays after school, instead of going with the
other kids to the playground, I'd strike out on my own and get
on the bus. I'd let it take me wherever piqued my interest from

inside the dirty, overcrowded bus where I stood peering out. I'd get off and wander around the neighborhood for hours, then ride the same bus back home in time for dinner. Mother never asked questions.

It was a strange time—soldiers stationed at street corners, siren calls for midnight curfews, nightly news of the military coup following the assassination of the sitting president, the news blaring on our new black-and-white TV set, even small children debating the ins and outs of 1970s South Korean politics over recess. Of course, I didn't think any of it was strange at the time.

Every time I took the city bus—dubbed the Sprout Bus after the cheap, ubiquitous vegetable that grows an inch overnight—a harrowing, high-flying adventure ensued; my small body and my will for survival would be tested to the brink. Every day the streets were crowded with a horde of pedestrians, frantically crossing this way and that like an untrained school of mice looking for their lost children. As the smallest of fries, I would run, run harder than any adult, to catch the Sprout Bus, not distracted by the cacophony of ambulance and siren calls, kids' wailing, mothers' howling.

The day after the president, Park Jung Hee, was assassinated in 1979, I rode the bus to city hall, where an overnight vigil was being held for him. I don't remember telling my mother where I was going before I set out. I ran for the bus. I ran and tripped and fell and got back up and ran again—almost flew—then, miraculously, mightily leapt aboard the already moving bus like some mythic bird. The bus attendants knew me as the "milky-faced girl" who always had the right change. *Ory, Ory!* (All right! All right!), the bus operator would holler, a signal to speed up after letting in the last of the stragglers. It was the job of the bus operator (an assistant to the bus driver) to manage the flow of body traffic onto and off the bus, one of the few jobs available then for young women. She always had half of her body out the door and half in, with arms outstretched in the air, the length of her leaning perilously against the moving vehicle, an elegant *V* flying through traffic.

Once aboard the Sprout Bus, it was impossible to move your body, only your eyeballs. So, you looked around, left, right, front, back; every which way you looked, you saw—no, you felt—the bodies touching you. That day, there must have been a hundred people, maybe a thousand, sprouting by the minute on this bus, this clunky old, reverse-centrifuged tube filled with humans, all of us headed to the vigil. Its walls could stretch only so much; the shoving, the kicking, the thrusting, the violence from all directions bruised my arms and torso, my sphere of vision dimming as more and bigger bodies piled on. Soon, even gravity would give, and my legs, twiggy and short, slowly as if by a spell, lifted off the ground; I was levitating. Levitating!

By the time our bus rolled in, a throng of people had already gathered on the grounds of the city hall, which had by then transformed into a massive wake to pay tribute to President Park. I had no clue what "assassination" actually meant, how it was any different from a regular death or killing, or why anyone would want to assassinate anyone, let alone the sitting president, who, by the looks of him, seemed like the good guy. Why would the military coup that followed his assassination then be quickly followed up with more couplike uprisings by fresh-faced college students, who also must have been the good guy? Surely, someone other than my mostly absent mother must have had something to say about all this; surely, a teacher, newscaster, or scholar could have explained the complicated backstory that led up to this historic moment, which would change the course of our shared history. The way they taught us early on to hate the North had been so clear-cut. All those anti-Communist drills we used to sing in first grade were so catchy, so memorable, making their message clear. This time, not so much.

None of it mattered, though. The only thing that mattered in that moment was that I had survived another ride on the Sprout Bus, and that I was among the spectacle, mired in this seemingly historic, hysterical moment together with *my people*. It is the way of the Korean people, I would learn, that we weep and we wail and we wallow deeply in mourning for a communal cause, that we touch and we feel the bodies of our neighbors with our own bodies as we mourn, and whatever the source of their suffering becomes our suffering.

As the night approached, hundreds of men, women, and children filed in line, one by one, to light incense on the altar next to the deceased, their inconsolable moans, sobs, and howls filling the evening air with burden and beauty at once. Under the evening's glow, I moaned, I sobbed, and I howled with them. I understood none of their pain.

V. The Small Dreamers

The gye would persist in America. My penny-wise, pound-foolish mother, and later, my grandmother, too, would export their trade and join forces with other aggressively saving Koreans in the area. By 1983, when our family moved across the great ocean and into a one-bedroom bungalow in Staten Island, New York, my forty-something single mother, who could never shed her impossible habit of saving and counting down to the last cent, would faithfully make her monthly gye payments, just as she did with her monthly tithes to the church, on a tiny salary earned from her job as manager of an ice cream store.

The meetings moved downstairs. The band of church ladies dressed up as the Bible-reading club, or as the prayer group doubling as the children's scholarship fundraiser club, or the hiking-without-husbands club, or whatever other Korean groups my mother belonged to, often ran their gyes out of church basements over potluck dinners. Because I was a girl I was allowed to tag along to these exclusive clubs. Over bibimbap and tofu jjigae and a dozen other dishes spread out over the Ping-Pong table, the ladies with their perfectly coifed ajumma perms would sit around mulling over their days. Hardened as they had become, they had small albeit real joys, like their children making honor roll even as they were made fun of for their accents or the pungent-smelling lunches their mothers packed for them. Every now and then there would be some whiz kid who got into Harvard or Juilliard on full scholarship, a cause for both celebration and intense envy. Sometimes, there would be a woman who stayed grim-faced and quiet in the corner, her cheating husband the subject of vicious gossip. *Who did he run off with this time?* There was that one time when the husband had second-mortgaged their house to pay off his gambling debt and ended up losing the house. The wife never left him, though, because kids, because house, because money.

Because money.

Always, there would be someone in the group who had come down with cancer or some other terminal disease and who was now in the hands of the Lord almighty, but who would come to the meeting anyway to make the payment. My mother, too, did her part; even after she was let go from her job scooping ice cream, even after she started complaining of headaches, body aches, un-explained fatigue, nausea, and bleeding, she came to the meetings to make the payment some-damn-how.

My mother turned to Jesus for answers to her sundry symptoms, to seek all that was earthly: a job, children who made honor roll, a healthy body. *I owe as much as I'm owed,* she'd say, a refrain she must have heard her mother say so often back home. Only now, the debt obligations of those words came crashing due. The money she had been saving and saving into her sock drawers would not save her body, not even her spleen; it certainly would not save her soul.

It would be the ladies, with flyswatters and pots and perm solu-tions in hand, the chorus who would chant a welcome, the ladies who had been waiting and waiting over the Arirang pass for their turn, as it was now her turn, and soon it would be mine, to settle the accounting from our lives, here and beyond here.

I remember the last time my mother came home from meeting with the ladies of the Korean-American Women for Home Own-ership Gye. It was the night of her payout, with her own deck of cash finally dealt. She had been waiting, holding her breath, for this thing to come through; she'd planned to put it toward the down payment on a house that wasn't to be, alas. I'd learn about her cancer diagnosis only weeks later. The pile of all that cash, the money she'd saved and saved with exacting calculus, bulged inside her palms. She shuffled the deck, counting and counting to make sure it was the right amount, the merciless sounds of her shuffling slicing the night precisely thin. I watched her face become flushed as if with fever. Something had changed; nothing in the pile of cash meant anything to her anymore. In the hollow of our dimly lit kitchen, I heard a low hum thrumming inside my mother's sick body, as her words, *I don't know what to do with this much money,* ric-ocheted off the kitchen walls.

JUSTIN TORRES

It Had to Be Gold

FROM *Los Angeles Times Image*

TODAY I FOUND myself standing at the window, half in a dream, my hand at my neck, fingers searching absently for a cross I'd lost more than a year ago. This keeps happening; muscle memory. I'd worn and worried that cross back and forth on its chain for some two decades. Over time, I added two other gold chains, both of them gifts, but the cross I'd found, on the street, and managed to keep for twenty years. This is significant because I'm not a finder, I'm a loser. A *chronic loser.* A term I discovered only a couple of days ago, listening to the writer Adam Phillips give a talk on an essay by Anna Freud. A chronic loser constantly misplaces everything— watches, phones, keys, wallets, gloves, hats, sunglasses, eyeglasses. Sometimes they are recovered, mostly they are not. From what I understand, this is a symptom of altered libidinal processes; some- thing misfiring in the deep, where desires are formed, making attachment difficult. Am I reenacting some infantile drama of neglect? Perhaps, who knows. But this made sense to me: In our attachments, whether to objects or others, there exists a continual fluctuation of our energies. We wish to possess, to be possessed, and to be relieved of our possessions all at once. The hoarder solves the problem of value and attachment by holding on. The chronic loser lets it all go. Not only do I routinely misplace every- day items but essentials as well; I've lost more than one passport, my birth certificate, Social Security card, numerous licenses, an entire library worth of books. None of these things were lost to- gether, mind you, not all at once, in a fire, but one by one, piece- meal. I once left a laptop on a train; it contained the only copy of a manuscript I'd been working on for years. But never in all that time did I lose any of my chains, or my gold cross. Until one day, I did.

Only when the cross went missing did I even realize I'd held on to it. I hadn't been careful, or clinging, or conscious of the value and meaning I'd bestowed. I simply never took it off. Now that it was gone, now that my fingers habitually reached up to play with it, and found absence instead, I came to feel the cross helped me to think, and daydream. I realized, too, how ridiculous this was; I'd never considered myself a fetishist, but as it turns out, I've got a thing for chains.

My father was a man who both did, and did not, wear chains. I must have been around eight years old when he found work which, for various reasons, involved him accentuating his "roots," by which I mean, it was necessary and expected of him to perform a kind of ghetto authenticity; to speak Spanish and Spanglish and jive with the older generations and a less poetic, more vulgar contemporary slang with the young ones; to embody the intimidation and charm of a gangster. His work car, which my brothers and I loved to sneak inside, had tinted windows and was pimped, as we said at the time. My father was not an actual gangster. In his home life, and in our white working-class town, he was aspirational, busy elevating his station, keeping up with the neighbors. He left the house and returned dressed like all the other dads. We rarely saw him in his work costume. Only on the rarest of occasions, for reasons unknown to us, would he break out the flash: the diamond stud earring, the gold chains, the gold cross, the medallions, the gold watch. (When alone in the house, I used to hunt for this jewelry, unsuccessfully. Eventually, I gave up, assuming it must all be kept in the lockbox under the bed, next to his gun.) He'd sag his jeans, and we'd imitate his strut. "Put some stank on it," he'd say, and we'd try and mostly fail. The persona that floated up to the surface in those moments was uncanny, this other, gangster father, drawn from both stereotype and some mysterious essence he kept hidden from us. Upstate, I was used to everyone projecting cool onto my father, no matter how corny he might act, due simply to his Brooklyn accent and brown skin; but in those moments of transformation—in the flash of the flash—an actual, almost tangible coolness radiated, emanated from inside.

My father was a proud man, and moody. He could be sentimental, loving, hilarious, but he could also explode into violence. My mother explained this had to with the prejudice and indignities of poverty he'd dealt with in childhood. Explaining away the "bad father" and redirecting us toward the "good enough father" was one of my mother's covert responsibilities. Yet whatever or whoever flashed in these moments, when he wore the charms and called forth this other persona, with both self-mockery and reverence, this trickster figure, hard and cool—well, I did not want this man explained away. I wanted him to stay. And to my child mind it seemed the charm of the shadow father had everything to do with all that bling, with the charms themselves, the most mystical and magical of all, which I was not allowed to wear, or handle, being the crucifix.

Then two, maybe three years later, something happened both mundane and terrible, which altered my relationship to this form of ostentatious, hardened masculinity. Here's the memory, present tense: We drive down from our home in the boondocks six hours south, making the pilgrimage to the three-bedroom Brooklyn apartment where my aunt and uncle and abuela and five cousins all live. Other tíos and cousins are there when we arrive, and more shuffle in behind us. It's crowded, loud, the air thick—people still smoked indoors back then. I'm forced through hellos, reintroductions, prods to speak up; I'm shy. On the living room floor the younger cousins press up close to the television, watching cartoons, which they turn louder and louder to battle the noise. Commercials play for toys and sugar cereals. I want to join the little ones, though I'm too old to do so unselfconsciously, so I inch closer and closer, when in walks a young man I've never seen before. He's beautiful. Apart from the uncles I know, in Brooklyn there are always new men, second cousins, half siblings of half siblings, somebody's boyfriend, who are introduced as "uncle" so-and-so. I don't remember this uncle's name or relation, only that I never saw him before, and I never saw him again after that day. He is beautiful. The soft luster of his skin only accentuated by his rather severe nose and brow. Everything is crisp: his fade, the lines shaved into his eyebrows; jewelry glints all around him, a diamond stud earring, chains, a gold watch worn loose. So beautiful the men are unafraid to acknowledge the fact, as they do now, whistling through their teeth and naming him pretty boy. He is probably only a teenager, but he very coolly makes the rounds of handshakes, daps, and benedictions. I stare, nakedly, as he unzips and removes his jacket. Underneath is a T-shirt printed with a cartoon rabbit, whom I recognize as the mascot of the kids cereal Trix.

Silly Faggot, the shirt reads. *Dix are for chix.*

I don't gauge any other person's reaction, though it's safe to assume some laugh and some chastise. This is the very early nineties. What do I know then? I know that the hatred of faggots has to do with AIDS, and in a deep and unformed way I know that the hatred of faggots has also to do with me; I know it is time for me to leave the world of cartoons and sugar cereals, and I am embarrassed by the fact that I am not ready, that I keep looking backward. I know that it feels dangerous, now, to look at this uncle, but still, I want to. I force my gaze into the middle space, below his eyes and above his message, where a crucifix hangs—and it's an exact replica of the one my father keeps hidden away somewhere in the house. That's the point of fixation, where the memory short-circuits, overloaded by the sudden double awareness of something burning in me, and a new depth to the ugliness burning out there, in the world. The memory ends.

How do we survive our own ambivalence? One way is to fetishize. Perhaps the chains, and especially the crucifix, became totems, able to neutrally absorb both hatred and desire. Perhaps in their glimmer and weight I saw a reflection of all that I wanted, and all that I feared. I don't know. I certainly didn't think any of that at the time. My parents divorced, and I lost my father, a gradual process that was pretty complete by the age of eighteen; I was doing everything I could to shake my mother. That Wildean quip comes to mind: "To lose one parent may be regarded as misfortune; to lose both looks like carelessness." I was careless with my life and their care for me, and things came to a head in a dramatic rupture, until finally I left for the city, where I was very much alone, and very broke, and then one day I was mugged.

Another memory: I'm walking down some Chelsea block with a friend, heading home from a club called the Tunnel. This would have been September 1998, coming on five in the morning and still very dark. The kid has a knife. Other club-leavers mill around, though no one intervenes. The kid has a knife, but he's shorter and probably younger than my friend and I. We must have looked like easy marks, vulnerable, newbies to the city, eighteen and piss drunk. We laugh, partly out of a kind of nervous terror, but also because we have nothing to offer up. I turn my pockets inside out, my friend opens her purse and pulls out various objects, a lipstick, a wad of tissue, and just keeps repeating, "Look, I have nothing. We have nothing." Neither of us have credit cards, or even wallets or phones. (No one carried phones in those days, at least no one like us.) Even our IDs are fake, we've left our real ones at home. We'd had just enough cash for the cover charge and had spent the night downing the dregs of others' abandoned drinks. The club kids ignored us, they were all so sophisticated in their debauchery; we were bumpkins. "Bumpkins but not for long!" we had vowed, yelling into the night, stumbling down the sidewalk, into the tip of the knife. I don't remember the mugger's reaction, I don't remember how we got out of it. The memory ends with the image of my friend squatting, crapulous, and dumping her purse on the sidewalk. "I have nothing. We have nothing," she says. And it's true.

A couple of days later, I found the gold chain with the gold cross on the sidewalk, in a kind of reverse mugging, a gifting; the city, it seemed, might make or unmake, possess and dispossess at will, but would never leave me alone. At the time, scrawny as I was, my uniform consisted entirely of printed secondhand T-shirts from the boys' section, usually with messages about Little League or summer camp or, ironically, D.A.R.E., and I began to wear them inside out, which I believed made me look more mature, and better displayed my gold necklace. I never took off the cross, not to shower, and certainly not when—as finally, finally, began to happen—men picked me up in bars, and brought me home for sex.

The very first line of one of my short stories—the first piece for which I was paid real money—begins with the main character, a young hustler, finding a gold chain on the ground. I was thirty years old when I sold that story and I used the entirety of the money to buy a designer suit, Prada. I wanted something extravagant and utilitarian; something that would help me transition into adulthood; something that would last. I lost the suit within a week. That year, for my birthday, my boyfriend bought me a silver feather necklace. (The necklace in the short story had been a feather, not a cross, though gold.) It had to be gold, it's always had to be gold, but of course I couldn't tell him that. I lost it.

But the loss I've been trying to figure out is the loss of the gold cross. So here's a final memory: I'm thirty-eight now, my man and

I are on vacation in Berlin, staying in a hotel room with too many mirrors, two of which face one another on the bias. Walking in one afternoon, I'm startled by my own reflection, only from an angle I've never seen before. By this time, along with the gold chains, I've added other adornments, everything plated, gold wire-rim glasses, and an inexpensive gold watch, worn loose. Recently, billowy short-sleeve button-up shirts have come back in style, and the one I'm wearing looks very much like the guayaberas worn by the older relatives. My forearms are tattooed.

"Jesus," I say. "For a second I thought one of my uncles was in the room."

"What, you mean in your reflection?"

I lean into the mirror, looking at the doubled image, turning and inspecting as one does in the barber's chair. "The back of my head is . . . messed up."

"No comment," my man says, moving past me. He falls down into the bed, and is soon napping peacefully.

Later that night we're walking from one gay bar to another, drunk for sure, but not too messy, swerving a bit, talking in English, probably louder than we realize. Alone on a wide, brightly lit block, we stop, both of us looking at one phone, to make sure we're headed in the right direction. When I next look up, two young guys stand before us, not two feet away, as if they had appeared from our shadows. They both offer greetings and smiles, ask us where we are from—the US, England—and we ask them in return. Another country, they say, originally, but they live in Germany now, in another city. English is clearly a third, maybe fourth, language; we don't push for clarification.

Somehow, we make small talk, one is cute and the other just impossibly sexy. The cute one does all the talking, presses up close, flirts, and very shortly suggests we take them back to our hotel. We laugh. The sexy one is quiet; he seems to be largely just indulging his friend. He absently lifts his shirt and runs a hand across his body, up to his chest, down, tucks the thumb of his other hand into the waistline of his jeans. His body is more than a little distracting. I feel the shorter one kiss my neck and politely pull away. All the while a conversation is going on, the short one asking us questions, flirting, lightly fondling, and finally seeming to give up. He asks for directions to the bar we had just come from, which we show them on our phone. We part laughing, the four of us. We have no idea what they wanted. We have a hard time believing they actually wanted to sleep with us, especially the hot one; standard protocol would have been to just join us for a drink first, before proposing some kind of group hookup. I suggest maybe the short one is on ecstasy, or something, and his friend's just along for the ride, he seemed sober. Certainly, more sober than we are. Whatever they were after, they took our rejection well.

It isn't until we arrive at the next bar and order drinks that my man realizes all the money is gone from his wallet. Nothing else, no cards, just the cash. I have my cash—I always carry cash in my front pocket, and instinctively keep my hand on it when any stranger approaches (especially in gay bars and cruising spots)—but the gold chain with the gold cross is missing from around my neck. It's all so clear in retrospect, the front man, standing slightly aloof, teasingly lifting his shirt and running that thumb along his waistband at porn-slow speed, while the other one, the cutpurse, worked us over.

"At least they were nice about it all," my man says. We laugh and marvel at the dexterity, the Dickensian nimbleness of his fingers, this other, better, sense of digital theft. There seems something quaint and decent and forthright, and relatively harmless, about a good old-fashioned hug-and-mug. At that moment I don't mourn the cross, I don't think about how much time and meaning I've invested; instead, I feel something more beguiling, a kind of giddiness, relief.

"Really," I say, "I was asking for it, with all these damn chains on."

"You know," my man says, "he looked like you."

"The sexy one?"

"No," he laughs. "The little one. Like you, but smaller, pocket size. A mini-you."

We drink, then head homeward, lighter. When I stumble, he reaches out to balance me, like Dorothy does for Scarecrow in *The Wiz.* I sing the number, *Don't you carry nothing that might be a load,* but can't get him to join in. The mirrored hotel is farther than remembered, or maybe we're lost, but I'm following now, in silence. I'm trying to remember a line from a book, something triggered by an answer the little one had given to our questions. Then it comes to me, Hartley: *The past is a foreign country . . .* but I'm too blurred to remember the other half. I'm thinking about mini-me, how much he would have liked to caress the uncle, who was not really an uncle, the beautiful man in the Trix T-shirt, to kiss his neck, to slowly and carefully unclasp the chain, to slip off the crucifix, palm it, and ease away to the sound of laughter.

ALEX MARZANO-LESNEVICH

Futurity

FROM *Harvard Review*

1. ON A morning early in the second month of the unprecedented
time, I rise to the sound of the birds and pad to the kitchen in
my slippers. The air smells of hot coffee. Snow blankets the roof
just outside the window, the light glinting off it tracing swirls on
the wall. I pour the coffee: roasty, familiar, constant. A few weeks
ago, I would have carried the cup to my writing desk, there said
a short prayer to the god of creation, pressed my pen to the
page, and tried to listen. But now I carry it back to my bedroom,
where the curtains remain closed. I turn my bedside lamp on
and open the novel on my nightstand. I will be in its world. Not
this one.

2. My jawline has become covered in blond fuzz, and later, in
front of the bathroom mirror, I see it backlit, the fuzz so pale it
is visible only when struck by this light. I turn my head this way,
then that, looking. The fuzz wasn't there a month ago. So much
has changed. When my agent sent me notes on the latest writing
I've been doing, he included an instruction that I must search for
mentions of my jawline. *You mention the fuzz here, and here, and here,*
he says. He means: we get the point.

He means: the mentions are getting old. But I have lived all my
decades with a smooth jawline; to me, none of this is old. I think
of change constantly, and the way change implies progression, and
now, looking left and looking right, I wonder what I am seeing,
what the fuzz is a harbinger of. Will it grow longer? Will I grow
a beard? Or will it stay like this, so pale as to be nearly invisible,

prepubescent even as time goes forward and inscribes lines on my skin? The future is as unknown to me as the changed world outside my window, the present like a scratch in one of the records my father used to play.

3. At the start of the shelter orders, a lover texted me that *Fuck it, while we are all staying at home they will grow in their soul patch.* Shortly after we first met, and I told them I was on testosterone, they looked at me in envy. *I can't, my levels are already so high, I'll look too much like a man,* they said. *I'm like you, I don't want to pass. But you. Your body takes its time. You get to choose where you land.*

4. This lover will come back up, so let's give them a name. Let's call them D.

5. When I wrote that I'd just met D, what I meant was that we had recognized something in each other on a dance floor, the floor almost empty, the music so loud as to hold all the space of the place, and our bodies had begun a silent communication, me moving this way and that, them coming closer and then farther away. This was still, of course, in the before time. Disco lights looped the floor, some colored an ice blue. The beams cast like shadows had been shaped into snowflakes. Watching the swoop of the carved light, I imagined the sheets of colored polyethylene that had made it, that cool blue pressed to a burn like fire. The lights chased us and the music grew louder still, and I had grimaced, or D had grimaced. They said something, but I didn't hear. I shook my head, and they came in close, their mouth suddenly fitted over the shell of my ear. *Want to find some quiet?* I felt the sound lap in my ear canal, warm. Then the cold slap of outside, the sudden grace of dark, the stars above us so still. They pulled from their pocket a key. The key fitted the lock of their office, which turned out to be across the street. They knew where the security cameras were. The unlocked closet.

Afterward, the two of us a little punchy, maybe with drink and maybe with flush, we laughed at the irony of finding ourselves in a closet. We who have located whole lives, whole selves, in the stepping out of closets. There was a small red light like in a darkroom and I remember using its dimness as cover to look at them, really look: the hair, dark enough to be inky, clipped short as bristles. The jaw, square yet soft. Their shoulders. Their breasts. They watched me look, the white of their eyes pink in the light, the mirrored black centers. Beads of sweat had formed on their upper lip. Tufts of hair greeted me from their armpits. Their sports bra, two sizes too small, had left angry raw marks across their soft chest. I looked at the hair under their arms and the scores left by the flattening and they looked at me and I knew what they were seeing in me, too. Silence stretched into something sinewy enough to hold us. For the first time I thought how alike were the words *rapt* and *wrapped*.

When they spoke, their voice scratched the edge of tears. "I didn't know it would be so healing," they said. "I've never been with someone else who . . ."

I don't think I let them finish, my mouth over theirs.

6. An incomplete list of things I have heard called queer about the pandemic: the surge in people making their own sourdough starter out of nothing more than flour and water and time. The rise in "masc for mask" jokes. Or: what does a lesbian bring to a second date? No, not a U-Haul, a COVID test. Or: U-Haul-ing as a responsible public health move. Cuffing season. Sex pods. The New York City Public Health Department recommending people "make it a little kinky" with glory holes. The rise in OnlyFans and findom, which is to say, the rise in sex work. Thirst traps. Sexting, phone sex, Zoom sex, FaceTime sex, sleeping with your roommates. Spending the holidays with chosen family.

The very fact of a pandemic.

Loss.

Grief.

The impossibility of imagining a future.

7. Futurity, noun: yes, all right, future time, the sense that there will be a future. The very thing we are all trying to hold on to, as we wait for it to arrive. The projected shape that future makes. The shadow (or light?) it casts over the present.

But also: futurity, noun: a race for two-year-old horses, into which they are entered before they are born.

8. As a metaphor for gender, maybe that's a little obvious. But also: futurities offer some of the richest prizes in horse racing.

*

9. From the windows of my study, I can see the largest hospital in Maine. By law the ambulances must turn off their sirens this close, and so periodically when I look up from my desk now, two months into the at-home time, I see silent flashing lights. After a few days of this constant screaming silent alarm, and of the helicopters that land on the hospital roof at all hours, their thrum so loud as to consume me in the beat of metal wings, I write a prayer with a blue Sharpie onto a purple index card and thumbtack it to the wall between the two windows, right in my line of sight: *May they be safe. May they be happy. May they be healthy. May they live with ease.*

10. When we learn that men are dying at an exponentially higher rate than women from this virus, a friend asks me if I'll keep taking testosterone. I mutter something about how, well, I'm not going to go off a drug without medical advice, and my doctor has other things on her mind right now.

That answer, I know, is bullshit. One of the purported benefits of the daily gel I use, versus a weekly shot, is that its progress is slow, and each day I must choose to apply it, must reaffirm my choice of who I am, of who I am transforming to visibly be. I could choose no.

What I really mean, but don't say, is that men have shorter life expectancies, more heart attacks, higher rates of dementia, and that I already knew all that. The trade-off did occur to me.

But I do ask the doctor if I will lose my hair.

That's what Rogaine's for, she says. *It's not a reason not to live your life.*

Obviously, I want to live my life. I'd just like to live it with hair.

11. Here is how, researchers say, we slot one another into genders with a glance: the shape of the hairline, the shape of the eye socket, the ratio of hip to waist, the shape of the jawline, the shape of the chest. Clothing, hair length, manner of standing. Where fat is distributed. Quickness to smile.

You Can Tell by the Nose: the title of a 1995 study.

We look for patterns. We look for what we know how to see.

And I get that with the bodily factors, I'm talking about *sex,* not *gender.* But what I am really speaking of is how people perceive. The slotting, the conflation, that happens the instant they perceive.

That instant's what I keep thinking about. Just an instant—but in it, a whole narrative (my life) unfurls.

12. Imagine the horse's owner perusing the pages of racing magazines, loading websites late at night in an office tucked in beside the tack room in a stable, the smell of sweat and dirt thick over the printouts of lineages that litter the desk. Perhaps there is a cup of coffee beside them. Perhaps a pregnant mare whinnies from down a long line of stalls, pacing before settling into her bed of hay. The owner sips from the coffee, clicks the mouse to scroll down the page, searches the list of the races in several years' time. (You have pictured the owner either male or female; which? Doesn't matter, the owner is not the one we care about here, but—which?)

Shadows pool around the blue light of the laptop. At the foal's birth, and then regularly thereafter, there will be fees to pay for each race in anticipation of when the horse will be ready. There must be a budget, calendars to be planned, a choice of projections in which to invest, the mapping out of finances and a life.

13. Imagine, too, that equine fetus, long limbs folded beneath it, not yet ready to run; tiny hooves still soft and shredded, not yet hardened by the pounding of movement; how now it rests and grows curled in the warm wet womb for eleven months. The owner clicks and sips and allots money and decides which racing ovals will inscribe its future path, where bets will be placed, where its hardened hooves will someday run. I have a twin brother. We had a triplet sister, a sister in chromosomes at least. She would die too young for any of us to know anything about her, so here is what little we knew; the blue eyes of a baby, tiny like us and like us premature, *girl*.

One of each, and me.

Two girls and a boy! the announcement.

At eight, I became aware I wasn't a girl.

14. One of the first known people to use testosterone to alter his body was British twenty-four-year-old Michael Dillon in 1939. He'd sought the treatment nominally for his menstrual periods but already wore the clothing of a man. Before Dillon, men had grafted slices of chimpanzee testicles to their own; they had attached

snippets taken from the genitals of goats; they had had the tubes that carried sperm from the testicles blocked, in the hopes that stopping its movement would create a surplus of vigor. Even William Butler Yeats underwent that surgery, hoping to keep up with a younger lover. Freud, too, and he demanded the doctor not disclose that until death.

Dillon simply took pills. In writer Pagan Kennedy's account of his transformation, it is one-way and absolute and the hormone is what achieves and legitimizes it, upholding the sanctity of the binary. Of Dillon before he was Michael, Kennedy writes, *She became the first woman on record to take the drug with the intention of changing her sex.*

A sentence elapses, only a sentence.

As soon as Dillon could look entirely male, he became invisible.

15. My writing seems to come out these days like my thoughts do: in snippets, disconnected, seized up. The thoughts don't—can't—adhere. I try to make a narrative line but only these dots appear.

Even D and I don't see each other anymore. I am alone in my apartment, no one to witness me or me them.

We are all social distancing from one another.

16. *We need a sense of what you want your body to look like,* my agent writes. *You tell us what feels wrong, what you want to change, but you don't tell us what you want to change to.*

He is asking me to imagine what comes after.

17. Levels of testosterone for those assigned female at birth generally stop at 60 or 70 nanograms per deciliter of blood. Levels for those assigned male at birth generally begin at 270 or 280 or 300.

Note the vastness of the unnamed middle.

When I began taking testosterone, my own levels fell very clearly on one side of the divide. Now I am caught in that middle, a sentence without knowledge of its end.

18. At times I try to imagine what I want this country to look like, when all this is over. I try to imagine us taking care of one another. I try to imagine my relatives and neighbors not reacting to the virus as though it is political.

I try to imagine 343,593 (today's count; tomorrow it will be higher) people not dead, so many of them Black and brown, and so many of them economically marginalized. While I'm at it I try to imagine Black men and women not killed by the police; immigrants not hunted at the border; a nation not founded on genocide; the erasure of the violences that make this place.

19. And, okay, I try to imagine what I want to look like, but I grew up in the same damn binary everyone else did. The same damn America.

20. The truth is, I don't know how to answer my agent.

It is easier for me to say what I don't want. Harder to say what I do.

21. *Queerness is not yet here. Queerness is an* ideality. *Put another way, we are not yet queer. We may never touch queerness, but we can feel it as the warm illumination of a horizon imbued with potentiality. We have never been queer, yet queerness exists for us as an ideality that can be distilled from the past and used to imagine a future. The future is queerness's domain,* writes José Esteban Muñoz.

22. There was a year, once, when I pricked myself 144 times with needles. I had known that my body could not cradle a baby (historically a mark of womanhood, but my body has always been made to fail that part), that to do so might endanger my life. I had assumed that there would be some future solution to this—maybe a partner would carry, or maybe science would catch up. (A bit of regression to how I soothed myself to sleep when I was a child: no need to be afraid of death, for science would surely solve it before I grew old. My belief in science more potent than that in magic, any dream, any god.)

But I had aged, and the future had arrived, and there was no solution beyond pulling forth what was inside this body, my body, and so I went to doctors and had a probe inserted in myself and saw my own insides on the screen and the nascent beginnings of the material that would go into making another person. Every morning, and every night, I drew clear liquid into a syringe and injected it into the ring of fat around my belly button, moving the needle clockwise to a new site, mimicking the march of time. My abdomen puffed. I grew nauseated, which seemed only fair—if my

child would come into the world without me ever having morning
sickness, shouldn't I be paying that debt forward now.

23. After each shot, I ate a cracker spread with the cheapest caviar,
the kind you can get at the supermarket for six dollars a jar. I had
begun the ritual as a joke, a need to find joy and inject levity into
the process. A need to disrupt how medicalized the whole thing was,
how sterile, all those foreign objects I used to break my skin. We
were trying to coax my body into such a high estrogen level it would
release more eggs than the usual monthly one; I would, therefore,
eat tiny eggs. Rhyming action: a move familiar to any writer.

But what began as a joke was soon overcome by sensation: the
smoothness of the hard little eggs between my palate and tongue,
the salty pop as intense as the sea. The joke became a prayer. The
taste as much a benediction as tears.

24. The drug I injected myself with arrived by manila envelope
from Israel, ordered off a spare website with a sketchy, straightfor-
ward name: 1800IVFMeds. In the United States, my dose might
have cost me a thousand dollars every two days. From the website,
more than a week could be had for that amount. The drug was
precious, befitting its fairytale origins: synthesized now, but once
distilled from the urine of elderly cloistered Italian nuns. At their
age, they had too much of the hormone needed to be pregnant.
How infertility works: too much, not too little. That too-muchness
could be harvested, the wealth spread.

Why nuns? Because the nuns had (presumably) not had sex,
because they had (presumably) never seen their body reflected
back in the body of another, because (presumably) there was no
chance they could be pregnant.

25. Only writing this do I realize that my gay self would have been
as safe a bet as those Italian nuns.

Pretty funny.

26. One morning in the middle of the year of injections, I went
to the doctor for a monitoring appointment. I did this a couple
of times a week each cycle and had long since asked to insert the
probe myself. A small bit of agency claimed. On the screen, black

fuzz resolved itself into the shape of the follicles inside me, the spaces growing larger to shelter eggs.

That afternoon, for a class I was taking, I went to a laboratory as sterile and white as the exam room I'd left. There, five dead bodies were laid out on slabs: two men, three women. I put on a plastic butcher's apron and clear plastic goggles and nitrile gloves, and my partner handed me a scalpel and pointed. I brought the blade to the body's fallopian tube.

That's not quite right. I don't want to say *the body*. Not doing something as intimate as slicing her up.

But there, there, you see the problem again. *Her.* I know nothing of this person, only the shape of their body; from this I have deduced a pattern. I have no other word to choose. I don't know who she was beyond the mark of those ovaries.

With my scalpel I split them open, pale pink and the size of green cocktail olives. I saw the tiny hard eggs within. Larger than a pinprick, a pencil point, the period of a sentence.

Futures that had never been.

27. The drug worked; my body released eggs. Never many, but enough. These were injected with sperm, grown for several days, and then frozen. The cycle repeated once, twice, three times again.

28. Still I waited. That fertilization had happened was no proof life could ever take root. It seemed likely I would be told it was all for naught, that the child I had wanted since I was a child was not possible. It seemed impossible that I would get anything I wanted that much, as though the act of wanting made it impossible.

Does everyone carry such felt knowledge of doom inside them, such belief in the impossibility of a future? Or only those of us born into bodies that cast us into a narrative that doesn't fit?

As though having the audacity to want, and to act on that want, would itself be a trick, the coin proffered by a magician that vanishes with the opening of the hand that ought to reveal it.

29. So I remember the *whoosh* in my chest when, over the phone at the end of the year, I was finally told that some—five—of the embryos were viable. How in that instant, a path opened to a door that opened to a future.

*

30. Maybe I only ever write about the problem of how to believe in the future.

31. I was ready to hang up then; I remember that, too. I was awash in glee, as though all at once the blood of my body had been rinsed in relief. The sensation was overwhelming, light-flooded, alive. I wanted to get off the phone, away from the doctor's voice and just feel.

32. But she kept on. *Of the five, there's,* she said, and told me the sex of the embryos. How many this kind. How many that.

A clear favorite. Not even odds. Not at all.

33. The child in my daydreams acquired a gender.

—. When I emerged from the restaurant where I'd taken the call, there was a child standing on the street, gripping a mother's hand. The mother—irrelevant to me, never what I would be.

But that child. Short blond hair, striped shirt, a smudge on its cheek. It appeared to be of the gender that matched the sex I had just been told my someday-child would likely be, and I remember how closely I observed it. I remember the feel of a daydream arranging itself, as though it were straightening its shirt hem, spitting into its palm, patting down its hair.

—. And sure, I do my best to note in my daydreams now that a child's gender is not known just because their chromosomes are. Of that, I myself am proof. And really, even those chromosomes may turn out to be more complex as each embryo grows more than the seventy to one hundred cells it has now. I know enough about sexology to know that the simplicity we've been bottle-fed is a lie, always has been a lie, that there are far more than two options and they are not as set as we might imagine. I do my best to imagine a doctor informing me of complexity. I do my best to imagine a child coming to me the way I eventually did to my parents. I do my best to imagine them speaking a truth about who they are, and it not being the truth I expected. Or—conversely, the queer version of the unimaginable future—I do my best to think that perhaps they will be the most gender-conforming kid around, and I'll have to wrap my mind around that.

I do my best to hold space for every possibility.

—. But I still can't imagine *child* without imagining *gender*.

—. And what is a dream if not a narrative?

—. And what is narrative if not constant foreclosure, *this* instead of *that*?

—. What is the future if not the thing that replaces all other possible worlds?

34. Nine months into the pandemic—the gestation of a body—I decide to switch from the testosterone gel to the shot. The gel is inconvenient, sticky. Often it runs in rivulets down my shoulders. And I no longer need to make this decision daily, if ever I did. I know it is the right one. But also, I am getting impatient.

So one afternoon I sit in my study, alone in front of the computer. On the screen, my doctor appears, from an ivory office where she also is alone. Yes, she says, it's likely my body will respond to the shot more quickly. The term she uses is *masculinize*.

35. *I may pass as a man someday, but I will know in my gut that I had to convince myself that I was allowed to have that passing,* writes Cyrus Grace Dunham. *And maybe I will always wonder if that passing is just a trick, a lie.*

36. And I do want to change, but I don't want to pass. Not as a woman, not as a man. I go back so often to that moment with D on the dance floor, when our bodies recognized each other. When, in the closet, we looked and we saw. "I've never been with someone else who . . ."

I kissed them then because I wanted to kiss them but also because what they were saying, what they meant, was so true I couldn't bear to hear it said. I knew what they meant because I felt it, too.

Someone else who. Someone else who exists in the in-between. Someone else who, with my body, could make them feel seen in theirs.

*

37. What did we see, that lay beyond sight?

38. D wasn't quite right, those months ago, when they envied me for getting to choose where I land on a gender spectrum. The effects of testosterone are cumulative. For as long as I use it I will—to use the doctor's parlance—masculinize myself. Were I to stop entirely, some effects would remain: the thickened vocal cords and thereby (still only slightly) deepened voice; the spread of bodily hair that has now overtaken my legs; the enlarged clitoris, called bottom growth. Others would recede: the increased libido, the increased tendency toward muscle. To take a smaller dose, as I do, is just to bring on these effects more slowly. Whatever time has felt like during this pandemic, there is no actual way to stand still.

39. Except, perhaps, for the embryos. They exist in a suspended state, frozen at negative 321 degrees Fahrenheit, the temperature at which biological progression pauses.
   I like that neat countdown, three-two-one.

40. I suppose I like the way numbers imply order.

41. After all: narrative is order.

42. After all: don't we live always anticipating the next step.

43. For a while, the embryos were kept mere miles from where I lived; passing by them on the highway, I would lift my left hand off the wheel to wave at the gray building, as nondescript as any warehouse. But I moved, and that warehouse was expensive, and now they are hundreds of miles away in a town, in a county, in a state I've never seen.

44. I think of them often. I try to visit the future.

45. I had decided I would do the first shot the evening of my birthday. Why not begin a new year with this becoming. And a practical reason: I had been warned that the hormone would likely hit all at once, twelve hours or so later, and so to do it earlier in the day might disrupt my sleep with desire. I have grown accustomed to

these wakenings; to say I don't mind them would be an understatement. What a gift, how amazing, how alive, in the midst of a time of stalemate to ceaselessly *want*. Still: the need for rest.

46. When I finally did the shot that evening, it was—no way around this—no big deal. I pulled the liquid into the syringe, less than a centimeter's worth. I twisted off the needle and replaced it with a finer one. It is not hard for me to find fat, for in this way, too, pandemic time has been working its way on my body. Most days this new curviness, gendered as it feels, is hard for me. But it makes injection easier. I pressed the needle's point against my skin and winced at the bit of pain. Inhaled, pushed. The 145th shot toward a future I want.

47. I suspect I had more pain than this once. I suspect I had less certainty.

48. The future is not yet here. Last week marked one year since the night on the dance floor. Nine months have passed since we all began staying home. When I pulled on my winter coat yesterday morning, I was startled to discover a bottle of hand sanitizer already in it, the mark of time's loop. *Oh yes:* we have been here awhile. *Oh yes:* for a while, here we will stay.

49. When I pass the small mirror I keep by the door, I see my reflection: a little more of that blond fuzz on my jawline. My skin texture a little coarser. To me my nose looks the same, but who sees change when they watch for it every day.

50. And I wonder each time if it is ever possible to break free from time. If and when and how the future becomes the now.

NAOMI JACKSON

Her Kind

FROM *Harper's Magazine*

THREE SPRINGS AGO, I lost the better part of my mind. I remember it starting with my feet. I woke up one February morning in the South Bronx apartment I'd just moved into with my husband, and my feet were so swollen I could barely fit them into my roomiest sneakers. I called in sick and rode the train downtown to the doctor, who told me my blood pressure was perilously high.

The news didn't come as a shock. I had been working and worrying nonstop. I was in my first year of a new job at a nonprofit; during breaks I called the cable company, the gas company, and the furniture store. I wanted everything to be just right, for the apartment to look instantly lived-in and spotless, and I was sleeping less and less in pursuit of this perfection. I spent an excessive amount of money on linens for a dining table we didn't yet own. I imagined parties in a backyard that was home to both bountiful collard greens and stray cats. My doctor prescribed a five-day course of water pills and told me to cut down on salt and fast food.

I didn't know it then, but I would never return to that nonprofit. I missed a deadline to submit an important grant application. I stopped responding to emails and soon stopped working entirely. I called my boss's cell phone on a Saturday morning. Eventually, I think, she blocked my number. I was paid my salary for a while, and then went on short-term disability leave. That leave was extended once. When I tried to extend it a second time, I received an unceremonious email terminating me from the job. I had been consistently employed since I was fourteen years old. This was the first time I had ever lost a job.

I was once someone people would describe as steady, the kind of friend you turned to for advice on buying an apartment or negotiating your salary. The year before I became sick, I started tumbling, transforming from a high-achieving, fiscally responsible, and thoughtful person into someone you might call "messy." From February to May of 2018, I felt profoundly unmoored, alternately joyful and inconsolable, fearful and invincible. I had never felt so free or so impulsive. My whims and emotions led me; my feelings were snakes that whipped me around. Some days, having a cigarette and a cup of coffee from the bodega—light with milk and one teaspoon of sugar—was the only thing that could cheer me up.

What the world saw most was my rage. I am typically a mild-mannered person who is slow to anger and patient to a fault—a pushover, even. I hate confrontation. But that spring, I was furious. It was as if the weight of every unsaid thing and every unaddressed slight had built up in my body and was being released in one intense burst. I was mad, and I had a lot to say. A wrong look or word was an invitation to spar. I cursed people out across boroughs.

I was angry, but also afraid. My old fears—of bridges, dogs, fire, things around my neck—were joined by new ones, including a fear of riding the subway. For six long months, I couldn't travel underground: a twenty-minute train ride to Manhattan became an hour and twenty minutes by bus and foot. I started having panic attacks almost every day.

I know I could have crumbled, receded into the plush silence of my illness. I recognize myself in Anne Sexton's poem "Her Kind," from her 1960 collection *To Bedlam and Part Way Back*. Feeling out of her mind, she imagines herself a "possessed witch" who haunts the night: *A woman like that is not a woman, quite. / I have been her kind.*

As winter turned to spring, I slept less and less, sometimes only three or four hours a night. To pass the days, which stretched long and formless, I talked on the phone. In the early morning, while my husband slept, I called friends in Barbados. I called acquaintances and ex-lovers around the world, people I hadn't spoken to

in years who were kind and patient but unsure what to make of
my ramblings. They listened and grasped for polite ways to end
our calls. I wanted to talk about my wedding, which had been
held the summer before at city hall with only a few witnesses.
But mostly I wanted to air out my wounds, to talk about who had
hurt me.

My husband was at a loss for what to do with me, how to keep
me safe, so he sent me to spend time with my parents in Brooklyn.
When I wasn't talking on the phone, I sulked, watched basketball,
and skulked around the house in a white nightie. I took long walks
to the mall, where I got into arguments and one-sided conversations with strangers. I tormented my parents and demanded that
my father, a deacon, pray for me.

One night, I babbled nonsensically and crawled on the
second-floor landing of the house, wanting to stay low lest the police see me. I heard my family start talking about taking me to the
hospital, which unraveled me further. I lit a cigarette in the living
room, an act of war in their tidy West Indian home. My father, who
rarely raises his voice, yelled at me to get in the car; I tried to jump
out of it as it was moving.

My parents, stepbrother, and cousin drove me to an emergency
room in downtown Brooklyn. I rambled about *Saturday Night Live*
and *The Cosby Show,* about Oprah, Toni Morrison, and Rihanna.
By the time we arrived, my mood had shifted again. I was elated.
As we ascended the steps to the entrance, I jumped with joy and
clicked my heels together, telling everyone within earshot that I
was pregnant with twins. (I wasn't.) The last thing I remember is
a nurse with dreadlocks asking me questions and then administer-
ing medication that knocked me out. I woke up the next morning
in a different hospital. My husband and stepmother were in my
room. I joked that this wasn't how I'd planned to spend Valen-
tine's Day.

It was either during this hospitalization or during one of the
three that followed that I was diagnosed with bipolar disorder. I
wasn't sure what the diagnosis meant, or what it had to do with me
and my life. That morning, I was furious that no one rode with me
from the emergency room to the hospital a few neighborhoods
over, that they'd left me alone with strangers. When my sister visited, I asked her how she could be certain that the medical staff

hadn't raped me. She said it was unlikely, but admitted that she couldn't be sure.

For weeks afterward, I couldn't write because my hand shook too much when I held a pen. I was terrified. I had written the entire first draft of my novel longhand, and I couldn't imagine not even being able to jot down ideas.

A week after being released, I had an appointment with an endocrinologist. My family floated theories about a thyroid storm. Mercifully, no one said the obvious: that I was acting like a crazy person. But when the time came, I couldn't get myself to the appointment for fear of being readmitted to the hospital.

I left the house that morning determined to walk to Harlem instead. I wanted to see my hairdresser on Lenox Avenue, and was somehow convinced that I'd be safe there. But again, I couldn't quite make it. I called my sister-in-law and an old colleague's husband for help. I called my husband from a funeral home on East 149th Street. I made it most of the way to the salon but couldn't cross the Harlem River, about a mile from my house. I think I knew that if I got to the river I might jump. Finally, I called a childhood friend from a Dunkin' Donuts on the Grand Concourse, and she told me to stay put. She picked me up in her car and drove me across the river. I remember that drive feeling like a marvel, the water a surprise.

In 1972, my beloved maternal grandmother was admitted for the first of many times to the psychiatric hospital in Barbados known colloquially as Jenkins, after the former plantation on which it sits. "Everything that is old is evil in Barbados," someone once told me. Nowhere is the truth of that statement more evident than at Jenkins, officially Black Rock Psychiatric Hospital, where patients in varying stages of distress and dissociation wander the same grounds their ancestors may have toiled.

My grandmother was a loving, generous woman who doted on me and my older sister. She was always the first person to call us on our birthdays and insisted that people traveling from Barbados to Brooklyn bring us her exceptional Bajan sweet bread. She was also intense. On an intake interview for a nursing home, she described herself as "aggressive," one of many reasons why her stay there was short. Granny called my father and stepmother's house at all hours of day and night, looking for somewhere to park her worries.

My sister and I didn't have a name for Granny's ailment until after she died. On a visit to Jenkins, we met with a psychiatrist who had cared for her, and she showed us records that stretched back nearly forty years, to the early seventies. My mother has the same diagnosis; her stays in American psychiatric facilities began in the nineties, not long after she lost custody of my sister and me.

In her best moments, my mother was an attentive parent with serious ambitions for her children. She sewed Black dolls, assigned summer book reports, and took us to the library religiously. But she struggled through a contentious divorce from my father in the eighties, and the stress of raising two children alone in New York City and her emergent mental illness caught up with her. By the time I was eight years old, my mother was no longer herself. Sometimes she was a carefree spirit who blasted Peter, Paul, and Mary and the *Amadeus* soundtrack while we cooked on the fire escape of the small apartment she'd bought in Crown Heights. At other times she was catatonic, a present absence who barely responded when we needed her and occasionally disappeared for days on end.

That summer, my mother lost custody of us. I will forever feel guilty for telling the family court judge the truth when he asked which parent we wanted to live with. *My father,* I said, hoping my mother would never know that I had betrayed her. At Daddy's house, the fridge was full, and there was always an adult around. My mother would cycle through homeless shelters, group homes, the streets, and the occasional apartment for the next thirty years, traversing Atlanta, Seattle, Boston, and Barbados in search of something or someone, I'm not sure exactly what. I do know that I inherited my mother's hot foot. And that Mommy, Granny, and I all belong to the same strange club of the severely mentally ill.

My own story starts when I am a child and a seizure interrupts my nap. It is one of many somnolent afternoons in Antigua, the island my father hails from and where our parents ship me and my sister every summer. We stay in a four-bedroom house whose walls end just before the ceiling to let the air circulate, with a ragtag band of cousins, uncles, and tanties—our paternal grandmother presiding. I am sleeping next to my favorite girl cousin and having a bad dream about something that happened to me the summer before.

The bad dream, which I know is real, is about a boy touching me on the school bus that takes me from a street corner in Brooklyn that smells like August garbage to what will become my prep school on the Upper West Side. The boy says that if I say anything, he will tell everyone that I wanted it.

I was having a nightmare about the boy and the school bus, and then suddenly I was awake, unable to breathe. My tongue was impossibly large in my mouth and the metal fan turned and turned and turned while I tried to find my breath. I remember what felt like an endless ride between our house and the hospital, and that somewhere along the way, or maybe even after I arrived, I peed myself. I remember my cousins' brown, mosquito-bitten legs folding over one another in the back seat of the car. Later, I will get a CAT scan at a hospital in Brooklyn, my parents concerned that perhaps I have epilepsy. All the tests will be inconclusive.

For the rest of that summer, and for months after we returned to Brooklyn, I did not want to sleep alone. I was convinced that my cousin who ran to get help when I couldn't breathe saved my life. I couldn't risk falling asleep alone again. I mark the seizure as the first taste of the anxiety and depression that would haunt me in the years to come. I was a brooding, melancholic teenager and young adult. I was at once angry with and yearning for my mother, whom I didn't have any contact with between the ages of fifteen and twenty-five. In my twenties, I cultivated coping strategies— therapy, music, meditation, prayer, yoga. In my early thirties, after I published my first novel, the anxiety and depression I'd felt as a child resurfaced. In 2016, a combination of work stress, heartbreak, and isolation pulled me into a suicidal undertow. I understand now that this was likely the prodromal or warm-up phase of my bipolar disorder, which preceded my full-blown psychotic break two years later.

One day in February 2018, I almost lost myself. It was unseasonably warm. I left the house in the early afternoon, the front door wide open behind me. I wore a black dress coat that I'd bought in France on top of a matching soccer jersey and pants that my husband had given me. As I walked up the Bronx's Third Avenue, I became taken by the idea of trying to prove how difficult it was for a woman to use the bathroom. I asked to use the toilet at a dry cleaner, a day spa, and a State Farm agency, making scenes each time I was refused, sometimes claiming that I was pregnant to see how far I could push the experiment.

When I grew tired of the game, I stopped for a slice at a pizzeria, where I met a nice Black woman and her little girl. The woman had just picked up trophies for a soccer program she ran with her husband. She told me all about it as we walked twenty blocks north into a neighborhood I'd never visited before. Along the way, I yelled in French at a Togolese man. I could tell that the woman was worried about me, and perhaps a bit afraid, but she was kind.

Before we reached the southern edge of Crotona Park, I bid the woman and her daughter goodbye. I had what felt like an endless fount of energy. I wanted to play. I saw a pit bull I liked, and followed the dog and its owner into a building that I later found out was a homeless shelter. I walked to the top floor and rang a few doorbells; no one opened up, though one lady spoke to me kindly in Spanish through her door. I ran outside, where I saw a few kids. I introduced myself to one of them, who looked to be about eight years old; within a few minutes we were shadowboxing. I asked him whether he knew about Muhammad Ali and Malcolm X, quizzed him between feints and jabs until we both grew bored.

I told the boy that President Obama was going to officiate my wedding that evening on the Harlem River, and that Rihanna would be performing. I told him he should come along and bring his crew. A dozen kids amassed to follow me. Then they realized that I was lying. The mood changed. One of them, the oldest, cursed me out and chased me. I ran, weaving between parked cars, yelling back at him. I avoided a fistfight only because someone mercifully called the kids back inside.

A tall, scruffy man who had been watching the scene pulled me into his apartment about a block away. I had to get ahold of myself, he said. I looked around his apartment, which smelled like cats had been peeing in it for centuries. There was a punching bag in the cramped living room. His girlfriend was a Black woman whose skin seemed to glow in the dim light. The man said that I was too much, that I was upsetting her. She looked high. She looked like she had the same kind of problem as me. I told the man I couldn't stay long because I was running from the FBI. As soon as I said that, he shoved me out into the dark night that had descended.

I headed to the Cross Bronx Expressway. I ran alongside cars on the highway for a while, stuck out my thumb for rides. I may have been trying to get to my wedding; I can't remember. But no one would stop for me. I thought that the United Nations was in session, and I was convinced I saw Robert Mugabe. Soon I was playing a game with myself, trying to see which African dignitaries I could spy on their way into the city.

Suddenly I was unbearably hot. I stripped, peeling off my layers until I wore only a white tank top and green sweatpants. In doing so I became my grandmother, who'd been known to stand on the road in Barbados in her slip until an ambulance came to take her away. That night in the Bronx, I waved my blue hoodie at a helicopter circling overhead. I was tired, and though I didn't want to go home, I knew I needed help. I sought refuge at a community center with a lactation station just above the highway, the woman with her babe a beacon. A man there called the police.

I had enough presence of mind to know to be afraid when the cops arrived. I knew that when mentally ill Black people spiraled, sometimes they didn't make it out of encounters with the police alive. In 2012, Shereese Francis took her last breath in her Jamaican parents' Queens basement after she was tackled by four police officers. In 2013, Miriam Carey, a Black woman with postpartum psychosis, was killed by police officers after driving her car into a restricted area near the White House. Her thirteen-month-old was in the back seat. In March 2020, Daniel Prude was pinned to the ground and died of asphyxiation after the police stopped him as he ran naked through the streets of Rochester. And that October, Walter Wallace Jr. was gunned down in Philadelphia while his wife tried to stop the cops by telling them he was "mental."

By the time the police arrived, I was cold; February's chill was wrapping its arms around me. I spoke rapidly in what I learned later was clinically known as "pressured speech." Though I'm unsure now of what I said, I remember putting my hands up to show I was unarmed. I told a female officer that I had once wanted to attend medical school, but had quit a premed program to follow my dream of becoming a writer. Even as I unraveled, I tried to present my most well-mannered, professional self, hoping that my credentials might protect me. I got into an ambulance and talked with the medic the whole way there, grateful for the way he treated it like a taxi ride.

It was four o'clock in the morning when I called my husband from the emergency room. When he answered the phone, I could tell he hadn't slept at all. Later, I found out that he and my sister had called the police when I didn't come home, that they had combed the park near my house for signs of me. I want to cry when my husband describes how he and my sister looked in garbage cans, hoping and not hoping to find something that belonged to me. Even now, I am only dimly aware of how my sickness has affected them. I try to be grateful and not to feel guilty, not to be the burden I am convinced I always will be to them.

The early signs of my illness—impulsivity, reckless spending, defensiveness, sleeplessness—alarmed the people who loved me. One morning, my best friend at the time sent me an email suggesting that my behavior might be the result of a psychiatric issue. My doctors eventually agreed, but when she wrote it, it felt like an accusation, the withdrawal of her friendship a punishment. After that, she became more and more distant. A year later, when we were trying and failing to reconnect, I sent an email expressing my anger with her. In response, she said she needed to protect herself from me. While her words wounded me, becoming a parent has made me vigilant about who and what I allow into my own life, so in some ways I understand.

This was only one of the many friendships I lost. Even as I mourn the loss of these friendships, I also know what it's like to be on the other side of mental illness. Having watched my mother and grandmother come undone by their illnesses, I know what it's like to feel helpless, angry, and sad in the face of what often looks like self-sabotage and narcissism. I know that self-preservation can require setting boundaries, keeping distance, looking away.

There were others who stuck by me. Friends and family formed a kind of safety net that I fell against but never fell through. They visited me at home, and in the wards of each of the four hospitals where I was admitted. Friends in Santa Fe, Barbados, New Orleans, and Kigali called and wrote. A high school friend I hadn't spoken to in years checked on me after seeing some of my alarming social-media posts. We made lunch dates around which I organized weeks that were otherwise spent sleeping, watching *SVU* marathons, and avoiding the shower. I wanted to talk, to know that someone I loved would pick up the phone and listen without judgment. I wanted to know that I was deeply loved. One day, a friend walked me slowly around my neighborhood while I smoked and stopped every few minutes to put my back against brick walls because I was convinced that the fire department and the FBI were hunting me down. Somehow the surety of a wall at my back made me feel invisible and safe.

My illness unfolded seven months into my first year of marriage, but my husband stayed steady, even as members of my family and his friends told him to cut his losses and run. Once I was home, and the hard work of rebuilding my life began, he made sure I took my medication every day, cooked and cleaned when I couldn't bring myself to do much of anything, shouldered the weight of our bills while I was unemployed. Later, when I was well, he asked me whether I still wanted to be married to him, whether I was sure that our relationship wasn't another impulsive decision I'd made as I was losing my mind. I told him that even if it was, it's a decision I stand by.

In March 2018, a month after the first hospitalization, my therapist, my sister, and a friend convinced me to admit myself to the psychiatric ward of a hospital on the Upper East Side. I arrived with a stuffed overnight bag, shaky and afraid of nearly everything. In the spare intake room, a Black girl, a high schooler, was brought in for fighting. I was afraid of her; I saw in her wild eyes and hair the girls who bullied me when I was a chubby kid in Brooklyn. I worried that she would beat me up.

That night, I sat with the other patients in plastic chairs and washed down my meds with ginger ale and graham crackers, which I'd gotten from another patient in a trade for a PB&J. One of the patient-care associates sat down next to me. He asked me whether I was a frequent flier at the hospital, whether I'd been there before. I didn't know until that moment that I looked deranged to people outside my family. Finally, I had a sense of how far gone I was. I think I frowned and shook my head no, but it's possible that I didn't say anything. At last, I understood the line that ends an Edwidge Danticat story: "Shame is heavier than a hundred bags of salt." That long winter into spring, shame sat atop my chest, heavy and unmoving.

Shortly after I was released from the hospital, my mother came to visit. She had moved back to New York City the year before, leaving a stable but imperfect living situation in Boston to start over again in the city's byzantine shelter system. It had been months since I'd seen her, a year since she'd told me, over a lunch I could barely afford, how little she thought of my "yuppie novel." We walked in circles around my block. We shared a cigarette. She was the first person to accurately describe the way that a coffee and a smoke takes the edge off the emotions swirling inside me. When we spoke that day, we didn't say the word "bipolar" or mention the diagnosis that belonged to her. I'd never acknowledged my mother's illness to her directly; she is fiercely proud and private, like my grandmother and my sister. There is dignity in allowing ourselves to be more than the clinical language that describes how our minds work. I believe she asked me how long I was in for. We knew without saying it aloud how much being on a psych ward felt like being in prison.

Since then, I have been on a steady, slow journey back to myself, or more precisely, toward someone new who resembles the person I was before. I stopped taking psychiatric medications when I got pregnant in the summer of 2019, and I have remained off them while I breastfeed my child. I landed a tenure-track teaching position when I was thirty-nine weeks pregnant. After two years of not publishing a word, I saw my byline appear in print again last year. I am somewhat in awe that the postpartum months have not plunged me into another crippling depression or sent me flying into another bout of mania. Talking with an acquaintance who also has bipolar disorder and a child of her own makes me think that perhaps the simultaneously monumental and simple task of keeping another person alive has steadied me.

Some parts of the year when I was sick are fuzzy. But there are echoes that reverberate still. I developed a stutter that resurfaces when I am tired or nervous; some nights, I struggle to say simple sentences. The vestiges of an insidious self-doubt remain— the inability to fully trust my instincts and decisions; a constant wonderment about whether what I want is what is good for me; a persistent, draining interrogation of the lines between my highest self and my illness. The period after my intense recovery has also required that I reset the boundaries in my relationships; I am still working to discern what is appropriate concern and what is inappropriate meddling in my affairs.

Feeling better makes me wonder what's changed, and whether and how the sickness will come for me again. Although I hope there won't be a next time, I'm not naïve enough to believe that

I am so exceptional as to be spared. A study in *The American Journal of Psychiatry* indicates that the likelihood of relapse within five years for people with bipolar disorder is more than 70 percent. This illness is the sixth-leading cause of disability for young people throughout the world. Before I fell ill, I identified as able in both body and mind; my life was a testament to privilege, luck, and a voracious appetite for achievement.

Now I identify as a person with a disability. This marker is more than a new box to tick. Becoming a disabled person has been alternately confusing and empowering, a source of new connections with people who are physically and cognitively differently abled. It has also surfaced a new kind of stigma. The material consequences of my illness continue to be grave. I couldn't secure life insurance until a year after my psychiatric hospitalizations, and I am facing an uphill battle to stay insured now. It took two years to pay off the more than thirty thousand dollars in credit card debt I racked up during the manic phase of my illness. I'm profoundly aware both of my own resources and of the financial insecurity that too often defines the lives of disabled people.

When the next time comes, as I know it will, I pray for the patience and presence of my beloved community. I pray that I will not alienate my friends and family, that they will still want to walk with me, sit with me, listen to me. I know that what I needed the most when I was sick were compassionate, alert witnesses, people to listen and help keep me out of harm's way.

Recently, a friend asked me how I came to be doing so well. The answer is deceptively simple: rest, childcare, therapy, meaningful work, healthier relationships. It matters that my therapist is a Black woman to whom I don't have to explain certain aspects of my selfhood. The cultural shorthand that we share affords trust, intimacy, efficiency. A 2018 American Psychological Association report indicates that only 4 percent of therapists in the United States are African American; Black people's lack of access to high-quality, affordable mental-health care is well documented. For my part, I see my therapist only once a month, because she doesn't accept health insurance.

Most importantly, I am writing again. What was disconcerting about being sick was that it robbed me of my focus, attention, and creativity. When I was manic, I had many ideas, but I was too wired to write; sometimes I couldn't sit still for more than a few minutes at a time. When I was on high doses of medication, I was finally able to sleep, and my emotions were in check. But everything besides the most basic acts required immense effort. I had few ideas and no motivation to write them down. I felt as if I were crawling through quicksand, or perhaps more accurately, viewing the world through a scrim. Now I am reacquainted with myself as a writer, which is to say that I am reacquainted with myself.

Since the birth of my son in February 2020, I have been writing with ease and urgency for the first time in years. I am almost scared to say so, lest I jinx it, but I am even more scared to stop writing. More than ever before, I am aware of the sanctity and precarity of my life. I have been working six days a week. I have written reviews, essays, and pages of a novel. I know that I am courting danger by working nonstop and caring for a baby who does not sleep through the night. I know that just below these heights of creativity, there is a winding staircase that leads to mania. Still, I write as if I may never write again. I want to get it all down. In case my mind betrays me, let me say one last thing.

ANGELIQUE STEVENS

Ghost Bread

I

I WAS ALMOST sixteen when I ran into my biological father, Reggie, at a Trailways station. My friend and I wanted to see some boys
an hour away in Geneva, so we concocted a scheme to tell our
parents we were each spending the night at the other's house. We
were in line to buy our bus tickets when Reggie walked in. He was
broad shouldered and dark skinned; even from across the room,
I could see that he was over six feet. His cheeks fell heavily into
frown lines just underneath tinted glasses. In my young mind, I
had imagined him with long black hair like the Indians on TV that
I grew up with, but this man's hair was short and neat.

My sister Gina and I had been maybe eight or nine the last time
we'd seen Reggie. He had been sober long enough that my mom
and dad (my stepfather) were letting us visit him on weekends. He
and his second wife, Pat, and their three-year-old son, Sean (my
half brother), picked us up at our little apartment in the city and
drove us the two hours to an old farmhouse nestled in a valley. A
pond rippled just beyond a clearing. A horse pasture and barn
marked the yard's boundaries. They had a big mutt of a dog that
bounded up the gravel drive when we pulled in.

Reggie let us ride Vail, their horse, around the pond while
he walked along the side holding the reins. At night, Pat helped
the three of us kids get into our pajamas. After dinner, we ate

chocolate-chip-mint ice cream on beanbag chairs in front of the TV. Some days we'd all pile into the car and go hiking to a local waterfall swimming hole. Other days, we would go out for a pizza dinner. It felt more like a normal family than anything I'd ever experienced, but their family life could not have been as ideal as I imagined because Reggie went off the wagon and got arrested again after only a few months of those visits.

This man who walked into the Trailways station was older, resigned somehow. I said to my friend, "That looks like it could be . . ." She stopped me before I could say it. It was our turn at the counter. After we got our tickets, I looked for him, but he was gone. I was thinking maybe I had just dreamed him up when I felt the tap on my shoulder. I sensed him before I turned around—an embryonic line connecting our tissue, his skin just a shade darker than mine, his hair black but spotting gray, and the parentheses around his mouth deeper.

"What's your name?" It was a question otherwise unforgivable from a father.

I started to say "I'm Ang," but he hugged me before I could finish. I couldn't remember the last time I hugged him. I wanted to bury my head in his chest and tell him I loved him, that I missed him, that I didn't care about all those lost years. I wanted to hear his voice say all the things that fathers say, "It's going to be all right," "We'll make it through somehow."

"I'm heading over to Clifton Springs to do some rehab. I'm trying to get better," he said, like we were longtime friends.

"I'm glad to hear it," I told him. My mom and stepdad ran in the same circles as he did, so even though I hadn't seen him in years, we had heard about his life regularly. He would do well for a while, like the time he, Pat, and Sean moved to California so he could attend Berkeley for his master's degree in alcohol counseling. They had stayed in California long enough for him to get his degree. When they moved back to Rochester, they had another son and we had another half brother, named Tim. But that didn't last long, because soon he was drunk again and passed out in a local diner.

I grew up hearing stories about him and his grandfather, Henan, who was a dropout of the Carlisle Indian Industrial School in Pennsylvania. Carlisle, the first of its kind, was built on General Richard Henry Pratt's philosophy, "Kill the Indian, save the man." It gained its reputation for taking Native children from their homes and assimilating them by cutting their hair and forcing them to speak English. The children who were sent there were often beaten for speaking their languages. Sometimes their skin was scrubbed raw in order to make them white. Many, including my great-grandfather, were sent out to work on local farms. But Henan didn't lose his Indian identity. He became a Seneca chief, one of the last ones, in fact, who could "read" the Haudenosaunee wampum, the messages that were woven into belts through a series of purple and white shells.

Reggie and his brother came home on the reservation one day to find their parents, Henan's daughter Rosella and her husband Ulysses, dying in a convulsive fit from wood-grain alcohol. Years later, Reggie ran away from the Indian boarding school that he and his brothers were forced into. In his twenties, because of his alcoholism, he was admitted to the R-Wing, the same psych center where he met my mom. She had been living there over ten years. They fell in love and left the ward and got married.

"I'll be in rehab for ninety days if I'm lucky, then maybe we can get together?"

I nodded.

"Where are you living now?" he asked.

"In a foster home in Hamlin, but I'm on a home visit for the weekend." I pulled out a piece of paper from my purse and wrote my foster family's information on it. He asked me if Gina was at the same foster home.

"No, but we're trying to get her moved in with me."

"Maybe when I get out of rehab we can all get together?" He smiled when he said this.

"I would like that." I moved in to hug him again, and for a moment I remembered the weekend, years earlier, at his old house in the valley when I had a broken leg. I was stuck inside with my casted leg and asked to go outside and watch Gina ride Vail around the pond. He scooped me up in his arms and carried me out the door. He was so close that I smelled mint Barbasol shaving cream intermingled with Old Spice. I put my arm around his neck and he kissed me on the cheek, like fathers do with their daughters.

2

Four months after that day in the bus station, he called. I had turned sixteen in the meantime and he had moved into a halfway house. He was going to volunteer at a soup kitchen for Thanksgiving and asked if Gina and I would meet him. Over the holiday weekend, when Gina and I were both on home visits, we took the bus to the soup kitchen, the same one our stepdad had often volunteered at. We didn't eat because Mom had a turkey in the oven, but we worked side by side with Reggie and it felt good just to be near him.

Shortly after Thanksgiving, he called again wanting to get together, maybe to go to dinner or a movie. I said no, giving him an excuse about a friend needing help. What would we talk about? I hadn't seen him in years. He didn't know anything about me. When he called again, I turned him down a second time. I didn't want to see him without Gina, who was still in the detention home. Then I feared he would stop calling altogether, so I wrote him a letter and told him that I was anxious. In his letter back to me, he said that he was proud to be my father and maybe someday I would allow him to be just that. Then he said,

> I don't have much to give right now, but I'd like to be a part of you. Without each other there is an important part of us missing. We need to be whole. Let's salvage all we can . . . I know I have a lot of strong feelings for you both . . . I could feel it when I seen you . . . I'm glad to hear you're working on yourself, changing for the good, "I'm growing up," you said . . . you have to . . . life is not always easy . . . I know how it is to be away from your parents. I was in a boarding school for eight years.
>
> Your mother is a good woman; she stuck by you against a lot of odds. She says John is a good man. He works hard—if it has been good for you, then I thank him too . . . I have no immediate plans except to get myself together. . . .
>
> I have a master's degree. So I can get a job when I get ready. I'm not rushing it . . . I can't afford to . . . I didn't mean to rush you. I must be like a stranger to you and it must be tough for you . . . take your time . . . write again. . . .

We wrote back and forth two more times before Gina and I started visiting him. One Saturday afternoon, we were all drinking coffee in his kitchen apartment when he took two big bowls down from the cupboard and put one in front of each of us.

"Today is a good day for you to learn how to make fry bread."

"I already know how to make bread," I said.

"Not that kind of bread. This is ghost bread, the bread of our ancestors."

"If it's ghost bread, then shouldn't it be invisible?" Gina asked, and we both giggled.

He ignored us.

"The government gave Indians commodity foods, like white flour, cheese, meats, and lard, so that they could live after being forced onto reservations." He took the flour and Crisco out of the cupboard.

"Is commodity cheese like government cheese? Because that cheese is the shit!" Gina said.

"This is not funny, Regina. This is your history," he said, taking two spoons out from the drawer.

Gina and I snuck glances across the table at each other. He made us prepare our own batches as he scooped flour into each of our bowls. I was about to pour the water into my bowl when he snapped at me.

"You're doing it wrong! You have to hollow out the center first to make room for the water!"

"What difference does it make?" I asked. "It's all going to the same place. This ain't my first rodeo, you know."

"You need to let the flour fall from the sides a little at a time." He slammed the Crisco down on the counter. "This is the matter of life! All of it. This is how we remember our ancestors, the ones who died before us. Those who are still connected to us."

"I thought it was just bread," Gina said. But she had gone too far because Reggie didn't say much after that. He began ladling the Crisco into the pan and then showed us each how to make the little saucers with our dough before placing them into the oil.

Later, when we were eating the warm rounds of fried bread, Gina made a joke about how she couldn't taste the ghosts in the dough. "Maybe we should put some of that government cheese on it," she said.

Without words, Reggie left us in the kitchen to go watch TV.

Over the next few years, as Gina and I were moving out of our foster homes and into our own apartments, the three of us saw each other often. Sometimes, we'd drive out to the reservation to visit his uncle. Other times we'd all go out to eat and see a movie. The first week in my new apartment, he came over with Pictionary. I made a casserole and fry bread, and we all sat at the table and played games.

3

The summer I was eighteen, the three of us drove two hours to Salamanca for a powwow. It was at Veterans Memorial Park, big enough to handle thousands of people who came from all over the country. At the heart of the powwow was the large dance arena, where several categories of competitions in all age levels, for both male and female dancers, took place. Hundreds of craft and food tents circled the arena. Native vendors sold silver jewelry, paintings, woodwork, and handmade regalia like embroidered shawls, jingle skirts, and headdresses, each signifying a particular tribe and clan. There were buffalo burgers and Indian tacos and fry bread stands. Campers and tents for the vendors and dancers were spread in an outer circle around the food.

When the grand entry started, Reggie explained the intertribal dance that opens the day's competitions. "This is the dance that everyone shares," he said. "It doesn't matter if you don't know how. It's simple." He made us go into the ring with him. At first, we were embarrassed, but as he pointed to the circle of people around the drum, he said, "Just listen to the drum and follow me." We watched him move—toe heel, toe heel, in the same clockwise direction as the rest of the crowd, some who were in full regalia, but many, just like us, in everyday clothes. Gina and I picked up our feet and moved them to the beat of the drum on either side of him, and then the crowd fell away and it was just the three of us and that drumbeat guiding our bodies.

We stayed all day watching the competitions, eating fry bread tacos, and meandering around the craft booths. At the end of that first day, there were fireworks just as the moon came up. It wasn't until very late at night that we all got back into the car to drive the two hours home, exhausted and full.

Over the next few years, we went to several more powwows: Niagara Falls, Canada's Grand River, Toronto. Gina and I learned new dances each time we went. When the competitions were going, I'd stand on the sidelines feeling the beat of the drums, sometimes moving my feet, sometimes lifting my arms high, sometimes twirling, sometimes pretending I could fly.

Reggie must have seen how much I wanted to dance, because one day he took us to a craft store together to pick out the calico fabric and ribbon that we could use to sew our own powwow regalia—a long dress shirt, a skirt, and leggings. Then he connected me with a women's singing group. He gave me tapes of social songs to memorize. It was mostly a series of chants like yo ha ya wayo, and I couldn't understand it. Still, I listened to them every day, rewinding and playing and rewinding again, trying to get the intonations down right. But Reggie's drinking continued, and though I memorized the songs, I never showed up to the group, and we never made our dresses either. That calico cotton sat in the Jo-Ann Fabrics bags for years before I finally threw it out.

By the time we were twenty, Gina had already been arrested for prostitution a number of times, spending three or six months in jail, after which she'd be sober for a while before going off the wagon again. When she got out, she moved into a tiny little studio over on Spencer Street. It was a sober time for both Gina and Reggie. At a garage sale, he found an oversized wooden rocking chair, an Aztec blanket, and some kitchen goods for her place. He'd stop by her apartment now and again to check on her. She was so much like him. I told myself that I understood why he did those things for her and not for me when I got my first apartment. Months later, when Gina went into the R-Wing and Reggie went on a bender, I cleaned her apartment alone and took that chair and Aztec blanket for myself.

The last time I saw him was at a Seven Clans picnic in the Finger Lakes. Someone he knew owned a big cabin on a mountain. We drove separately, Gina and I in one car and he and his brother, Les, in another. The cabin was on the top of a mountain. The trees in front had just been cleared so that from the porch we could see for miles and miles.

"This is all Haudenosaunee territory," my father said as he made a sweeping gesture in front of him. Then he walked inside and left us rocking on the porch.

In the afternoon, somebody pulled out a game of Pictionary and Gina and I played with Reggie and two of his friends, a man named Bill and a medicine man named Ted. In the evening, after we were all stuffed on a big dinner of fry bread, corn stew, and sweet apple crisp, a bunch of us gathered in the living room and someone pulled out a water drum. Some of the men began to sing. I watched Reggie look down at the floor at first. Then, as the music poured out of him, I saw his head lift and his eyes close and I heard that voice, his voice above the others. It was a voice I had never heard before.

4

Shortly after I turned twenty-two, Reggie called me from Syracuse, where he was living. He was plastered. I asked him what he was doing. He said, "A little wine, a little women, a little song." He had married another woman named Pat, one who kept him swimming in alcohol.

"You know I love you," he said. But the word "love" sounded more like "luff." "You wouldn't know it to look at me, but I luff my kids. All of them." He laughed a little. "You never met your brother Tim, did you?"

"Not yet." I remembered the letters Reggie had written me when I was in foster care and thought I always knew, even when I was very little, how much that disease had a hold on him, had a hold on his parents, how much it now had on Gina too. I wondered then if my brothers would follow in the same footsteps.

"You will someday. Your brother Tim is maybe eleven now." His words came out slurred, like he said "eesh mabeh." He talked like this for a long time and I didn't say much but yes and okay and unhuh. It wasn't the first time he had called me drunk. I wondered how many times he had called my mother drunk over the years. Mom told us that when she was leaving him, when we were just babies, he'd come to her apartment and pound on her door calling for her. Once, she said, when she didn't answer the door, he stood outside her window and sang.

Then the phone went silent and I couldn't tell if he was asleep or if he just needed a break.

"Reg," I said.

"I'm sorry." He paused. I heard a whisper or a gurgle, a sound like maybe he was talking to his new wife Pat or maybe he had laughed. "I'm sorry I'm not the one you called Dad."

I realized then that he was crying.

"I love you, Dad," I said. That title felt funny coming out of my mouth. Though he was always my father, he had never been my dad. My mother had been with my stepdad, John, since Gina and I were babies. John had been with us all of our lives taking care of us. Drunk as he was, John still went to work every day. He took us to our doctor's appointments. He stood up for me at school when I was bullied in the fourth grade. He took me to emergency when I fell on the playground and got a concussion. He taught Gina and me how to ride a bicycle. When I went into foster care, John was the one to write me twice a week to check in and let me know what was going on at home. He was the one to give me money to get new shoes or school clothes. Because he ran in the same circles, he was often the one who told us news about Reggie throughout the years.

John had earned the title of Dad. But when Reggie was around, I felt it in my bones. Every time I looked in the mirror, I saw Reggie's face, those lines around my mouth, the heavy cheeks, the black eyes, my skin the color of earth. My body, I knew it was an Indian body, broad shouldered and strong on top. It didn't matter to me, the stories about him being drunk and violent, about him coming home incoherent. It didn't matter to me that he called me wasted and never remembered afterward. It only mattered that he was my father, beautiful and proud and Indian.

In October, I had just come home from shopping, bags still in my hand as I entered my apartment, when the phone rang. It was my mother calling to say that Reggie had died. It was Columbus Day weekend. He had been in an aneurysm-induced coma for a week and no one called to tell us. It was almost seven years after I had run into him in that Trailways station.

Mom, Gina, and I drove to the reservation together for the funeral. Not much had changed on the Rez since the time that my grandparents had died. Even in the early nineties, there were still many houses without potable water. Reggie's wake was held in a small shack owned by my great-uncle. There was a three-seater outhouse just outside the back door. When we arrived, there were people all around the house outside in jeans and T-shirts, drinking coffee from Styrofoam cups. Inside, women were elbow to elbow, making corn soup and ghost bread and baking roasts in the cramped kitchen. Resting near the sink in an awkward spot was a full-size garbage pail full of water for cooking and cleaning.

When the three of us walked in, one of the women pointed to the living room. "He's in there." Mom stayed in the kitchen to offer help and Gina and I walked into the living room.

His casket was wedged in between a woodstove and the wall. Aluminum chairs were lined in rows facing the casket. There were a few people sitting. Gina and I walked up to his casket and felt the warmth of the woodstove on that early October morning. He wore a bolo tie and a gray suit. His hair fell in black strands over his shoulders. I remembered him saying, "I'm sorry I'm not the one you called Dad." Gina grabbed my hand and I put my head on her shoulder. From the chairs behind us, I heard a voice, "Oh my god, is that . . . ? Sean, Timmy, come meet your sisters."

After the wake and the funeral in the longhouse, I gave Sean my address and phone number. Months later, I still hadn't heard from him. But he was sixteen, I told myself. I wrote a long letter to their mother, Pat. But I never heard from any of them.

Years later, Gina called me up to tell me she ran into some lady in the laundromat who had known Reggie. The lady gave Gina an old picture from 1976. I was six years old when the picture had been taken. In the picture, our father was with a group of Indians signing some proclamation with our city's mayor. That afternoon, Gina and I canceled our plans and took the bus downtown to meet at the library and scroll through old microfiche. From a Thanksgiving-week newspaper article, we learned that Reggie had been part of an activist group advocating for Native American Awareness Week in Rochester.

I had been going to the local community college then, and it was around the same time that my anthropology professor asked me if I was related to Reggie. He told me that in the seventies Reggie had been a consultant on a number of projects related to Native American issues. Even later, after I got my own master's degree and started teaching Native American literature at the same community college, I learned that Reggie had worked at the local museum developing materials for the Haudenosaunee exhibits.

After Reggie died, Gina and I still went to powwows. Even when we were dead broke. We'd scrape up the gas money to drive to Salamanca for the day. On Friday night, we'd make a gallon jug of iced tea in my apartment and the two of us would each pull bowls out of the cupboard. I grabbed the Crisco. Gina took out the flour and other dry ingredients. Each in our separate bowls, we made a well with the dry ingredients so that the water could be poured into the middle. Then, stirring, we let the soft powder fall from the sides deliberately into the liquid. Little by little, it formed the pliable dough we would use to make the ghost bread.

I still have that photo and newspaper article, maybe four or five pictures given to me from people who knew him. I have the three handwritten letters from 1986 and 1987. Sometimes I wish I still had that old rocking chair that I dragged around from apartment to apartment for years, repainting and reupholstering, until finally I left it on the curb, or that Aztec blanket that I kept right into grad school only to lose it in a park somewhere, or that calico fabric left in a plastic bag, long gone. Sometimes, he himself feels like an artifact to me, a man who exists in a photograph, who signed a proclamation somewhere with someone long ago, who tried, who really tried to pay tribute to those ancestors long gone. But then, I look in the mirror and I see my skin, just a shade lighter than his, the lines around my mouth deepening with age and my hair spotting gray.

The Gamble

FROM *Freeman's*

I REMEMBER THE first night my father came to us and said: tomorrow we will be millionaires. We believed him. That was back when we still believed most of the things my father said.

We must have been in Montreal only a few days at that point, in that furnished apartment where the kitchen was not so much a kitchen but a counter overhanging one of the couches in the living room, and the living room was barely big enough to sit all five of us at once. The carpet in the apartment was an overcooked pea green and the curtains had large ugly flowers on them and the view was of a redbrick wall, though I didn't mind that part because it reminded me of the buildings on Sesame Street. My younger brother and I were still zinging off the furniture into the wee hours, sleepless with excitement and jet lag. Why do I immediately think of tiger stripes when I remember that night? We may have asked him if we'd be rich enough to afford a tiger. He may have said yes.

My father was a great teller of bedtime stories though he never told them often enough for our liking, because he was rarely present, or able, at bedtime. These stories were serials that each took place in their own universe, but there were tantalizing promises that they might spill over into our own. For example, there were the stories about Ringo fi bilad al bingo, where Ringo had adventures in the faraway lands of Bingo as he searched for his best friend, traveling from place to place looking for him in a great contraption that was essentially a ball inside another ball. The interior ball, with its captain's seat and gleaming, bleeping electronic dashboard, like the inside of a spaceship, stayed upright and steady while the outside one was transparent and coated with a scratch-proof, dirt-proof polymer, so that Ringo could look out the front windshield while his vehicle rotated on well-oiled bearings, rolling over any sort of terrain: mountain, desert, and sea. My father took as much care describing the mechanics of that contraption as he did Ringo's various adventures, maybe more, because I remember that ball better than I do anything else about the stories. He promised he could, and in fact would, build us one of our very own. In Australia, he said at first, and then when it became clear we weren't going to Australia, in the United States, and then when it became clear that a US visa was going to prove impossible, in Canada. We believed him. We believed almost anything our father said because he was a genius. It's not just that our mother repeatedly told us that he was a genius; we could see it. My father could draw an eye that looked so much like an eye you kept waiting for it to blink, and he could play the violin and keyboard, and could fix the keyboard when it short-circuited by welding tiny wires to other tiny wires, and he could do math sums in his head, and he read fat science fiction books by Isaac Asimov and talked about space travel and faster-than-light vehicles and how the future would be a wondrous place of shuttling back and forth between the earth and moon. "Your father could have been anything he wanted," my mother would say. An artist, a scientist, an inventor. If only, if only.

Growing up, everything I knew about the past, personal and historical, was inflected with that melancholy of the perfect, rendered in the grammar of regret. It was not just my father's bright dreams that had been thwarted by the fates—it was this whole region into which we'd been born. Had it not been beset by occupation; had it not been claimed as a spoil of war by the British and French; had they not signed declarations and agreements that carved up the territory as they saw fit, sidelining our own leaders, installing rulers, and making way for settlers as they pleased; had they not, with all this, crushed any hopes of sovereignty and self-determination. Had our liberationist movements been given an honest chance to succeed; had our best and brightest not been imprisoned or assassinated; had every dictator and despot and occupying force not been given arms and financial support and moral backing for the most egregious crimes against humanity by the United States or else the Soviet Union. And in the midst of it all, there was little

Lebanon, every utterance of its name always accompanied by lamentation, either in tone or word. Ya haram ya lubnan, oh, poor Lebanon, once so beautiful and cosmopolitan, with its ancient ruins and modern cities, its snowcapped mountains and deeply blue sea. So many resources, so much potential, had the French not crippled it from the outset with a system of governance that meant success and positions and hence money were only attainable not on the basis of merit but on sect and connections alone. Had it not, by virtue of its location and famed openness, become the proxy battleground for greater powers near and far. Had this not meant that it, too, would be rent apart, tearing at the weak seams that had been sewn into its fabric from the very beginning.

In the face of such great forces, arrayed against you from the outset, what could save you? Certainly not will alone. It could simply never be strong enough to power you through. What was required, rather, was wit. Cleverness. You had to take the unexpected path between these giant obstacles. You had to take bold risks. You had to outwit the fates, because you couldn't fight them head-on. They were too big.

My paternal grandfather taught every one of his eight children these lessons. Born on the bottommost rung as far as both sect and class were concerned, he died—after years of swaying wildly between fortunes good and bad—in a middle-class home, in a middle-priced bed. He'd pulled himself out of the muddy fields he'd been working for a pittance since the age of seven by teaching himself how to read and write, which eventually helped him make his way out of the valley, up the hills, and down the mountain into the great port city of Beirut, where he found a job peddling gas from a donkey cart up and down the length of the old Sidon road. He would move from Beirut to Baghdad to Tehran and back, his brood of children, and hence mouths to feed, multiplying along the way, chasing the right connection that would lead him to the right business deal that would make him rich forever, and, as the Arabic expression goes, "bury poverty for good." But things would never quite work out in his favor. In Baghdad, the cargo of sugar in which he'd invested all his money, that was certain to make his fortune, sank in the river before ever docking. In Tehran, the mass arrests following the US-orchestrated coup against Mossadegh included his business partner, and he had no choice eventually but to pack up the family and leave.

I didn't learn any of this from my father, nor did I ever know his feelings or his place, as the eldest of the eight, in any of it. I sensed only the burden of it, embodied in the halting vocabulary of his movements and gestures: the expectation that he would have to do even better, depart even further from the position in which he'd been born. In no other way, however, did my father ever speak of the past. Instead, he was a great believer in the future. For himself and the world at large. It was the promised land where everything we'd ever wanted would come to be. It was his favorite tense. When we are; we will; we'll have; you'll see. I used to think that belief in a shining future was a way of refusing to dwell on the failures and disappointments of the past. A form of resistance to it. Now I think the opposite. I think the past and future are the same place, taking long refuge in either the same thing. A way of avoiding, not living in, the present.

Here's the one true thing I know about my father's childhood, one of the rare things he told me himself: when he was eleven, or fourteen—no one seemed to remember exactly—he survived a fall from the fourth story. He had just showered and gone out onto the balcony to hang his wet towel. Somehow his hand touched one of the wires that crisscrossed the narrow skies in such neighborhoods. This wire happened to be live. The current grabbed hold of his body and flung him clean off the balcony and down onto the pavement below. Is that how it happened? Is such a thing even possible? In any case, he fell from on high, and against all odds, he survived. He survived, even after the doctors told my grandmother that she had better call the sheikh and begin preparing the shroud. He spent months and months recovering. His jaw was shattered and had to be wired shut for the better part of a year. By the time I knew him, the only physical trace left of it was a thin, crescent-shaped scar on his chin, white against the brown of his skin. His upside-down smile, I called it.

My father hated religion, hated mumbo jumbo: he believed in science. He saw religion as the purview of the dull-witted, those who weren't brave enough, intellectually speaking, to strike out into the unknown. I also think it's because religion necessitated a belief in fatalism, in the idea that everything that comes to pass comes to pass because god has written it so. This meant that the future, too, was already decided, as irrevocably locked-in and unchangeable as the past. And when the past was all doom and defeat, the highest probability was that it foretold the same about the future. Thus, no one wishing to make their way forward and upward in the world could afford the indulgence of such a thought. To shed a belief in fate was somehow to shed the weight of the past altogether.

And yet, despite his rejection of what he called nonsense, my father also had faith in the strange, random, improbable, and unpredictable possibility called *luck*, which is different from the set of fortuitous circumstances referred to as *privilege*. A lot of what looks like luck on the surface is in fact, upon further scrutiny, privilege. And my father, though he would never learn of that particularly modern word for it, knew very well how to recognize privilege, for there is almost no one to whom it has been denied who cannot identify the halo of its blessing—always hovering above someone else's head. But luck, real luck, can happen to anyone. Real luck, in fact, is the only wild card that can trump privilege.

This possibility, I think, is what my father gambled on his whole life, even as he convinced himself that beneath it all was simply a code of probabilities that could be cracked given enough determination and smarts.

If my father's beliefs sound contradictory, that's because they were. All addicts exist inside a contradiction, at an unmappable crossroads between the forces of fate and individual will. Fate (genetics, circumstance, hard luck; not I) made me an addict. Will (power, determination, pure self) will allow me to overcome it. Perhaps that's why twelve-step programs, instead of employing linear logic to lead people out of addiction, simply flip this contradiction around. Will, choice, made me an addict. Surrendering to a higher power—not I—will allow me to overcome it.

My father was a happy drunk, or at least, the drink undid a sort of tightness, heldness, around his eyes and mouth, and this made him appear happier. When he was surrounded by people, as he was back in Beirut, he was only one of many drinkers in the evening. His voice would ring out from the living room and into the bedroom I shared with my brother at the end of the hall. We'd listen to him tell stories to other people, regaling *them* with his quick wit and clever ideas. There would be roaring laughter and the slap of cards, or else the clatter of dice on the backgammon

board. My father was equally loud and good-natured in his excla-
mations whether he won or lost. He never, ever let the resentment
of the sore loser dull his tone, but he definitely always played to
win. Even when he couldn't manage to gather a large group together, there was always someone willing to share a drink and a
laugh and a game with him in the evenings, as often as shelling or
checkpoints would allow.

It took a long time for the facts to add up, for me to even think
the word *alcoholic*. There were many reasons for this, the most obvious being that drunks on TV were mean and violent, all their
held-back ugly thoughts torrenting out the minute their lips were
loosened by drink. My father was the opposite. When he was drunk
was the only time he let himself express, with abandon, affection
or love. "I love you so *much*, Baba," he would gush. Encouraged by
his mood and words, we'd ask him if we could, say, take a trip to
the mountains that weekend, or if we would have a swimming pool
in Canada, or if he could finish tomorrow the story whose ending
we were dying to know. "Of course, Baba," he'd say. "Tomorrow
you'll have anything, everything you want." We believed him. Only
later, after we'd been in Canada for a while, would we come to understand that when he smiled like that, blinked like that, smelled
like that, he never really meant, or even remembered, what he'd
said the next day.

Many things were revealed in Canada. I suppose, in that way,
Montreal was exactly the fresh start it was intended to be. The
strike out into new territory, the bold move West, where each of us
could be free to realize our potential, taking any road we pleased,
without the countless restrictions that narrowed our possibilities
back home. Everyone knew anyway that Lebanon, the entire Arab
region ya haram, was a lost cause—there was no future for anyone there. We left behind the civil war, all its fear and common-
place horrors and discomforts, and went to a place where waking
up to see the next day was a certainty rather than a question of
odds. My parents bet everything we had—the money we'd saved,
yes, but also our friends and family and language and geography
and weather—on this flat, cold, very cold place where they had no
idea that the system was gamed against them from the start. Where
connections and insider knowledge and perceived class were just
as important as they'd been back home, only in this new place
my parents didn't understand the underlying rules that governed

them. Where even the cleverest person could be deemed stupid, slow-witted, and unfit for the level of employment their experience qualified them for if they were struggling to master a third language. And where, cut loose from all support systems, it was revealed that those alone had been propping up the illusion of a happy family, more or less united in cause and purpose. We fell apart from one another like so many loose twigs and my father, always slightly at a remove from us, always slightly unattainable, retreated into his own world entirely, lost in his own calculations. As though living in a parallel timeline. A hologram, there in body only, like a character from one of his science fiction novels.

With the fates arrayed against him, you see, my father was not about to let them win. He was going to outwit them, take the unexpected path, the shortcut that would shoot him past all the obstacles and into the shining future he'd dreamt of all his life.

My mother says he was pretty much hooked from the very first night. We'd barely put our bags down, so to speak, in the furnished apartment on Boulevard de Maisonneuve before he went across the road to the dépanneur to buy milk (and also whiskey, and cigarettes), and returned with a fistful of lottery tickets and shining eyes, asking my mother if she knew, could she even *guess* what the grand prize was for the person lucky enough to win the pot?

And that was the other reason it took me so long to identify my father as an alcoholic. It was that his drinking problem was the least of ours.

My father claimed he had a system, that he could crack the code of the numbers. It was all a game of probabilities. He would go no farther than this in his explanations. He would sit at the dining room table, at which we never ate because it was always covered with papers, and all the papers covered with columns and rows of numbers, some of them with little sketches and caricatures of people he knew in the margins. He bent over them like a medieval scribe, writing out numbers in his neat hand, sometimes punching furiously into a calculator.

Occasionally he would quiz us on our dreams, listening for anything that resembled a number.

"I dreamed I was being chased by soldiers!"

"How many were they?"

"I dreamed I was older and living alone."

"How old were you?"

"I dreamed we traveled back to Beirut."

"What was the flight number? How many passengers do you think there were on the plane?"

"It wasn't on a plane, Baba, we just suddenly appeared there, and we all liked it much better than here."

The lottery results were always read out at some point late in the evening, between 10 p.m. and midnight. Close to the magic moment when today becomes yesterday, tomorrow becomes today. My father would have spent all day poring over his numbers, smoking cigarette after cigarette as he filled out the lotto cards carefully, circling six, or was it eight, numbers out of sixty-nine, barking out reprimands if anyone got too loud and distracted him. At some point in the late afternoon, after taking a break to watch *The Simpsons,* which was the only activity we did together, he'd leave, his one outing of the day, to go to the dépanneur and hand over money we didn't have, money he'd borrowed, to exchange those cards for electronic versions of themselves, where the choices were made irrevocable. His fate sealed. Then, if he happened to be out of whiskey, he'd go to the SAQ and pick up a bottle—Black Label when he wanted to splurge, J&B if he couldn't, the same two brands he'd drunk in Beirut. He'd come home and pour the first glass out for himself, settling into the living room couch, his head hunched over the Game Boy, which he'd bought for my little brothers but quickly claimed for himself. He was especially good at Tetris, calling us over excitedly to see the pixelated celebrations when he beat all nine levels, doing it so often our enthusiasm quickly wore into eye rolls and sighs.

When the hour came for the results he would always stand, never sit, in front of the TV. Onscreen there would be a man and woman, the man in a suit, the woman in a lovely dress or tasteful skirt. The very picture of respectability, both. Nothing sordid or hopeless here. The man and woman would be on some brightly lit stage somewhere against a stark white backdrop, the logo of the provincial lottery behind them. A great transparent ball would turn, like Ringo's magic ball, filled with smaller, colored balls that bounced crazily about inside, sometimes revealing flashes of numbers. Then they'd roll out of a tube on the side, one by one, and the woman would hold them up, smiling maniacally, her long nails gleaming, while the man read the number out. What feral, furious, ferocious optimism must have gripped him as he stood there, waiting! He never betrayed any hint of it, only sometimes swaying slightly, but that also could have been the drink. I can only now imagine what must have bounced and roiled behind his set features: possibilities as bright, as wild, as buoyant as those dancing balls. In that moment before the first number came out he was always a potential winner, always seconds away from an eternally changed life.

What did he think he would win?

What did he imagine he could afford to exchange for that money? Our house, surely; the car. The country in which we now lived? The expectations that had been placed on his shoulders from the outset, being the eldest of eight, being so smart, being now the unwilling patriarch of his own disappointing family? Perhaps he thought he could exchange all of us for happier versions of ourselves. Perhaps he imagined he'd wake up the next morning, and, rich, we would all be thinner, gleaming, well-behaved. A family of whom he would no longer be ashamed. For this is what he blurted out one day—stone-cold sober—when my mother confronted him during one of their many house-shaking fights, asking why he couldn't be more present, why he couldn't set the lotto cards and whiskey bottle aside for one goddamned day so we could all go out together as a family, enjoy the things we'd left everything behind in order to be able to enjoy, namely parks and open spaces you didn't have to pay for and afternoons that could unfold at leisure without chaos or curfews. "Because," he said, "I am ashamed of all of you." We were not the family he wanted. We were not the family he ever had in mind.

Here's a thing my father blurted out to *me*—drunk as a skunk—late one night when I was the only one around. I forget what prompted it; most likely nothing. My father's conversations and confrontations were all with himself. We just sometimes got to hear the odd snippet of all that mental chatter, on the very, very rare occasions he let his guard slip.

"*You,*" he slurred, pointing unsteadily, "you don't know what love is."

I remember my breath catching, both enthralled that my father was trusting me with something adult and also terrified of what he would actually say. I was seventeen, molten with first love, ablaze with feelings I was certain no one else on earth had ever felt or would ever feel or could ever understand, so great and grand and sublime were they. My father knew nothing of this, of course. He went on:

"*I* know what love is. I know love like you can't imagine. It makes everything possible. But maybe you can answer this: If a man has been able to experience the kind of love that makes everything possible, but then he loses it, does that make him lucky or unlucky?"

Hard-core gamblers are always willing to stake everything on the bet, but can rarely pay up their losses. To avoid the acceptance of loss you must be ready to gamble again. And again. And again. It's like any other addiction. To avoid reckoning with the price it has exacted from you, you must continue allowing it to return you to that place of refuge, from where it is possible to dream that this is it, the last time, the final plunge before a triumphant emergence. From inside addiction, sobriety seems like the place where all your possible selves can come true. But sobriety itself is a slog, because it is a place of daily reckoning. It unfolds minute by slow minute, in the present simple. The only place where a real sense of the future—the future continuous—exists is inside addiction, that magic moment that comes every day, when you decide to succumb for the very last time. And so you surrender to your fate, assuring yourself that it was, in fact, an act of will.

In any addiction, the debt you incur is always owed to yourself; the debt you incur is that of time. You borrow from the future to forget the past, to make the present easier to bear. Tomorrow you will be the winner. Tomorrow you will pay it all back by living as fully, as happily as you can.

When all the givens were aligned just right, my father could be extraordinarily fun to chat with. He did hilarious, merciless impressions of all the Lebanese people that Canada had forced him to befriend for lack of any other options. He whistled distorted versions of famous tunes and tried to get us to guess what they were. He was always making jokes and puns by creating mixes of Arabic with English with (terrible) French.

His favorite thing to talk about was how technology would solve every problem humanity ever had. He spoke confidently of the day when computers would be small enough to be carried in people's pockets wherever they went; when robots would take over all the hard labor and save so much time and money that it would shift the culture from one where people had to work to live to one where they could pursue whatever they damn well pleased. He liked to speculate how there were probably entire other universes inside black holes, where life was so different we couldn't even imagine the rules that governed it.

He was especially wildly excited about the internet. Said he'd predicted it all along. A global information network that would make laughable all borders. He died shortly after it came into our household. In the era of Netscape and Hotmail, long before Gmail or YouTube. After the paramedics left our house, while my mother waited for the sheikh to arrive, to perform death rites my father would have rolled his eyes at, I sat in the basement and listened to the keening howl of the dial-up and then tapped out an email from our AOL account to my friends back in Beirut, who were all spending the summer together without me. *My father just died of a heart attack,* I wrote. Or maybe: *My father just died. He had a heart attack.* Something as short and sudden and quick as what had taken place that August morning in an upstairs bedroom of our house. I couldn't tell if I was being overdramatic in my wording or not dramatic enough.

For the longest time I didn't know what to feel. Or rather, I could not identify any of the sharp specifics inside my general, awful sense of loss. My father had not so much left us as completed, made visible, an absence that had been present among us all along. He had postponed the business of living until he'd simply run out of chances and time. Anyone could have seen it coming. Anyone could have predicted he'd die of a heart attack. He ate badly, smoked too much, drank too much. What strains, too, that nightly anticipation must have placed on his heart. He hoped too much. He wanted too much. He carried more sadness than should be allowed and never shared it with anyone.

But even while he was actively killing himself, I'm sure he never truly believed in the possibility of his own death. For there are many like him who don't die. Who carry on, despite all odds. Who survive the first heart attack and go on to live better, healthier lives, having been scared straight. There are also others who do everything right, and then one day collapse just as suddenly and finally to the ground as he did. There are those who trip on a step and fall at such an odd, improbable angle that it kills them instantly. And there are those who fall from the fourth story of a building after having been electrocuted and live to tell the tale.

I don't know how he mythologized that survival for himself; how he explained it in his own vocabulary of belief. I know my grandmother said it was because god had decided it was not his time to die. I know that my grandfather said it was because he was clearly destined for a great future. I also know that when my father tried to kill himself one drunken night before I was born, it was by attempting to throw himself off the balcony before he was wrestled down into submission.

But he did not die either of those times. Instead, he died in Canada, in a bedroom of our suburban house where we were behind on rent, far from anywhere he considered home, almost exactly three weeks shy of his fifty-fifth birthday. He died and left us to sort through piles and piles and piles and folders and boxes of papers scrawled with numbers, an incomprehensible code known only to himself. And with forty thousand dollars in credit card debt.

When someone dies, the only way to give condolences in Arabic is to hope that, despite all this, god smiles upon the future. There is no way to say, "I'm sorry," or "my condolences." It seems ridiculous, in fact, to offer up the smallness of individual contrition in the face of this, the grandest of all things. There is no "I" in any of the words offered up as consolation to the living over the departure of their cherished dead. Each dialect of Arabic has its own call and response for this occasion. A rote script that also gives the grieving something to say back, when they might otherwise have no words. In the Levant we say, "el 'awad bi salemtak." May the compensation for this loss be found in your own health. Or else, "el ba'iyyeh bi 'omrak." May the lost years of the deceased be added to your own life. The Syrians say, "inshallah khatimat al ahzan." May this be the last of all your sorrows. And the response for all of these is to wish the blessing back, always accompanied by some variation of "inshallah." If god wills it. Death is the greatest of obstacles, the strictest and most unchangeable of fates. It is the single certainty, written from the start. In its face, this truth must be acknowledged by all. When it comes to death, a surrender to fatalism is a great comfort. Otherwise the *if onlys* might shackle themselves to your feet, tripping you back into the past every time you try to move forward.

Years later, long after I'd left my mother and brothers in Canada and moved back to Beirut, as I'm sure my father would have wanted for himself if he'd had the chance, I was flipping through one of the countless photo albums at my grandmother's house. I went through them every time I visited, always paying close attention for sightings of my father. Rare were the photos in which he looked truly happy; even as a child his face was guarded and full of sorrows. One day, I came across a picture of him with a woman so white-blond the blob of her hair was almost like a burn in the black-and-white photo. She wore a mod little dress and thick-framed glasses. My father looked both shy and terribly pleased with himself.

"Who's that?" I asked my aunt.

"Oh," she said, as though I knew this, as though she and everyone else had not been keeping this from me my whole life, "that's your father's first wife, Anke."

My aunt wouldn't really tell me more. Every question I had—How long were they together? How did they meet? Did they have kids? What happened, why did they divorce?—was met with either a shrug or the briefest and most untelling of answers. It would take many more years to piece together what had happened, and even still I don't have any clear picture. The only person who was forthright with me about it was my mother, but even she was never allowed but the smallest, blurriest glimpses into my father's past or inner life.

They were together for two, three years at most. She was Dutch. They fell in love when she was married to someone else; she divorced him and immediately married my father. They were crazy about one another. They had no children of their own but she had a young daughter from her first marriage. His family disapproved. They never said so outright but made it icy clear. She was foreign, divorced, older. He was the eldest; he was expected to shoulder the heaviest of the family's expectations, the entire weight of all the sacrifices my grandfather had made to give them all a better future. My father was torn between loyalty and love. He was given, not in so many words, a choice. He chose wrong. He regretted it for the rest of his life.

*

In North America my father became openly taken by the idea of individualism: that a man could be whatever he wanted, that his fate could turn on a dime (or a million), that he alone was responsible for his success. "You are the master of your own destiny!" crowed any number of the sparkle-toothed maniacs he liked to watch on TV. "Today is the first day of the rest of your life!" And he believed them, or at least I know he wanted desperately to believe them, I think because that would have been the ultimate way for him to make a fresh start, to prove that he was truly able to leave the past behind.

But none of these wild-eyed gurus, the chanters of North America's siren song, ever mentioned the way a person could be fettered by circumstance; acknowledged that one could be anchored to the weight of family or country or class or body or war or history in such a way that made it not only impossible to attain success by being the master of one's own destiny, but outright ridiculous to even think it possible. Those weighed down the heaviest would have to muster all the forces possible to be able to pull forward: will, yes, inhuman will, which is what this philosophy mandates—but also cleverness, brilliance, wit, talent, and even then, none of these might ever lead anywhere without the magic boost of that powerful, unpredictable little engine called luck.

But as I assess the lost potential of my father's life, I always find myself asking: Where is the line drawn between personal responsibility and collective circumstance? Between fate and individual will? Between irrevocable past and open future? Between the hand we are dealt, and how we choose to play it?

This line, like the present moment, is a slippery thing. Ever-shifting, ever-changing, moving elsewhere as soon as it is grasped.

My father would have hated me writing this, hated me revealing anything about him at all. But where does a person's jurisdiction over their own story end? Is it with death? Or is it when a person has children, and their story becomes essential to the way someone else might understand themselves and their place in the world?

In every sense, my father's story is also mine, and that of my brothers. It is both the burden we carry, and the material from which our own fates are made. Each of us can only try and chisel it for ourselves into a shape less severe, both for his sake and ours, but its facts, now that he is gone, are set in stone.

I am old enough now to understand this very simple truth: that because my father's story is my own, to be compassionate with him is to be compassionate with myself. Likewise, to hold him to account is to also do the same for myself. And again, I find myself lost between poles, between distinctions that might be obviously identifiable to other people but which have always been so difficult for me.

A view that I hope maintains some balance, calibrated to the lesson I wish most to take for my own life: my father was dealt a mixed hand, but what hindered him above all was that he was a fearful player. He was also never allowed to reveal that fear, not even to himself. Being a man, being an Arab man, being a man of his time and place and origin, he was not permitted to ask for help; he was not permitted to fail. As such, he never let himself take the boldest risk of all, which was to bet on his own talents and see where they might lead. He saw his cleverness only as a means to an end, a tool that was worthless if it didn't produce wild success, and wild success, for him, could only be measured in money. He rarely allowed himself the simple pleasure of creation, just to see what he might make, or what it might make of him. He rarely, in fact, allowed himself any pleasure, except the pleasures of addiction, which come with harsh punishments built into them. He had, like many people—like me when I don't catch myself— a simplistic view of what it means to win, and what it means to lose. As though life has some final score, some moment of arrival at a finish line that isn't death.

I wish there were a system to follow, a code that could be cracked. But I wouldn't even know how to go about finding it. My beliefs, like my father's, are a contradictory mess of cold logic and riotous feeling, of magical thinking coupled with disdain for certain kinds of faith. Like my father, I carry the vast histories of my region and my country, as well as the smaller histories of my family and myself, each of them inflected by tense, aspect, mood, and voice. Out of this chaos I must every day try and make a story to best serve my purposes. That is all I can do. I know that what I write today is not what I would have written yesterday, nor is it what I might write tomorrow. I might regret the things I've revealed, or the things I failed to say. I am choosing to write it regardless. The only real truth that can ever be told, anyway, is that of the continuous present.

The Wrong Jason Brown

FROM *The New Yorker*

IN THE SPRING of 1994, I was driving back from running an Alcoholics Anonymous meeting at a prison in Orange, New York, when blue lights appeared in my rearview mirror. I had gone through a rural intersection and taken a right onto a narrow road. I might have rolled through the stop sign. I took off my seat belt so I could dig through the glove compartment for my paperwork. After years of driving illegally, I now had a license, registration, and insurance. The officer approached. I rolled my window down and placed my hands on the steering wheel. A young guy around my age, mid-twenties, with the same kind of pizza-dough face as mine, asked me for my documents. Hoping for a warning, I handed over my information, and he returned to his cruiser.

I went back to staring out the windshield and thinking about a poet I thought I was in love with, who wisely saw me as trouble. The light had just started to fade in the tall oaks and maples. When I checked the rearview mirror again, I counted five police cars, with twice that many officers gathered nearby in a huddle. One of them spoke on a radio and relayed information to the others. I stopped breathing, and, every time one of the cops glanced in my direction, the muscles in my neck ratcheted tighter.

The prison, called the Monterey Shock Incarceration Facility, was where young offenders, almost all of them Black or Hispanic and from New York City, marched around a military-style campus wearing olive-green fatigues, some of them carrying eight-foot logs, while the guards, all white, barked orders. Then the young men sat in neat rows in a cinder block room and looked at my friend and me, two white guys from a college town who had come to share our "experience, strength, and hope."

This was how it had started for them, I thought now: waiting to be surrounded. Except this couldn't be happening to me, because I was Jason Brown—I was innocent. One of the officers produced a bullhorn, while a half-dozen others approached my car in a crouch, their hands on their guns. From what I could see, the remaining officers seemed to be taking up positions behind the cruisers and preparing for battle.

The officer with the bullhorn raised it to his mouth and yelled, "Jason Brown, get out of the car with your hands in the air."

They split into two columns on either side of my car. Though I knew I should follow the orders of the officer with the bullhorn, I no longer had any control over my arms and legs. My thoughts spun out of my head and flew into the air, leaving my body behind. I felt as if I were watching a TV show about someone named Jason Brown who was about to be arrested for crimes he claimed not to have committed. The Jason Brown in the car was starting to hyperventilate, while the Jason Brown watching this on TV was curious to see what happened next. The approaching officers froze, and the voice through the bullhorn repeated its demand. Either I would step out of the car, or they would drag me out. I understood that if they dragged me out they would be angry, yet I was no more willing to open the door than I would be to shove my hand into the mouth of a shark.

The guy with the bullhorn told everyone to hold on. I sat with my hands molded to the steering wheel. One of the officers ran back to the cruisers. After a minute, the rest of them joined him. Another minute passed. The officer who had originally pulled me over approached my car. He tapped on the roof, handed my license back, and looked around the interior.

"We had the wrong Jason Brown," he said. "There's another Jason Brown with an arrest warrant. He's very dangerous."

My forehead collapsed against the steering wheel. When I eventually leaned back, the officer held a yellow sheet of paper in front of my face.

"What's that?" I said.

"A citation for not wearing your seat belt."

We had been married a year when my second wife told me she had dated another Jason Brown, a helicopter pilot. I asked her if she was sure she had married the right one. "I do like helicopters," she said, and smiled.

When I published my first book, a man wrote to me and said, "My name is Jason Brown, too, and I am a writer. What are we going to do about this?"

To me, the name Jason Brown sounds like an amateur golfer. In the 1980s and '90s, a spate of future athletes were born with the name Jason, including Jason Brown the professional football player and Jason Brown the figure skater. Another Jason Brown, born either a month or two years after me, became a fugitive wanted for murder, in Phoenix, and appeared on the FBI's "Ten Most Wanted" list. That Jason Brown was born in California, which I was not. He had a master's degree in international business, which I did not. For a while, he was a Mormon and owned a business called Toys Unlimited. At one point, Jason Brown took a firearms class; at another point, an eyewitness claimed that Brown had accidentally shot his truck. A little while later, he allegedly shot an armored-truck driver five times in the head and made off with fifty-six thousand dollars in cash. He hasn't been seen since.

I wish I could tell it straight through, but that has never worked out. Too many pills, too much booze, born missing a beat or a bearing—often I come to the end of a sentence not knowing where I started. Frequently I read Camus, Arendt, Baldwin, many others, but I always come back to Camus, looking for a road map I can recognize. I can go a week, sometimes a month, and I feel almost engaged, motivated, invested. Then, without warning, I'm frozen. The muffled voices of my family, students, and others seem to come from down the street. For long stretches of time, I can't move.

"Well, you were born late," my mother once told me, "and before I even laid eyes on you, the doctor told me that you looked like a Neanderthal. I didn't think that was such a nice thing to say. We couldn't separate you from your bottle for at least four years, until you developed trench mouth, and when we brought you to preschool you curled up in the corner and moaned until the teachers made me come back for you. Also, for a long time, you would only play with orange toy cars, and then, one day, you found your father's hammer and smashed all your cars to pieces."

Like teenagers from any generation, I suppose, my friends and I wanted everything destroyed and remade in our image. But we were the last generation for whom there were no rules. Pretending to be undercover police, Dan and I borrowed a friend's blue Chevy, put a flashing light on the dash, and pulled people over. Once, when I picked up a job crewing on a sailboat going from Florida to Maine, I left school for three weeks and told everyone my godmother had died in a plane crash. I was going to Florida to sprinkle her remains over a coral reef. I told kids that I was from a rich family and even had them drop me off in other neighborhoods, only to have to hike halfway across town to my house.

Already drunk and driving with a guy from my high school whom I didn't know very well, I stopped at a 7-Eleven to buy beer. After we loaded the back of the car, everything went dark until sometime later, when I came to naked in a one-room cabin. I was lying on my back, and a woman I had never met was sitting on top of me. Apparently, we were having sex. A dozen or more people sat drinking in the cabin. "Who are you?" I asked. Her eyes were closed.

In my last year of high school, my father moved out and my friend Tom moved in with me. My parents' house, in Portland, Maine, had a windowless, dank basement apartment where Tom and I lived.

"You know, he's very, very handsome," my mother said one morning, while I was pouring myself a bowl of cereal upstairs. I supposed there wasn't much I could do about that. There were handsome people out there. That I might be one of them, as my mother had said many times, in no way canceled out the existence of other handsome people and of the desires that ripped through our lives like the wind. My mother blushed, as if she were fifteen. She put her hand on my arm, smiled, and raised her eyebrows. I poured my cereal into the sink.

In the spring, a month before we graduated, my mother, Tom, and I were drinking in the kitchen and we ran out of beer. I took Tom's car to get more from the corner store. The name on my fake ID was Bob. Bob Brown. On the way back, I crashed into a fire hydrant and slammed my forehead into the windshield. The car wouldn't start, so I left it there and walked home with the beer under my arm. It was dark by the time I reached the house. I sat at the kitchen table as blood dripped down my cheek, along my neck, and into my shirt.

"What happened to you?" my mother asked. Tom took a beer out of the case, and she looked at him the same way she looked at me. Or she looked at me the same way she looked at him. He looked at the floor.

At the end of the week, Tom and I were buying a slice of pizza downtown on Exchange Street. We only had enough money for one slice and were trying to split it evenly in half as we stood in an alley.

"Your mom asked me to have sex with her," he said, and shrugged. This wouldn't have been an unusual thing to say. Not for us, not in our world. He was just keeping me informed. I waited for him to say more, but he didn't have to. Sex was not something we could say no to. It was all around us. My mother shared whatever sexual thoughts passed through her mind.

Maybe the context started when I was ten. That's the age that makes sense from other proximate evidence surrounding my memory of getting out of the tub and turning to my mother, who held a towel. Instead of handing it to me, she dried me off: first my head, then my chest, then below. I turned in a circle in front of her. She said, "You're big down there."

It would be helpful, in a way, if there had been one particularly heinous act I could point to—one act, that is, that stood out from moments like that one, in which I stood next to the bath and she smiled as her hand lingered on me. The same smile, coy and embarrassed, that she would flash in the future when she would come into the bathroom to dry me off, or touch my arm as I passed her in the kitchen, or tell me about the men she liked and why. The same smile she would later offer Tom, my other friends, other men, me.

For Tom and me, our mothers' sexuality was like the coastal fog of our native state: everywhere, in our lungs, slowly suffocating us, though we didn't know we were suffocating. We didn't know what was happening to us when it was happening to us. A person's hand on your body is like a word. It has no meaning—doesn't even exist—outside of context. Once the context is set, once the fog settles in, anyone's hand on my body would feel like her hand. Every woman who ever smiled at me with desire was my mother. If I was drunk or had just met a woman, there was a chance I could make it work, but not for long.

"To those who despair of everything, not reason but only passion can provide a faith, and in this particular case it must be the same passion that lay at the root of the despair—namely, humiliation and hatred." Camus.

In college, while blacked out, I took off all my clothes and walked across campus to a party where I started talking in a soft, serious voice about certain key passages in Nietzsche's *The Gay Science*. I had blackouts all the time by then. Many of them were not really drinking blackouts. I would lie down and fall asleep after a few beers, only to wake up sometime later as someone else. This other Jason Brown liked to be on the move. One night, I threw my clothes and furniture out the window and had to see the dean. I woke up in the bushes; I woke up in hallways. Once, I was down by the Androscoggin River and found a pair of pants hanging from a branch, with the name Jason Brown written on the tag.

In 2002, when I was thirty-three and coming out of another failed relationship, I paid for a five-day codependency workshop at the Caron Foundation, in Pennsylvania. A number of people from AA had attended, and they spoke highly of the ability of the therapists there to take you back to the origin of your damage. By the time I arrived at the orientation, I was sure I had made a huge mistake.

The program was designed for people who were still having trouble with relationships. Our group of twenty was mixed in gender and appeared to range in age from sixteen to sixty. After we got to know one another, we broke into small groups of five or six to talk in therapist-guided sessions about the problems, most of them sexual in nature, that had led us there. Then we were handed foam bats to wield against furniture, the floor, walls— anything but the other participants. We were supposed to expunge our rage. That was the plan, I was told.

The food was great, and the therapy didn't work at all. I sat in a circle on the floor with my small group and narrated what I knew about what had happened between my mother and me—a part of my life I had never talked about before, not like this. I wasn't describing anything I had somehow repressed or forgotten, but, in telling it to all these strangers, I felt as if I were talking about someone else's life. That person, the person in my story, didn't sound like me.

When I finished, I took up the foam bat and pounded on the chairs and tables and walls while the strangers watched. It was satisfying to beat on objects while the strangers (two of whom, a teenage girl and a forty-two-year-old wife and mother of three, I found attractive) watched me pretend to lapse into a rage storm. For their benefit, I contorted my face and clenched my fists. I grunted. I wanted to be a sensitive but explosive Jason Brown. Misunderstood, sexy—the James Dean of damaged lovers. I had worn my tight black shirt for the occasion. But I wasn't enraged, not in the slightest. When, at age twelve, I had put my fist through the windshield of our car, I was full of rage. When, during my first year of sobriety, I picked up Dan and threw him across the room, I was enraged. I knew I was supposed to get back there now, but I couldn't, not while I was working the audience.

Having relinquished my bat, I returned to the group, curled up into the fetal position, and pretended to cry. I hadn't been told that this was expected, but I understood the script. The mother of three rested her head against my back while the teenager pressed her warm lips against my ear.

Later, in a private meeting with the therapist, I confessed that I didn't think I was supposed to be there. I was a fake. In the same way I had faked my rage in front of the group, I had faked everything else in my life. Starting when I was twelve, I had spent years guzzling booze in a periodic way, but I didn't think I was really an alcoholic. I went to the meetings because I needed somewhere to go. I needed someone to be, and "alcoholic" fit better than anything else.

"It's not like anything *happened* to me," I said. Nothing, I meant, that justified how I still felt, years after giving up drugs and alcohol. In other words, my mother hadn't had sex with me, so I didn't see what I had to complain about. I was sick of my failed relationships and of how I felt, but, mostly, I was sick of hearing myself complain—yet here I was, complaining again. The more we talked, the more he nodded. I imagined that he could see that I was terrified of myself. I had tried to halt for good all thought, desire, rage—everything—once by slicing up my arms and once by throwing myself in front of a bus. In the latter case, I was wasted and fucked up the timing. The bus stopped and waited for me to pick myself up and get out of the way.

Then the therapist used the word I couldn't apply to my experience with my mother. No one had ever said this word to me, about me. He used the word again together with the words "emotional" and "covert." According to the therapist, all three groupings—the word "incest" alone and the word paired with the other two words—described what had happened to me, which I found impossible to believe.

I have the ability, always have, of not being wherever it is that I am. I see, I hear, but I am not there, not anywhere. This was the case for me now as he explained how my personal context overlapped with the diagnostic context. On one level, these were all just words, like the words of my name. The therapist finished his discussion of my new context and asked me what I thought.

I told him I had no idea. I didn't think anything.

He leaned forward. He had a perfectly manicured dark-brown beard that matched his eyes. "I don't think that's true," he said.

"But nothing *happened*," I said. "She didn't . . ."

"Didn't what?" he said.

"Do anything to me."

"She did," he said calmly. "Based on what you've described since you got here, she did."

The therapist thought I was trying to avoid the truth, but that wasn't the case. I'd heard other words and acronyms: ADHD, dyslexia, bipolar disorder, alcohol-use disorder, major depressive disorder, generalized anxiety disorder, suicidal ideation—not a disorder but a symptom. Abuse. Survivor. For my mother, what they used to call borderline personality disorder. Maybe we had been winged by some of these, I told myself—my family tree on her side was riddled with examples—but I was no hard case. I knew how these things went. First came the category that only half fit. Categories like footprints in a field. Our lives poured passively into the molds. Then the narrative to support the category. Then maybe medication that would make me feel less like me than the booze and drugs I had taken to medicate myself in the first place.

The bearded therapist with coffee breath didn't understand that part of me wanted to believe what he had said. If I could accept his word—if I could only agree that something had *happened* to me—then my life would no longer be my fault. Not just parts of my life, certain mistakes, but the whole thing. That was the promise as I saw it. What an incredible relief that would be. The trouble was that I resisted the tools that psychology and academics had given me to explain everything: by absorbing statistics and micro-categorizations of pathologies, traits, and isms, my feelings had become a function of systems, diseases, genetics, class, race, gender. Even if I could put a name to what felt like my true story, it might not be true at all. It might just be the story that made me feel better. I had a sense that there was a disturbing parallel between my desire to obliterate the pain and confusion of my experience with booze and drugs and my desire to extinguish my uncertainty with the totality of interpretation. Maybe both were ways of trying to make the real story disappear.

I left the therapist's office with his words lodged in my brain. A handful of words to describe what was wrong. No words can bear that burden—but when you're drowning and words are all you've got, then words are better than nothing.

Over supper that night, I sat across from the mother of three, just the two of us, not talking, looking at each other between bites. When your context is set early on, you don't feel attracted to the people you are allowed to be attracted to. Only the people you are forbidden from touching can break the spell. I said I was going to the bathroom and slipped out the back of the cafeteria. When I reached my dormitory, I found the teenage girl standing in the hall outside my door. Her room was just around the corner. She hadn't noticed me until my performance, until my fake rage and grief. Now she noticed me. I recognized the look on her face when she raised her chin. Her cheeks were burning, eyes watering. The heat of her sorrow passed right into me, and I understood that she didn't want to talk or play with foam bats. We'd done enough pretending. I shook my head, rushed into my room, shut the door behind me, and turned the lock. Now I was feeling something. Terrified of my bottled-up desire and the certainty that I would always be alone, I stood sobbing at the window and looked out toward the dark woods.

Camus again: "A man who says no, but whose refusal does not imply a renunciation. He is also a man who says yes, from the moment he makes his first gesture of rebellion . . . He means, for example, that 'this has been going on too long,' 'up to this point yes, beyond it no' . . . In other words, his no affirms the existence of a borderline."

When one becomes the sexual object of one's parent—or, I imagine, of any member of the close family—there is a part of oneself that becomes sealed off like an insect in amber. Over time, one begins to suspect, especially during important moments in relationships, at work, with friends and family, that one is not fully present, not wholly there. Finally, it is impossible to avoid the feeling that this sealed-off part is the real self and therefore the source of all our fear and all our desire. Then it becomes impossible not to feel that this part of us we cannot touch, cannot know, determines who we are and how we see the world. It explains, maybe, why other people never seem quite real and why we never seem real to ourselves, as we pass through the world speaking, acting, desiring. This explains why when I meet people I often have the strange feeling that I am them and not me. Then they walk away, back into their own lives.

A local woman found my mother's father where he had killed himself, in the garage attached to the barn, in New Hampshire, in 1996. He had pulled his car inside, connected a hose from the tailpipe to the interior, and gassed himself. Assuming, as people do, that his pet would not want to go on without him, he died with his cat, which had been a present from my mother. They passed away listening to the rumble of the engine of the car.

One of his daughters (my aunt) disappeared—I have no idea what happened to her. One son later served time in Sing Sing for molesting a boy. His brother, when he was about fifteen, supposedly chased his father through the house blowing holes in the walls with a gun. He was trying to kill his father but was too drunk to aim. I don't know what happened back there, in that family, not exactly. History is a thunderhead passing over the earth. We are the lightning that touches the ground.

In 1991, I lived in Portland, in a condemned apartment next to a sex shop and across from the Nu Body Health Spa, a place that had nothing to do with anyone's health. I lived with Dan, and we were both three months sober. Behind the apartment was a funeral home. Frequently smoke poured from its smokestacks. One day, a voice told Dan he was Jesus. I asked him if he believed the voice, and he said that at first he did but then he thought about it. I suggested he write a note to himself, *I am not Jesus,* and leave it next to his bed.

It was a Saturday in May, and I wanted Dan to go with me to some kind of gathering. Maybe with AA people at Denny's, I can't remember. I never wanted to go anywhere by myself. I was lucky when I rolled with other people, especially with Dan. He had a motorcycle, and I had a broken VW Rabbit.

He said he was busy with his old girlfriend. What happened next didn't happen, not in the usual sense. I only know what happened because Dan later told me about it. I lost time as completely as if I had blacked out from downing a fifth. Dan and I weighed about the same—between 190 and 200 pounds—but he was twice as strong as me from lifting weights. Also, he knew how to fight and I didn't, not really. I lifted him off the floor and threw him against the wall. Then I jumped on his chest and tried to strangle him. He got off a good shot to my face at some point. When I came to—when I came back to myself—I tumbled off him, and he scrambled into the corner.

Unremembered acts that we learn about through someone else's report belong to a second self that lives slightly out of reach. Scenes from a novel we read years ago. Sometimes it seems as if we remember what we do before we do it, and our actions feel like the shadow of memory.

My mother remembers a time when she had just turned seven and had been given a litter of kittens for her birthday. She was always caring for some animal: bunnies, mice, pigs, dogs. That weekend, three weeks after her seventh birthday, she had to leave the cats with her mother and stepfather because it was her allotted time to visit her father on his farm in New Hampshire. It was the coldest weekend of the winter in upstate New York, where they lived. When she came back, she found the box of kittens outside by the shed stiff as wood with their eyes frozen open. "They were making too much noise," her stepfather said. I frequently think of my mother standing in a shed looking down at a box of dead kittens. She stood there until she stopped shaking. Then she walked inside.

I often have the feeling that I am unstuck in time and living more in the past and the future than in the present. More in her life than in my own. She has spared me the worst of what happened to her—I know that—but I don't know how. I can't say that either of us has changed. I don't know of anyone who undergoes fundamental changes because they want to. It may be possible to change, but not without becoming someone you don't know.

Our mothers are the first people we know, at first the only ones we can trust, our only gateway to ourselves. If my mother didn't recognize me, I would see myself vanish by becoming a stranger to her.

In Arizona, in 2001, my mother lived alone in a dirty apartment across town from me. Usually, she couldn't figure out how to make the internet work. Usually, the answer was that she had not paid the bill. When she called on the phone I had bought her, usually I didn't answer. When I talked to people about my mother, I often lamented the burden of looking after a lost cause. I liked to tell people that she couldn't live without me, but I had already begun to suspect that I couldn't survive without her.

My mother had her own lost causes: cats with terminal diseases, former show dogs abandoned in shelters, her boyfriend from the bus riders' union who slept in a riverbed and complained that the coyotes came at night to nibble on his toes. He saved half his supper from the shelter and gave it to them so they would stop chewing on him. "This probably was not the best idea," my mother said, raising her eyebrows.

She was also involved with a group called the Samaritans, who drove out into the desert south of Tucson to leave jugs of water at key points for people who had been abandoned by another kind of coyote. More than once, I saw her cruise by in the passenger seat of a white Toyota truck. She wanted to rescue people—"the people with dark hair," as she called them—from history. One jug of water at a time, she would be their savior.

I thought of the men at the Monterey Shock Incarceration Facility, in Orange, New York, years before. Most of the men had been under twenty-five, strong, tall, many of them handsome. They sat upright in their fatigues and looked at us. My friend and I always left the camp feeling as if we had helped those who needed it—those who had been forsaken by history—but I later discovered that we had the story upside down. They were dealers and kingpins, not addicts. They came to our meetings because they were forced to by a world that had given them few if any options. We came to them hoping to be saved from ourselves.

Camus: "Here ends Prometheus' surprising itinerary. Proclaiming his hatred of the gods and his love of mankind, he turns away from Zeus with scorn and approaches mortal men in order to lead them in an assault against the heavens."

I have a memory that feels more like a dream: I am young, I don't remember how young, and I rise from my bed before dawn and walk to the bathroom as if I am being led by someone's hand. I stand on the tub to reach the upper cabinet, take out one of my father's razors, and cut red lines lengthwise along my arms.

When I first stopped drinking, I had a recurring dream that my mother and I were walking through a narrow tunnel that led deep underground. We were being led by men with automatic weapons. The air was heavy, hard to breathe, and finally we came to a small room carved out of the earth. The room was lit by a torch, and at the center of the room, on a pedestal, sat a clay bust of a dog's head. The bust radiated an oppressive power that forced me to my knees, and I had to look away. Then I couldn't breathe.

It is only by applying a kind of constant pressure, as a compress is applied to a wound to stanch the bleeding, that one can keep from drifting away, even as it is impossible to say what one is drifting away from.

My mother told me fragments over time—handfuls of puzzle pieces dropped from a box. After divorcing my mother's father, my grandmother remarried her high-school sweetheart in Buffalo. A few times a year, my mother's father, a traveling salesman, drove over from New Hampshire (in that ocean-blue car) and took my mother back to the old farm in North Sutton. Because I have been to the farm and know the smell of must from the stone cellar rising through gaps in the pine floors and know the sight of crumbling horsehair plaster and the shotgun in the closet—because I have woken in the morning to stare out the warped panes at the lower field dotted with cows and descended the stairs to the kitchen to find my grandfather already drinking—I can see my mother, aged eleven, walking in the winter field below the house with her hands brushing through the air over dry grass.

I am going over a story, looking for what's missing so I don't have to see what's there. Her thin legs. She held herself taut, arms out to the side, and turned around. The cold dampness on her cheeks anticipated the storm. The limbs of the apple and maple trees bending in the wind. A knotted cloud grew closer as she climbed the front steps and let the porch door slam with a crack. The front hall steeped in a century of woodsmoke. Her father passed out on the sofa in the parlor. Her upstairs room remained unchanged. Across the hall, what had been her father's room was also unchanged. A skin of dust covered every piece of furniture.

She woke in the middle of the night and gazed out the window toward the snow-covered fields glowing under the full moon. A vibration in her chest rippled back to its source, somewhere out there. Before she saw the fresh tracks that led from the house to the opened barn door and from the barn door back to the house, she felt as if this were a story being retold without a teller. He wouldn't kill himself in the barn for another forty years, but what she didn't know, what she couldn't foresee, was already in motion. He was coming for her. She rushed to the door that led to the empty back room and turned the knob, even though she knew that the room on the other side of the door was the same as the room on this side. There was no inside and outside, not for her, not anymore.

Between These Lives, Azeroth

FROM *Wired*

MY COUSIN KANO emerges from the oasis water as something aquatic, fins where his feet used to be, tusks sprouted from his mouth, gliding. This is something he learned today, spent all day walking the endless plains of the Barrens, killing this and collecting that (with me healing him along the way) to finally complete his quest: A seer teaches him Aquatic Form, he surges with gold light and reaches level 17. This oasis is where he wanted to cast this spell for the first time. I sit at the edge of this shining pool, surrounded by palm trees and red centaurs in an expanse of cracked earth, and I watch him with awe. Through Ventrilo, the ancestor of Discord that compelled Kano and me to compel our mothers to buy spongy microphones from Best Buy, I hear his pride. *Watch me,* as he moves through the water, transformed. *Look what I can do.*

We were growing and learning what we could with these bodies. Eleven and twelve years old, with the chemical murmur of adolescence around the bend, our worlds were a string of question marks and exclamation points, from the acne on our faces to new dreams of becoming a doctor (him) and a writer (me). At this tail end of true childhood—before girlfriends and college, before quarantine, before the fires turned California into an orange world where the sky bled like a sunset all day—Kano and I spent thousands of hours together, living and dying in *World of Warcraft.*

Four years ago, Kano died from brain cancer. We drifted apart many years before, around 2009, when I began to show signs of addiction and my parents uninstalled the game from my computer.

We lived a hundred miles away, him in California's Inland Empire and me in Orange County. So Azeroth, the central planet of *WoW*, was our tether. Twelve years severed and Kano now gone, I wanted to come back and somehow find a way closer to him and the time we spent together. I wanted something worlds away.

Quarantine, so far, had brought horror into the mundane corners of my life: This March, while making breakfast, I accidentally cleaved my finger with a bread knife. I had to perform a home surgery with superglue, chopsticks, and my girlfriend's hair tie as a tourniquet—all to keep my asthmatic body away from the hospitals then brimming with COVID cases. When I was capable of putting both hands back on a keyboard, the first thing I wanted to do was trade this surreal planet for another.

I reinstalled *WoW* in May. To recover my old account, for which I'd long forgotten my username and password, I had to email Blizzard, the game's developer, with fragments of information that still lingered with me: I had a male Blood Elf named Otaru (an anagram of *Naruto* with the *n* thrown out) and then renamed Mizukage (named after the leader of the Hidden Water Village in *Naruto*, height of my geekdom) who was maybe level 80. I could not remember my server or my guild. I sent the email without a hope of a reply, but Blizzard said they found my old account. The names of my original characters had been wiped—retired and surrendered to new players—but those characters still lived. Blizzard logged me in and, seeing those characters as I left them over a decade ago, in the same armor I had grinded so many nights to get, I could feel the tether again, the distance closing.

I logged into my Blood Elf and, spawning on the snowy cliffs of Icecrown, it was like returning to your hometown. All the people are different and, as you walk again through this place, you remember everything you did there and everyone you did it with. I opened my friends list and I scoured the names for something that rang a bell. So many names grayed out, retired long ago and replaced with a computer-generated key smash. But I locked on one among them, still legible and not yet surrendered: Tahara. That one, I thought, could be Kano.

I searched the name on *WoW*'s character database. And there he was. I recognized that face. A white-haired Tauren, a half-human, half-cow hybrid with long horns. A druid, the class that shapeshifts into bears and birds and creatures that glide in the water, in the same realm as me. Growing up, I think I knew that face better than his real face. It felt like seeing him again.

I tried another route to him. From Icecrown, I mounted a dragon and flew across Azeroth. I went to the Barrens, where I first saw Kano in the oasis by the palms and those red centaurs, and now I witnessed a world upended. Since our time there, Azeroth had been updated and rewritten over with one expansion after another. *Cataclysm,* the third expansion, released in 2010, had literally cracked the Barrens open. Bits of earth floating without gravity. Fissures torn across the plains. Floods in the desert. New flora sprouting from new water. The wreckage of a hometown.

Beside me flew another player on a sunburst phoenix called the Ashes of Al'ar, trailing purple beams through the sky. I remember when Kano and I first saw that years ago. We were caught by surprise, hunting bird men for their feathers in Terokkar Forest, and I looked up for a moment. Through the treetops, I saw those purple beams. *Kano, look!* We'd never seen one up close, only online like a celebrity or the northern lights. It was like catching a shooting star before it disappeared.

Ezra Chatterton, a child with brain cancer, received this mount through the Make-A-Wish Foundation. He was the first in the world to get the phoenix, which had become his personal symbol. His middle name was Phoenix, and his *WoW* character was a Tauren hunter named Ephoenix. And in the green hills of Mulgore by Stonebull Lake, there's an NPC named Ahab Wheathoof, a farmer searching for his dog Kyle. Ahab bears Ezra's voice, which he recorded when Blizzard flew him out to California. *Will you help me find my dog? I miss my dog so much.* Just ten years old then, he deepened his voice to sound older, wiser, a fantastical adult. (Playing with people two or three times my age, I had done the same to seem grown-up. Kano would make fun of me for it.) When Ezra died in 2008, players around the earth ventured to Mulgore to complete a quest that reunites him with his dog. I imagine that feeling of finding something loved that was lost, that elation that stings your throat, on a loop forever.

Azeroth, over its sixteen years of existence, had become a place as complicated as any place. Where people meet and find love, actual love, and throw weddings. Where people farm gold over twelve-hour shifts, seven days a week. Where funerals happen. As I flew over Winterspring, I remembered this story of a woman, a Horde player and an officer in her guild, who in 2006 died suddenly of a stroke. So her guild planned a funeral in Azeroth. She loved fishing in the game, and she loved the snow, so they set the funeral by the lakes in Winterspring, where she spent so many hours. The guild spread the word throughout the realm. *We're going to honor our friend, at this location, and at this time.* The day came and people throughout Azeroth traveled to Winterspring, gathered in a massive line to pay their respects, one at a time.

And then, the Alliance stormed through the hills. A guild called Serenity Now caught wind of the event and came in droves. They rained down arrows and lightning bolts, hellfire. They smote the funeral-goers down, waited for them to resurrect, and murdered them again. The attendees tried to fight back but they were outnumbered. In a moment, the funeral became a war zone. And in days, story of the onslaught spread around the world, through hearsay on forums and YouTube clips, even a news article here or there.

The immediate take was that this was a travesty, condoned in the Player vs. Player boundaries of the game, but despicable at its core. But now I wonder if that's what the woman would have wanted. To become part of the lore, a legend discussed and debated, remembered and misremembered years later. To bring people together, by their love or their cruelty, some way. What more could one want from a video game.

But this game has changed. Beyond the floating debris in the Barrens, *World of Warcraft* had been redesigned to support less social play. Taking on dungeons had once meant intense preparation: Kano and I would shout "LFG" (looking for group) into regional chat forums, repeating it over hours until we found other people doing the same; traveling together across a continent or two to those dungeons; and slaying boss after boss, often wiping out and starting again. The people we found would stick with us afterward; monsters were hard to kill and questing together ensured fewer deaths. After years of playing, we formed a tight band of friends, all gathered digitally, who would talk about everything from their parents' divorce to football practice. When we leveled up, we congratulated each other like it was a birthday.

But now, the game is *efficient*. A dungeon finder tool enters you into a queue of other dungeon goers, and when enough people queue, you teleport there together. The monsters die easy. And the experience points come quick. When I level up now, I burst with gold light and it's quiet.

I flew into Orgrimmar, the capital city of the Horde, and I saw more Ashes of Al'ar, purple beams everywhere. I asked one of the riders where they got this, and they told me they bought it in one of the in-game markets for forty thousand gold—or about seven dollars, if you charged your credit card for an in-game voucher.

I wanted Azeroth as it was, where gold wasn't for sale and every achievement from a mount to a level up was something incredible, ground out over days and months, that demanded you sacrifice relationships and build new ones. Something deeper than seven bucks. So, I left that world, too. I installed *World of Warcraft Classic*, Blizzard's pixel-for-pixel restoration of the game as it existed in 2006, when the gold and XP came slow, when you died easy, when you had to call others for backup, but in the grind your world and Azeroth became indistinguishable. "Immersive" is selling the experience short. As I remember my childhood with Kano, I don't remember looking at a screen; I remember our avatars as ourselves, wandering the planet.

In *Classic*, I created a new character, a fresh level 1 Undead mage. Slinging frostbolts at bats and wolves in the night, more memories came back. I found myself slipping into a familiar trance—a fugue state killing one monster after another, loosening my grip on time, walking by foot from this town to the next, dying and walking as a spirit back to my corpse, resurrecting again and again.

I skipped meals to play with Kano uninterrupted. It was during those trances that we spoke the most. Forgot what our fingers were doing and we talked crushes and things unrequited. We talked about how to show a girl that you liked her (you make eye contact, and you have to smile). We stumbled into a discovery of the word *cum* when we tried an abbreviated way of telling each other to come over and help out—and the game's built-in censors turned the verb into a row of asterisks. I called my dad over to ask him why that was. He looked me in the eyes, straight-faced, and said, "Must be a bug."

Kano talked to me about his dreams. *I think I want to be a neuro-surgeon. Or a physician. I think I'd be good at that sort of thing.*

I told him I wanted to be a writer. Maybe live in a house by the canals in Amsterdam, where Kano could visit me someday. We fantasized together, our voices hushed in the night so not to wake anyone.

I once played fourteen hours straight with Kano and the next morning passed out in a Del Taco. While I slept in the booth, face-down on the table, my mother drew a smiley face on a napkin and draped the thing over my forehead. I glared at her with inky eyes as she sat across the table, grinning with her bean and cheese burrito. Fearing addiction, my parents uninstalled the game from my computer shortly after. But I wonder now what addiction to a game like this means. Maybe it is not so much an *addiction*, something prescribed away, but rather a symptom that your life—at least the fraction where your friends live, where adventure is possible—is more digital than it is physical.

Over a decade later, now twenty-four, I had another bender of a weekend, but this was lonelier and quieter. It's hard to kill a thousand boars by yourself. I died so many times. Dungeon groups kicked me out mid-run if I made a mistake and replaced me with someone else. But suddenly my reddened eyes were staring down that oasis again, the pool where Kano transformed in the water. Now approaching level 20, I remembered what we did after he learned to shapeshift into an underwater creature. *You wanna raid tonight?*

We walked from the Barrens to Orgrimmar, took a zeppelin from the city to the jungles of Stranglethorn Vale. I swam along the Savage Coast, as Kano sped along in his Aquatic Form. We passed the murlocs and crocolisks, and we hit the shores of Westfall. There, we marauded towns full of lower-level players, danced over their dead bodies. Waited for the spirits to return to their corpses and we'd kill them again. And then some players at a higher level or with better gear or more people would do the same to us. We'd flee and hide in fields, amateur villains. This became our Saturday ritual, repeated for years as we grew from level 20 to 80, ages ten to twelve.

And so I came back to Westfall, alone. I took the zeppelin and ran up the coast. I slipped between the trees in the night. I found another player slaying ghouls, perhaps in a trance of his own. I threw a fireball at him and another. I froze his feet in place so he couldn't run. I struck him down dead. And I sat on his body, waiting for his spirit to come back.

This, four years too late, felt something like a spreading of ashes. A journey to a place that mattered. Today, I hear his voice more clearly than I have in a long time. *Watch me, look what I can do.*

Among Men

FROM *Ploughshares*

YEARS AGO, IN the liminality of early transition, I worked a brief labor job. I hadn't started hormones and looked like what until recently I had been: a dyke. At the café where I hung out was a private contractor, with a crew of macho-seeming mostly Hispanic workers, doing construction and remodeling. He liked the Republican Party and surfing; hard work, hard rock, and weed. He hired me for a three-day trial, at minimum wage, to impress a mutual friend. He was sleeping with her.

I lacked the skills for complex or unsupervised tasks. Instead, he had me drive with him to different job sites, sometimes carrying things, while he smoked and expounded on life: Women should not do construction, because they lacked physical power. He hired a woman sometimes, an electrician, but she worked slower and cost more, so he only did it to mix things up. I wanted to be a man? I didn't want to be a man. Being a man was wanting to—he made a sound between a roar and a grunt, hitting the steering wheel—all the time. "You know what I mean?"

"No."

"That's being a man. You just—agh!"

He didn't want to use my new name (my current name), but I refused to say the old one. He tried to buy it. Anytime I wouldn't do something, he wanted to pay. At lunch, unpacking my vegetarian sandwich and salad, he offered me one hundred dollars to eat meat. I was making eighty-eight dollars a day.

I didn't want to admit the toolbox was too heavy, so I staggered forward, thrusting my entire body to move it ahead, breathing hard, and stopping when he couldn't see. The other men smiled and offered to do it for me. I put it down, picked it up, and lurched forth. Eventually, the box reached its appropriate shed.

Prep work went better. Sweeping, protecting the floors. Covering furniture and molding in plastic. I mixed grout and laid tile while he yelled on the phone.

On the next drive, through forested back roads, he talked about lesbians. It didn't make any sense, two women together. No meat, no substance: foreplay. Like air. He asked me about my girlfriend. He said we should have a three-way with him. If I answered, he spoke louder, crushing whatever I said. Finally, with the two of us alone on the long country road, with no cars in sight, no buildings or even hikers, this man, at least twice my weight, with a powerfully sculpted body, in long shorts and a ball cap and half-day's stubble, said, "I should pull the car over and ravish you until you like it." He looked at me. "What would you say?"

These interactions happened so often it didn't register as a threat. The hostility started when I was a teenager, as my chest developed, and became more pronounced as I edged into bastions of maleness—like construction—and favored men's clothes. Sometimes, it came with a complicated inverted kindness: I missed the gendered hazings of boyhood, the *agh* inserted in men. If I passed the test—which I often didn't—carried the heaviest objects, ignored the insults, they were proud. "This girl can drink any of your boys under the table." "This girl jackhammered that whole front walkway herself." In the truck, beside the contractor, I blanked my features, suppressing any natural emotional response, thinking: *If I'm stoic enough it might shift.*

But it didn't. He didn't think women—to him, I could only ever be a woman—belonged in the trades. I slogged through the rest of the trial, knowing he wouldn't give me the job and that I didn't want it, no matter how badly I needed money, because—fuck him. I'd spent the last years around butch working-class dykes whose dignity came from being tougher than men. They were proud of their size and strength; of picking fights, coaching sports, and working in trades, often with the same butch/femme rigidity that other people, like the contractor, brought to traditional gender roles. They wanted girlfriends in makeup and skintight dresses with stilettos, for the contrast to highlight and legitimize them. They weren't impressed with my bookishness or clumsiness, my inability to catch or throw balls. I would have hated them as men, acting like that, but they weren't and the stance seemed powerful; the only way to be respected, as a butch woman, was out-masculinizing the men. It meant taking labor jobs instead of customer service, doing the roughest segments without flagging or asking to rest. Instead of categories, manhood and butchness were goals.

Muscular Judaism, originally *Muskeljudentum,* dates to a speech by Max Nordau, at the Second Zionist Conference in 1898. A physician, Nordau diagnosed the nervousness, weakness, and passivity of Jews as the inevitable result of diasporic oppression: "In the narrow streets of the Jewish ghetto, our poor limbs forgot how to move freely; in the twilight of sunless houses, our eyes blinked nervously; in the constant fear of persecution, the power of our voices turned to frightened whispers, swelling only to a mighty shout when our martyrs cried the death prayer in the face of their executioners at the stake."

He came from a German culture emphasizing strength, honor, and fraternity—courageous masculine traits expressed through dueling and war. Burgeoning racial theories placed Jews in opposition to Aryan virtues; Jewish blood precluded honor, they were intrinsically malformed. Jews were borderline hermaphroditic: their women too active, their men too passive, subject to homosexuality. Like gentile Victorian women, Jewish men suffered hysteria. Ideas of impurity and femininity were deeply rooted: physicians believed, as late as the seventeenth century, in the menstruation of Jewish men.

Nordau did not argue with the stereotyping of Jewish weakness— but faulted circumstance, instead of racial degeneracy. With physical training, Jews could resurrect the warriorship of ancient and biblical times. He looked to figures like Bar Kokhba, who led a bloody revolt against the Romans, and the similarly ferocious Maccabees, encouraging a return to "our oldest traditions; once more becoming deep-chested, tautly jointed, boldly gazing men." He lauded the contemporary Bar Kokhba gymnastics club, proudly displaying both their Jewishness and physicality. Muscle Jews had "clear heads, solid stomachs, and hard muscles," exemplifying both Hellenic and Germanic ideals.

The wandering Jews, the ghetto Jews, were emaciated, exhausted, fearful, grotesque. The new Jew would build a nation. The new Jew was strong.

I shouldn't do manual labor. Ashkenazi Jews are at a higher risk for many genetic disorders than the general population. One of these, Ehlers-Danlos, affects connective tissue. My ligaments do not function. My right shoulder constantly slips from its socket. I cannot run or lift certain objects, several joints dislocate if you touch them, I cannot reach backward; I have chronic pain. High-impact activities, like using a hammer, ruin my body for days. My wrists are fragile; even typing can be too much of a strain.

For a long time, the genetic disorder seemed like my only connection to Jewish history. My family did not attend synagogue or read Torah, did not speak Hebrew or observe holidays. We lived in an immigrant district, with a few Russians, where most people were Chinese. My elementary school ran an English immersion program, most of the teachers bilingual in Cantonese. Most of the Russians were Jewish, having fled Soviet persecution. This fact applied to half my family, but seemed completely abstract. Surrounded by kids from China, I felt white: generically American. My relatives spoke Russian, German, and Yiddish, but I was born in San Francisco and their cultures seemed distant, external to me. (Kafka: "What do I have in common with Jews? I hardly have anything in common with myself, and really ought to go stand myself perfectly still in a corner, grateful to be able to breathe.")

Feeling male, I looked to generic ideals. I remember being four and five years old, insisting my parents call me Robin Hood, running around with a stick and shoelace bent to form a crude bow. The only woman I would be, for Halloween, was Joan of Arc, in chain mail. In middle school, I played sports—which I hated—despite incompetence and joint pain. In high school, I set on firefighting as a career.

At the same time, I loved books and hoped to write them. A vague thought floated of writing and firefighting. I heard firefighters had three days on and three off, meaning I could make a living and write when away. Nothing appealed to me about the actual job. I needed to earn an income and needed to earn my butch stars. I hadn't met anyone transgender and—though I knew they existed—did not apply their condition to me. I identified as a woman, but suffered beneath the perception and expectation of femininity.

At twenty, I moved to a smaller radical college town. The university had famous professors in Feminist Studies—Angela Davis, Bettina Aptheker, Donna Haraway. Many of the queer people I met studied in that department. They wanted to dismantle gender and capitalism, the criminal justice system, and all other racist structures. Names and pronouns shifted regularly, many identifying as neither male nor female, but genderqueer or nonbinary. This is when I got used to referring to singular people as "they." Some of the trans people (binary or not) pursued medical transition, showing changes wrought by scalpels and hormones. I rapidly chose a new name.

My brief career with the contractor happened at the same time. By then, I identified as transgender, though less as a man than not-a-woman, and thought I might stay, with male name and clothes and pronouns, in perpetual androgyny. I did not particularly relate to, or wish to simulate, men. When I thought of "men," in the abstract, I imagined people like the contractor and the masculinity of those hardworking butches in my teens. When other people (outside the Feminist Studies department) heard about my name change, they said the same things. If I was taller, macho, athletic; if I preferred dogs to cats, or knew how to shoot a gun, or *wanted* to hold guns; if I was aggressive, or louder, or filled any number of masculine traits, they'd understand. As things stood, how could I live as a man?

I studied as if for ambassadorship to a country whose customs I needed to learn. History, sociological and psychology studies, fiction, textbooks, memoir. At fourteen, grasping attraction to women, I did a key search for *lesbian* and checked every book the library had. Now, I did this for *transgender, masculinity, men*— eventually stumbling into a piece on Jewish men whose title I do not remember and have not been able to locate again.

The article said that in mainstream American culture, masculinity is expressed by stoicism, physicality, and the ability to provide for women. The ideals are expressed traditionally, in folklore, by Paul Bunyan—the lumberjack capable of extraordinary labor— and contemporarily by caped crusaders: impermeable supermen. Historically, Ashkenazi Jews have different cultural values, shown in folklore. The author recounted the Golem of Prague.

One version, briefly: In the sixteenth century, Rabbi Judah Loew ben Bezalel went to the river and fashioned a creature of clay. This rabbi was a great mystic and scholar; drawing upon this knowledge, he animated the hulking figure. Mute, strong, and stupid, the golem labored for the ghetto, doing brute labor and protecting them from the violence of Christians outside. Eventually, the golem becomes a danger—desecrating the sabbath or turning against its creator—and the brilliant rabbi removes its access to life.

The golem is not the hero of our story. Boys do not look to it as an example of how to be men. The central figure, with all of his maleness and power, is Rabbi Loew.

Across *Muskeljudentum* sits *Talmudjudentum,* the notion of Jewish culture centering Talmudic learning, Muscular Judaism opposed. By Max Nordau's time, Talmudic Judaism had a poor reputation for dis-corporeality leading to degeneracy and effeminacy, the weakening of physical and mental capacities leading to such psychological ailments as neurasthenia and the general nervousness of Jewish men.

The contemporary scholar Daniel Boyarin argues in his book *Unheroic Conduct: The Rise of Heterosexuality and the Invention of the Jewish Man* that traits historically derided by Christian Europeans were the same ones valued within the community. Ranging from antiquity to nearly the present, Boyarin paints a picture in which the ideal, for men, is the rabbi: gentle, intelligent, modest, "sitting indoors and studying Torah, speaking only a Jewish language, and withdrawn from the world," while women "were speaking, reading, and writing the vernacular, maintaining businesses large and small, and dealing with the wide world of tax collectors and irate customers," acting as primary breadwinners so their husbands could devote themselves to religious study.

Jewish men defined themselves against Roman and European models, against "violent physical activity, such as hunting, dueling, or wars—all of which Jews traditionally despised." Instead of becoming medieval knights or Roman soldiers, Jewish men (ideally) cultivated wisdom and sensitivity; pious submission to God. The same traits valued in desexualized Christian monastics were desired in Jewish husbands. Attractive men were pale and thin, delicate Talmudists with long side curls and fine hands.

Boyarin points out that these values date back, at least, to Babylonian records—and I see them today. (Philip Roth: "Physical aggression, even camouflaged by athletic uniforms and official rules and intended to do no harm to Jews, was not a traditional source of pleasure in our community—advanced degrees were.")

After four months of hormones, I looked like a thirteen-year-old boy, acne-ridden with the first sparse starts of a beard. In another year, I underwent a double mastectomy and passed 80 percent of the time. By twenty-eight, my hairline receded, my chest hair thickened, and bartenders stopped carding me. People started asking if I grew up in New York. It happened on the West Coast, where I lived, and in New York when I visited. By New York, they meant Brooklyn, and by Brooklyn, a Yiddish-inflected bagel-and-deli enclave. There are more Jews in the five boroughs of New York City than anywhere, outside of Israel, in the world.

It often seems that people are reduced to their most visible difference, that in the hierarchy of difference, something floats to the top. I think of friends who are Black and Jewish, and how the world tends to define them solely as Black. I used to be a butch woman; passing changed me into a small Jewish man.

The new perception is very convenient, justifying a number of standard masculine deficiencies. I refuse to lift many objects—but there are those Jewish genetic problems. I never learned to drive and probably never will—but Jews, as established, live in New York and take the subway. Clumsiness is, if not impressive, acceptable in weedy bookish neurotic American Jewish men. There is a basic assumption of intelligence (deserved or not) lacking before. I had excellent grades, from kindergarten to college, and people were often surprised. I remember being told, in a job interview, before transition, that I wasn't nearly as dumb as I looked. Was it being a woman? A butch woman? The mountain of studs and ripped jeans? The jump in perceived competence, authority, knowledge was phenomenal.

When I became indistinguishable, to most people, from any man born with a penis, who spent his life with a comfortable legal-and-birth-certificate "M," general perception, of the wisdom of my transition, pivoted. I didn't need to be taller, athletic, aggressive. Most men are not Paul Bunyan or Superman. Gay, nerdy, quiet, pacifist, feminist, celibate, academic, monastic, disabled men exist in this world—and people remembered the diversity of these subtypes, instead of measuring me to ideals. I looked like a man, and so a man I must be.

This acceptance, sudden ease, came from a fluke of hormones. I wanted hormones, had a body capable of undergoing the process, lived in a state willing to pay for the doctors and treatments, after the historic isolation and synthesization of testosterone. I started injections young enough that my body did not struggle to reshape. If I had started a few years earlier, before my growth plates fused—or even earlier, as many trans people now do, in first adolescence—I might be as large as my brother (who is younger, six inches taller than me). My brother lacks my genetic disorder; he is bigger, more mechanically apt, and served in the military. He has, unquestionably, in terms of the larger culture, greater masculine credence—but I don't remember that attitude surfacing, despite any difficulty with my transition, in our own family. They were concerned with our grades.

New York intellectual Jews were born, as a recognizable subtype, in the 1920s and '30s, coalesced around New York's heavily Jewish colleges. Ronnie Grinberg's study says "Prior to World War II, a CCNY education was to the New York intellectuals what West Point had long been to blue-blooded white Protestants: not only an elite educational institution, but also a place and a process of 'masculine' socialization. [. . .] Whereas elite Protestant constructions of masculinity stressed traits like strength and athleticism, Jewish masculinity emphasized intellect and combative debate— the mind over muscle."

In contrast to Nordau's muscular Zionism, they rebelled against the perceived weakness and effeminacy of Jewish men, through intellectual means. Like secular versions of the Talmudic scholars, they wanted to know everything, moving toward academics and public comment—without the old emphasis on mildness or delicacy. "Their ideology of masculinity was not fully bound by traditional Jewish gender ideals or antisemitic stereotypes, nor did it seek merely to mimic American middle-class ideals of manliness. It was new—both uniquely American and uniquely Jewish."

The early New York intellectuals were immigrants or children of immigrants. Their schools excelled at chess, not athletics. When CCNY acquired a football team and, eventually, had a winning

season, the players were noted for strategy and deceit, lightness
and speed, over brute physical strength. Their cohort produced
some of the prominent and influential American thinkers in their
generation—acerbic, ironic, ambitious, and agitating. They grew
up and trained others, leftists and neoconservatives arguing with
each other—and everyone else—in print.

Jon Lasser and Michael Gottlieb stated, in their paper "Gender
Role Socialization in Jewish Men":

> Jewish boys are encouraged by parents to be gentle, kind, and
> emotional. Contrary to the dominant culture's stereotype of
> masculinity, Jews' construction of boyhood is one of respect
> for mother and father, emotional sensitivity and kindness to-
> ward others. [. . .] Interaction with children at school who
> have been socialized by mainstream notions of masculinity
> may pose conflicts and create tension for Jewish boys. It is the
> Jewish boy who is likely to be targeted as sissy or girlish. Such
> teasing, which is viewed by majority children as a source of
> character building and a contribution to the development of
> coping strategies, may be experienced by Jewish boys as puni-
> tive and a dilemma from which they see no alternatives with-
> out violating cultural proscriptions. In order to compensate
> for perceived feelings of inadequacy, Jewish boys may actively
> involve themselves in fights or rough sports to demonstrate
> their masculinity.

They neglected to mention the simplest, quickest form of
defense—distancing women and the perceived feminine. The
military, Talmudic study, and New York universities traditionally
excluded women. Historic elevation of the gentle *mensch* didn't
eliminate sexism or domestic violence, and it is still too easy to
express masculinity, in all realms, at the cost of women. One
thinks of Norman Mailer drunkenly stabbing his wife and calling
the knife a symbol of manhood, of Mailer's summing up a screed
against homosexuality, masturbation, and un-guilty sex with the
statement: "nobody was born a man; you earned manhood provided you were good enough, bold enough"—speaking later of his
fear and distaste of being perceived as "the nice Jewish boy from
Brooklyn [. . .] the softness of a man early accustomed to mother-
love." Boyarin notes, throughout *Unheroic Conduct*, that insecure

rejections, among Jewish men, of the dominant culture's charges of effeminacy sparked some of their most toxic behaviors: from domestic violence to imperialism.

The queers I knew worried about this with trans men. Misinformation circled about testosterone, that it gave nice butches roid rage, turning them into terrible or boring men. I've known other trans men, with binary genders, for whom transition enabled hitherto buried feminine sides to unfurl, men who became drag queens or gender fuckers, wearing dresses beneath their new beards—and there was a period of strangely inverted pressure, in radical circles, that I should wear glitter, experiment as a femme. What they meant was: Don't leave your queerness (/visibility/community/shared risks) behind.

I felt safe, for a long time, from accusations of machismo—but in recent years, considering Jewish men, I'm not sure. After working with the contractor, I told myself not that he was a misogynist but that he was an idiot—which he wasn't. He taught himself Spanish, to fluency, as an adult, and ran a thriving business. Yet, faced with the accusation that I could not hope to fulfill his expectations of manhood, I responded by saying he couldn't fill mine.

At the time, this wasn't conscious. I wanted, like my early butch friends, to beat him at his own game—beat him in terms that he and those dykes would recognize, even if those terms had nothing to do with my specific family culture or models, even if it meant contortions my body literally could not maintain. I did not let myself feel the joint pain, carrying his stupid toolbox, or the envy, hatred, and fear simmering under my surface—envy that had nothing do with a genital lump, and everything to do with how easily his aggression and insensitivity proved a certain masculinity.

I had, by now, read about Loew and the golem—recognizing in it something about the men I grew up with and my own desires, buried under what I thought I should want (that impossible firefighting career)—but did not see this specifically Jewish vision helping my claim, in the United States, of manhood. I could not impress the contractor with rabbinic or scholarly erudition and felt trapped defending myself on his terms. Inevitably, I failed and, in defense of my own dignity, retreated to the meanest corner of inherited culture: telling myself I was smarter (read: better) than him. What did I care for that goy, that man, that idiot's opinions? What did I care for his threats?

*

Jews are, of course, as Nordau suspected and the Israeli military proves, as capable of physical and martial development as anyone else—just as other cultures produce intellectuals, and women, in modern Judaism, have proved as capable of Talmudic study as men. Boyarin asks not if Jews are capable of embodying muscularity but why we should want to, seeing it as a most profound assimilation when "Jewish heroes, whether of the Bible or modernity, are all transformed into mimics of gentile heroes." To him, the internalization is particularly disturbing when violent and hypermasculine postures led, in part, to the annihilation of a third of our population under the Nazi regime.

—And yet, I cannot help thinking of how often supposed passivity led to genuine threat. Jewish weakness, particularly male weakness, justified pogroms, attacks in turn-of-the-century American ghettos, and the Holocaust itself; it justified lack of aid or intervention—if Jews didn't defend themselves, why should anyone else? It's a worldview where victimization means weakness and weakness—no matter how unfortunately—deserves what it gets, that values the "passive" deaths of those who perished in gas chambers less than the "active" deaths of those Warsaw ghetto fighters in their hopeless revolt against SS exterminators. Martial power earns a respect that sometimes envelopes to safety. A *New York Times* article, following the 1903 Kishineff massacre, spoke admiringly of antipogromists' defensive valor: "The strength and courage displayed by these people who are generally taunted for cowardice was something astonishing. Even women fought. Their physical agility and the correctness of their aim was not at all that of a race of cringing peddlers."

I think of the story an older woman, an acquaintance, told me as a teenager. I was shyly/proudly/newly a lesbian, and this woman, in misguided affirmation, told me about her father, as a young man, going with his friends to bash queers. They got in the car and drove to bars and waited until a group (of gay men? Transgender women?) exited. To the father's surprise and chagrin, after getting jumped, the queers beat the shit out of him. She told me the respect he had for fairies after—that he never tried bashing again.

I remember how disturbing I found it that this was an uplifting story for her—but also the pride in queers able to hold their own, similar to the pride of reading about the American Jewish boxers defending their neighborhoods in the 1930s, and Max Baer, the heavyweight champion who put a Star of David on his trunks for the fight against Hitler's much-publicized symbolic favorite, Max Schmeling. Baer knocked the fascist out in front of seventy thousand spectators in 1933.

Nearly a hundred years later, Baer's victory gives me a thrill—the same thrill I wonder if Nordau felt reading about Bar Kokhba— of vindication. And yet the joy is tempered. Baer was six foot four, 220 pounds, reputed to walk sideways through doors (for the width of his musculature), to toughen his skull with an iron pipe; an incontestably powerful man. His existence rebutted the lies of Jewish degeneracy, his triumph symbolized Jewish defeat of Nazism—but Schmeling's defeat was not Hitler's, the Holocaust did not end. I struggle with sports as a metaphor. Not only do athletics seesaw too easily (Schmeling went on to defeat African American Joe Louis—an Aryan victory—before Louis beat him in turn), but their use as a moral symbol disturbs. Black and Jewish (and queer) people have value whether or not they win fights; we shouldn't judge the merits of Einstein or Rabbi Loew by another Jew's boxing prowess. Schmeling, for his part, refused to join the Nazi party, kept an American Jewish manager, risked his life saving two Jewish children from the Holocaust, and befriended Louis; decades after their match, Schmeling—a philanthropist—helped pay, and acted as pallbearer, for Louis's funeral. People transcend metaphor.

I'm face blind. It's a minor neurological difference: I can't always find my parents or brother or housemates in what, to me, is a blurred crowd. After transition, I started seeing a man in shop windows and mirrors, a man who startled me by being too near, and it took a moment for recognition, to realize we wore the same clothing, that the reflection was me.

This happened before transition, but accelerated after hormones, becoming constant—occurring, even, in my own bathroom, brushing my teeth—and never entirely left. The memory is too strong from the many years of living in a body that did not reflect my sense of self and the expectation of that gap—when the gap no longer exists—is like expecting a step, in the dark, that's not there.

As with many transgender men, hormones made me appear

much younger than my age. At twenty-three, newly on hormones, I looked twelve or thirteen. In my late twenties, when I started balding, when hair crept from my chest to my shoulders and out my shirt collar, when my chest barreled, that changed. Now, in my early thirties, I look at least my real age.

These vicissitudes left me with two seemingly contradictory theories, simultaneously true. The first, that appearance has no relation to the abstract sense of myself—to that voice, without gender or possibly even culture, that speaks in my head; the *I* transcending temporal corporeal worlds—and the second, that I am made of my body and context; that these create the substance of me. It is in this second category that we relate to other people, the category in which we are more than floating spirits communing with eternity; where we wish to be seen. There came a point where I needed, for any authenticity of relationship with myself or others, to live as a man. Only transitioning did I realize that this particular manhood was Jewish; that culture and history were not, in fact, external to me.

ANDREA LONG CHU

China Brain

FROM *n+1*

SHE GETS THERE and it's like someone's aunt has decorated the place. Big block colors and weird expressionist paintings, limbs and tits hanging out of color fields, but also an oriental rug on the wall, zigzag throw pillows, boho-Bauhaus. Orange, red, orange, orange. And then just attic crap: old chairs, audio cables, yellowing books, jigsaw puzzles, a Rubik's Cube. In the bathroom, she finds a porcelain replica of Fowler's phrenology head resting above the toilet. From where she's sitting now, in a big blue chair purchased at a discount from a folded dental practice, she spots a large model of a human ear covered in small Chinese characters, for acupuncture training. Her hanzi are poor, but she knows a few. Heart, eyes. 心、目.

It's her shrink who first recommends it to her. *Transcranial magnetic stimulation,* she says with her throaty uvular *R*s. Her psychiatrist is literally German. Frau Doktor explains that TMS is relatively new, a bit experimental, but the idea is to provide a noninvasive alternative to electroshock for patients whose depression has resisted medication, which hers has. But the procedure sounds like something out of science fiction. What they will do, her psychiatrist tells her, is put a big magnet on her head and shoot electricity into her brain. Like jump-starting a car.

She will try anything at this point. It's been two years since her first depressive episode and nothing feels good anymore. She doesn't want to have sex or see anyone. Her girlfriend takes care of her, and that's basically their whole relationship now. She can't write. She backed out of a bunch of gigs a few months ago;

gradually, editors have stopped asking her to do things. When they ask, she doesn't know how to say no. She hates to say she's sick, like she's trying to skip school. She eventually settles on the word *sabbatical,* because it sounds like a vacation. She is terrified of vacation.

The slightly nutty psychiatrist who runs this place goes by Dr. L. She is Italian, not German, but really Dr. L inhabits a tiny nation of one, her own private Monaco, from which she communicates by long-distance telephone. Despite appearances, it's a real clinic, at least in the sense that Dr. L is board-certified, and the bald, sarcastic technologist who runs the machines with his small team of graduate students claims to be among the most experienced TMS practitioners in the city. This man, it turns out, is Dr. L's husband, Dennis. The two make a strange pair, bright and gloomy, talkative and laconic; she stands like a bird in his crocodile mouth. Together they decide where to put the magnets. Opposites, something something.

They did an EEG last week, an electroencephalogram, to listen to her brain. The technician was a sweet pudgy man named Timothy who stuck electrodes onto her scalp with conductive gel. She had to scrub her hair hard to get it out, like bad sex. Today they give her the results: two sets of sine waves, one recorded with her eyes closed and the other with them open. "You have a high alpha peak frequency," says Dr. L. She compares this to the sampling rate of an audio recording. Her husband grunts from his terminal, "It means you're smart."

Above her head she can see the magnet itself, a large figure-eight coil attached to a posable black tube, which runs behind her chair into a generator with a display screen. When Dennis lowers it onto her scalp for the first time, it looks like a giant black butterfly has died on her forehead. Dr. L is busy explaining what an alpha wave is. "They're in the less-active range frequency-wise, between eight and twelve hertz," she says, unconsciously lifting her arm and resting it on her motor cortex. "Your neurons oscillate in an alpha rhythm when you're relaxed, or when you close your eyes." The magnet is heavy but not uncomfortable, and the machine chirps behind her as Dennis fiddles with its settings. Dr. L stares up at the ceiling. "Now alpha waves are perfectly normal," she says, "but in the case of a depressed patient like you, there's an increase in alpha band coherence in the left dorsolateral prefrontal cortex, which has to do with executive function—decision-making, planning, et cetera. And what we think is that this alpha coherence inhibits executive function." So that's what it is: her brain is walking around with its eyes closed. "It's like a tumor, but it's not made of tissue. It's a pattern of concentrated wave activity with a two-centimeter radius, give or take." Dr. L touches her pointer to her thumb. "About the size of a golf ball. That's what we're targeting."

Once the machine is ready, the first thing Dennis does is determine her motor threshold, which means he gradually increases the power until her hand twitches, like he's tapping her brain with a little hammer to see if it kicks. They run this test to make sure they don't give her a seizure. When her hand finally shudders like a dying spider, what's strange is that it feels like a choice. "Now what we're going to do," says Dr. L, "is send an envelope of electromagnetic waves into that golf ball at regular intervals, to try and break up the alpha coherence." It's like radio interference, she thinks; it's like in science fiction when they get in a space battle and somebody yells *Jamming their comms!* so the bad guys can't talk to one another.

Dennis fires up the magnet. It shoots seven pulses of electricity into her brain, then pauses, then sends another packet, then another. It sounds like the igniter on a faulty gas burner. It feels like getting flicked in the head with a pencil.

For a while, that's all it is. The machine keeps the minutes. Sunlight gently pushes through the blinds. Outside, summer is ending.

"So what do you do?" asks Dennis.

"I'm a writer," she answers.

"A writer?" He smirks, turning back to the glow of his computer. "Are you gonna write about this?"

"Maybe," she replies. "Probably a little fictionalized, some first-person stuff."

"First person? What, like you'll be the narrator?"

"No," she says. "The narrator will be my brain."

Hello.

Sorry for the runaround. I just wanted to make sure we could talk in private, you and me. Brain to brain, if that's OK. It's your brain that's reading this right now on your computer or your phone, or bless you, maybe in print, feeling the coarse weight of the paper stock under your fingers, which are your brain's fingers, with their thousands of nerve endings. The truth is it's always the brain, reading or writing. It's always the brain talking or eating, having sex, not having sex, lying about why, apologizing for earlier, walking around the apartment wondering where did I leave that thing, saying how could you do this to me, asking is this really happening, asking what will I do without you. Brains softly crying together. Brains kissing brains goodbye.

Now I've forgotten what I was going to ask you. Maybe it's, Have you ever been sick? I had this teacher in middle school, I can't remember her name. I can't even remember what she taught. History? She had this bit she would do where she would say something like, "And the Puritans said to themselves, *Self? Let us cross the Atlantic in search of religious freedom!*" That was so funny to us, the idea of someone addressing their own self. She was young and alarmingly bony, and she had this long, curly brown hair she wore in a homely ponytail. She had a piano in her classroom and a beautiful operatic voice. She loved music. Did she teach music? I don't know. Anyway, she died. Brain hemorrhage.

That's not what I meant, though—sick like that. I mean, I do mean that. That was the first funeral I ever went to. But I also mean my English teacher, who threw himself off an overpass a few years after I graduated. He was a bad English teacher. I don't know what his brain was like, if it was depressed or manic or just tired. He was young and energetic, and he was bald with a short beard, and he had a frenzy behind his eyes and a guitar behind his desk. He loved music too. He would bring in songs from rock bands and we would analyze them like literature. We did "Hallelujah" once. What he didn't love was English. He gave us vocabulary words: *harbinger*, noun, a sign that something's coming. But he pronounced it *har-binger*, like it rhymed with *folk singer*, which is what he should have been instead. I whispered to the other brains, it's a *juh* sound not a *guh* sound. *Harbinger*. Like *injure*. Like *jump off a bridge*.

Then there was my old crush's older sister. She said the word *fuck* like it wasn't anything, like she was flicking a ladybug off her arm, and she loved long words and *Star Trek*. I don't remember how she died, only that she posted a note to Facebook, which I guess is the world we live in, though she doesn't anymore. They say it's ruining us, the internet, melting us down until we drip out of our ears. We say it too, don't we? There goes our last brain cell, we tweet; this is what finally broke our brain. She has brain worms, we say, or we get our hands to tell our fingers to type out *G-A-L-A-X-Y B-R-A-I-N* when someone posts something so magnificently stupid it's like their brain has engulfed an entire star system.

Is that where they all went, brain? Where no brain had gone before?

Almost immediately she notices the effects: a jolt of energy in the afternoon accompanied by trembling agitation, like she's holding a hornet's nest in her cheek. This doesn't feel good, but it feels like something, which is more than she can say of the past two years. She goes in for half-hour sessions four, sometimes five days a week at first. They tell her this is normal; that once they've established a baseline, it'll be more like two or three days a week, until they hit remission—maybe eight to twelve weeks total if all goes well. She tells Dr. L about the buzzing in her mouth and Dr. L confers with Dennis, who adjusts the protocol to include something called a theta burst. To supplement, they decide to give her a ketamine nasal spray right before treatment. Horse tranquilizers. They tell her it's not to anesthetize her, just to make her brain more pliant, more plastic. The brain, like a horse, can sleep standing up.

She has never done ketamine before, or any drugs really. Does ibuprofen count? She's done a lot of ibuprofen. In high school she started to get debilitating migraines, especially after staying up late. It got to where she was popping a few ibuprofen before bed out of habit. Eventually her pediatrician wrote her a prescription for sumatriptan. At the appointment he joked—it must have been a joke—that maybe her brain was too big for her head. Now, when she's on the ketamine, it's the world that's too big for her brain. Her field of vision acquires a kind of curvature; the carpet curls up toward the wall, which is buckling into the ceiling. No hallucinations or anything, though. Beyond, you know, consciousness.

Dennis hates Donald Trump. He hates him rapturously. On the wall he has hung a bizarre plaque featuring a brass relief sculpture of the president's face and engraved below it the notorious lines about grabbing things. She would be able to see it from where she sits, this seditious monument, if it weren't for the fact that turning her head would allow the magnet to reach its fingers into her motor cortex and make her dance like a marionette.

Sometimes she argues with Dennis about Bernie Sanders, whom he also hates. This is a bad idea, but she can't help herself. Other times they discuss the science of the treatment. Dennis comes alive talking about the brain. He tells her that TMS requires you to think in terms of electromagnetic events, to treat the brain less like a computer and more like the weather. The target area, that two-centimeter golf ball? It *moves,* says Dennis. The golf ball moves around. Not far, just a few millimeters usually, wobbling around in her head thanks to minute variations in alpha activity. Waiting impatiently for someone to drive it down the fairway.

Dennis refers to this book a lot, *Rhythms of the Brain,* by a neuroscientist named György Buzsáki. Later she will flip through the busted copy that he leaves for her in the waiting room. The cover has this big gray brain on it, plopped down in a desert of red cortical folds; it reminds her of the evangelical space fantasy novels she was given as a child. The book is very technical, way over her head, but she gets the thesis from the introduction. "Most of the brain's activity is generated from within," she reads, "and perturbation of this default pattern by external inputs often causes only a minor departure from its robust, internally controlled program." She mentions this to Dennis, as he once again positions the magnet on her scalp, this idea that most of what the brain does is, as it were, business-facing. His eyes light up. "The brain is intelligence!" he says, and he says it in this booming, revelatory voice, and the thing is, for her it is a revelation somehow, to realize that the same intelligence that builds cathedrals and invents gunpowder is also, and in fact primarily, responsible for itself.

In 1978, the philosopher Ned Block put forward a thought experiment called the China Brain. Block was trying to settle a debate in analytic philosophy over the relationship between the brain and the mind. The dominant cluster of thought at the time was called functionalism; generally speaking, functionalists argued that mental states like perceptions or emotions could be understood purely in terms of sensory inputs and behavioral outputs. In theory, this meant that minds were "multiply realizable": mental states could be realized not just by the human brain but by *anything* capable of matching outputs to inputs—for instance, a silicone-based Martian brain, or a computer.

Block disagreed and proposed the following scenario: Let every person in China be given a two-way radio. Then let massive satellites be shot into space that can be seen from anywhere in the country. The purpose? For each comrade to function like a neuron: a billion identical Chinese in their little Mao suits radioing each other in response to the signals beamed down from the people's satellites in the sky. In theory, China would now be functionally equivalent to a brain if it were hooked up to a human body. Yet surely this strange dictatorship of the proletariat could not be said to have mental states, Block argued; hence, functionalism was false. Surely China could not, for instance, feel pain, or fall in love, or taste the sting of alcohol on someone's lips. Surely it could not wallow in resentment, or beg for another chance, or get a horrible sinking feeling way down in its Yellow River heart.

A few years later another philosopher, John Searle, put forward a similar thought experiment called the Chinese Room. (Analytic philosophy is nothing but this kind of stuff, brain.) Searle set out to disprove the functionalist view, popular among some researchers in artificial intelligence at the time, that the brain functions like a computer program. Here was his scenario: a hypothetical version of Searle finds himself sitting in a room, where he has been provided with several packets of symbols, as well as a set of instructions in English for how to relate the symbols to one another. A new packet of symbols is slid under the door by his faceless handlers, and by following the English instructions, Searle is able to produce his own packet of symbols in response, which he slides back out. The process repeats.

Now here is the trick: Unbeknownst to the man in the room, the first symbols form a story, the second symbols form questions about that story, and the symbols he sends out form thoughtful answers to those questions—all in Chinese characters. Searle argued that to an observer outside the room, the room's occupant would appear to be a fluent Chinese speaker answering questions in Chinese, thus passing the Turing test—Alan Turing's test of a machine's ability to imitate human language—all without the man inside understanding a word of Chinese. Hence, he concluded, the brain must not function like a program, precisely because a program can function like the brain without having any idea what it's doing. Interestingly, Searle was not arguing in favor of some kind of metaphysical consciousness, just for a biological explanation for intelligence. "Can a machine think?" he asked. "My own view is that *only* a machine could think, and indeed only very special kinds of machines, namely brains."

But why Chinese? Why China? It's a curious coincidence, which is to say, probably not one. Block said he chose China because the brain had about a billion neurons and China had about a billion people. I don't know if he knew about Lenin's definition of communism: soviet power plus electrification. I do know that Mao Zedong had only been dead two years in 1978; by the time Searle was writing in 1980, Deng Xiaoping had opened the country to foreign capital. Was communist China the closest Block could get to a red planet without leaving the atmosphere, its citizens as alien as the Martians in his colleagues' papers? The Chinese were already ideal for experimenting on. In the first place, they had that air of oriental mystery, just like the Mechanical Turk, the turbaned automaton that played chess for the Habsburgs until it was revealed to be operated by a chess master hiding inside. But they were also socialists, cogs in a giant organized machine that nevertheless could not yield a single blossom of intelligence. Did you know that the word *brainwash* comes directly from Chinese? 洗腦.

That's you, brain. That little *x* floating inside your skull, like John Searle locked inside his room. Searle, for his part, chose Chinese because it was all Greek to him, though he didn't use Greek, did he? "I'm not even confident that I could recognize Chinese writing as Chinese writing distinct from, say, Japanese writing or meaningless squiggles," he wrote. "To me, Chinese writing is just so many meaningless squiggles." A language with an alphabet would still have been too close to his native English, a code he might have accidentally cracked. But Chinese "symbols," as he called them, were perfectly cryptic, impossible to parse. Not true, in fact, since most characters are phono-semantic, connected by a loose threadwork of indices and rhymes. But true enough for Searle, for whom every word in the Chinese language could symbolize the same thing: the brain, the brain. Intelligence uncomprehending itself.

Let's try a different thought experiment. Suppose the year is 1900. Empress Dowager Cixi has just dispatched Manchu troops to support the Boxers' violent campaign against foreign missionaries. In Jiangsu province, my grandfather's grandmother is sitting in a room. In it, she finds several stacks of symbols. Thanks to her gentry family, she is literate. She reads the first stack, which turns out to be a story. She reads the second stack, which turns out to be questions about the story. She thinks for a minute, then writes down some answers and slides them under the door. She receives more questions; she sends out more answers. The third and tallest stack sits undisturbed on the table next to her, covered in strange symbols. She wonders, with a growing sense of dread, what they could possibly mean.

She asks the kid running the machine today if he believes in Chinese medicine. He's one of Dennis's master's students, early twenties maybe. He has one of those names, like Kyle or something. They struggle to relate to each other. He is from the Midwest. He plays fantasy football.

Kyle says he doesn't believe in alternative medicine. "Or," he qualifies, "like obviously if it works, it works, but I just think there's always going to be some kind of scientific explanation for it." This is the easy answer; she knows because she's often used it herself. Her ex's mother had trained in traditional medicine back in Beijing, so her ex grew up drinking these teas made with bark and herbs, which her ex always hated. This was the Chinese mother she never had, the woman whose jiaozi recipe she still uses. They are still friendly. Sometimes they text in squiggles.

"But that's the thing," she says to Kyle. "The whole 'if it works, it works' thing, that's how Western medicine works too." She once talked about this with the Chinese father she does actually have, that doctors like him mostly don't know what the drugs they use do. "They just make sure they do what they want them to do without doing anything bad," she says.

Kyle angles his chin toward Wisconsin.

"Also," she presses on. "These fields, like medicine or biology or whatever, they're historically located. Like the phrenology bust in the bathroom. The only reason we say phrenology is a pseudoscience is because it fell out of favor and got replaced by something else. Don't you think neuroscience is gonna get replaced by something one day?"

The magnet ticks away like a bomb.

"Maybe," Kyle says slowly.

"Science is just pseudoscience with a bigger budget," she finishes triumphantly. She prewrote this line in the notes app on her phone.

Kyle frowns. "Not necessarily," he says. "Take evolutionary psychology. They get tons of money, but it's all bullshit."

*

I have been thinking about the mad German scientist Mel Brooks plays in *The Muppet Movie*. Brooks does this zany caricature of a Nazi doctor, though that was lost on me as a small child. He has arrived to perform an "electronic cerebrectomy" on Kermit the Frog, whom the movie's villain has been trying to secure as the spokesman for his tacky chain of frog leg restaurants. The doctor wheels in a sinister machine with a small chrome seat, above which hangs the tiny, electrified dome that will be lowered onto Kermit's head. The villain asks what the machine does. "Vat does it do? Vat does it *do*?" scoffs Brooks. "It turns ze brains into *guacamole*."

But here's the thing: Kermit the Frog doesn't have a brain. Kermit the Frog has a *hand*—specifically, Jim Henson's hand, one of the greatest hands of his generation, which was his brain's hand, with its thousands of nerve endings. Go watch Jim Henson on *Johnny Carson* in 1975, operating Kermit in plain view of the studio audience, no camera tricks, no hiding that it's just his arm wrapped in some felt. "I got a bad throat," Kermit tells Carson glumly, "I got a person in my throat." That's frog humor, Kermit clarifies over the audience's laughter. Later Johnny ponders the experience: "It's funny the way that the fantasy starts, and you get so caught up—I'm sitting here talking to a frog!" He puts his index finger to his temple and twists it like a corkscrew. "You must know when you're ready for the home," he quips, as if talking to someone without a brain has made him question the integrity of his own.

It always terrified me to see Kermit clamped into that electric chair, the little transparent dome descending onto his Ping-Pong eyes. Brooks calls it an electronic yarmulke. It did put the fear of heaven in me, brain. I would cover my ears or leave the room until it was over, like the electricity might leap from the cathodes straight into my skull, and in a few irreversible seconds there would be nothing left of me, the only part of my body I had ever been taught to love. Each time, there was a chance, a real chance, that Kermit might not make it out, that he might finally become what he already was: a puppet, with someone else's hand up his brain.

They say we're muscles, you and I. It's not true; we're mostly fat. We think we're the ones pulling the strings, but if all it takes is a couple of strings, what's the point of having a brain at all? No heart, no eyes, no little calculi, just five fingers, a song, and a dance.

*

She is sitting in a noodle shop with a friend. They are talking about the philosophy of mind. She is saying something about how she doesn't want to believe that how she feels is just an effect of neurons firing or whatever. She tells her friend that she is trying to work out an ontology where everything is equally real.

"Let's say objects only exist within their own systems," she says, crunching black fungus between her teeth. "Like, alpha waves do exist, but only as objects inside of neurobiology."

"Right," says her friend.

"But at the same time, a catatonic episode is also a real object, but its reality is located within psychiatry."

"Uh-huh."

"So then it's like oil and water. Objects in the same metaphysics can act on one another, but not on other kinds of objects. Like, an antidepressant can block a serotonin transporter because they inhabit the same biochemical reality, but neither of them can interface with intrusive thoughts, which are psychological objects. And nothing is an 'effect'"—she does the air quotes with her chopsticks—"of anything else, there's just a massive number of these object systems superimposed on each other acting in parallel, and they're all completely blind to each other."

"Right," says the friend. "You can't drive a train through a field."

"Right."

They finish their noodles. 拉麵.

Later, she thinks things can't be that simple. Objects get lost or misplaced all the time. They wander, migrate from one reality to another, visit one another's dimensions. Isn't that what depression is? Electricity flaring into consciousness.

You *can* drive a train through a field, after all. It's called a train wreck.

If you are considering trying transcranial magnetic stimulation for yourself, I think you'll find that its appeal lies in treating your depression not as a psychological disorder, or even a chemical imbalance, but as a basically electrical problem. Sure, you can talk to a therapist or a psychoanalyst about all the things that make you want to die. They will help you narrativize your pain, or the jagged border around your pain; if they cannot stitch the hole inside you, then at least they can help you hem the edges. Or you can get a psychiatrist, and they will write you a prescription for an anti-depressant, and you can spend months or years negotiating a dose with the animalcules who operate your cells. But the magnets are different, brain. They promise direct manipulation of the voltages inside you, much closer to physical therapy than to an SSRI. What the magnets say is, it's just physics, dummy. What the magnets say is, what you need is a good kick in the head.

Of course, if it's direct intervention you're after, you could always get electroshock, like a sad lady in a movie, which could be fun. Electroconvulsive therapy is considered no riskier than general anesthesia, but the brochure points out that they anesthetize you because, no joke, they are literally going to give you a seizure. And so you settle on TMS, which is much less invasive and nominally cheaper, though that's just a nice bit of advertising, because who knows how long you'll be doing this. And I hope you have insurance, brain, because I know I just said it's cheaper than ECT but it's still a bitch, and honestly it helps maybe 60 percent of people. But here you are now, in the big blue chair, and while the magnet pecks away at your skull like a bird looking for worms, they're just gonna ask you some questions about how you've been feeling. But don't worry: they just want feedback so they can adjust the machine. They don't really *care.*

But you care. You care a lot. Way too much, actually. I know you feel like life is meaningless, but that meaninglessness is saturated with meaning. Nothing has ever felt more important to you than the waxing conviction, as the afternoon sun moves across your motionless body, that nothing fucking matters. So that's the promise of TMS: less meaning. The magnet will come for you with its little chisel, and bit by bit, if you're lucky enough to be 60 percent of a person, it will carve away the existential meaninglessness of your depression until all that's left is the electromagnetic meaninglessness of static on the radio. Whether this is something gained, or something horribly, terribly lost, will be up to you.

When I was a kid, my parents were regular listeners of *A Prairie Home Companion,* the variety show on public radio. My favorite bit was this fictitious sponsorship by the Ketchup Advisory Board. "These are the good years for Barb and me," a man named Jim would say, describing their mild suburban lives. But then Jim would find Barb softly crying in the garden or staring blankly at the wallpaper. And it was always something small at first—a rescheduled vacation, a misplaced pen—but really she was consumed with middle-aged malaise, middle-class void. So they would talk or bicker, getting nowhere, until finally a new thought would occur to him. "Barb," Jim would say, "I wonder if you're getting enough ketchup."

A reader once wrote to tell me that they'd been depressed for seven years when they discovered that they had a food allergy. They cut the offending item out of their diet—I think it was gluten—and just like that, the depression stopped. Seven years of suffering, from a protein. I told my therapist about this, and she asked me well didn't I think they might be exaggerating. Maybe, I said. But what an idea, brain, to reach down through that stack of needles and find a tiny piece of wheat.

"I always think of the Tacoma Narrows Bridge."

It's Timothy on the machine today. They are a little acquainted now. Timothy knows the Latin roots of things. She likes Timothy.

"That's how I think of thalamocortical dysrhythmia," he says. Timothy explains that this is an abnormal kind of brain wave oscillation that some researchers have proposed as a key element of depression, plus Parkinson's, tinnitus, and other disorders. There are these columns of electromagnetic resonance in her brain, he says—thalamocortical columns they're called, on account of they run from the cortex down into the thalamus, which as Timothy can tell her is the Greek word for chamber, and well especially a marriage bed, she says, because she knows the roots of things too. But sometimes the thalamus says, Do it this way, I like it this way, and the cortex says, I just don't know what you want from me anymore, and suddenly the columns start to vibrate all wrong, and now the whole house is quivering all the way up to the eaves because that's what columns do: they hold things up.

Treatment is not going well. It's exhausting coming in day after day. She can't take two days off without pitching back into despair. It's so imprecise; each session, the magnet wanders around her head like a cheap contractor, banging on the drywall. She begins to have these trepanation fantasies. Of taking a power drill to her temple and releasing all the spirit or phlogiston or whatever. Of a metal bar passing into one ear and cleanly emerging from the other, like the tamping iron that blasted through that railroad worker's skull during the gold rush. Meanwhile, Dennis grows more truculent with each passing primary debate on TV. "You

can't do anything to me," he cries during one of their arguments,
"I'm threatening my wife with retirement!" Autumn is waning, and
the trees in the park outside are giving up their leaves like joss
paper. One day, Dr. L abruptly takes her off the ketamine, without
explanation; somewhere, a horse gets its wings.

Timothy pulls up a black-and-white video on the big monitor
across the room and hits play. She remembers the Tacoma Narrows
Bridge now, from some physics textbook. What had happened was,
to save money, the state of Washington hired a big-time civil en-
gineer from New York who promised a sleeker design at a lower
cost. The resulting structure was especially vulnerable to what the
textbook had called mechanical resonance; when the wind was
right, the deck would oscillate at one of its natural frequencies,
like a musical instrument, producing visible undulations that led
the construction workers to nickname the bridge Galloping Ger-
tie. One day in 1940, a strong wind induced a new kind of motion
in the bridge, which began twisting back and forth in increasingly
violent waves. "Until it collapsed," says Timothy, which is what it's
doing now in the video, drowning itself in Puget Sound along with
a journalist's daughter's doomed cocker spaniel.

Curious, she looks it up on her phone. The internet tells them
that despite what they may have learned in high school, the Tacoma Narrows Bridge actually collapsed as a result of a much more
complicated phenomenon known as aeroelastic flutter, not mechanical resonance. Less wineglass, more plane crash. They agree
this is a less romantic explanation.

The magnet on her head is making her eye twitch. Timothy
restarts the video. Without speaking they watch the bridge writhe
in the wind. Silently singing itself to death.

I just want to check in, brain. How are you feeling? Do you need
some water? You always need some water. You know that thing
about how you only use 10 percent of yourself? That's because the
other 75 percent is water. I know that's only 85 percent. The last
15 we set aside, like the fiftieth yarrow stalk in an *I Ching* reading.
We reserve it for the Infinite. 無極.

Brains are so fragile, brain. How easily we break. China brains,
like china dolls, balanced on the shelf. One little bump and there
we go.

We're almost done now. I believe in you.

It's bitter cold. Timothy does a second EEG to see if the treatment has had any lasting effects. More crusted gel in her hair. Good news: she isn't pregnant. But the golf ball is still there. The trees outside are empty now. They reach their dendrites toward one another trying to synapse.

They are going to put the EEG results up on the big screen. Her girlfriend is here today, come to witness the science of her suffering. They are both suffering, and whenever she has pictured the bottle of bleach under their bathroom sink, holding it in her mind for a few seconds like hot toast, her girlfriend has pulled her close and rocked her away into the dark early night, but has she ever really done the same when her girlfriend was staring deep down into the down deep, and how long have they been doing this, loving each other away?

She's in the big blue chair. Her girlfriend is next to her. Dennis is on the machine. Dr. L is leaning back against the windowsill. Timothy is at the computer bank. Kyle is at home, dreaming of the open sky. The whole coast vibrates.

Timothy jumps the data to the television. This time they show her something new, topographic maps. There are these circles, like diving helmets viewed from above: little rectangular ears, little triangle noses pointing north. Inside them are the waves, which means the divers are dead. These bands of color in her head, they look like rain on the weather channel, going from blue to green to yellow to red, increasing in intensity. Dr. L points up at the circle labeled 10–12 Hz, which is within the alpha range. The top of the circle is fully engulfed in red, radiant burning red, and in the middle of all the red, a little to the left—right where they put the magnet—there's this prominent magenta spot, like a firepit, or a volcanic crater, or a cyclone on a distant moon.

"That's it," Dr. L says. "That's it."

She looks up at the moon. What she's thinking is, she wrote this book last winter, and it's coming out soon. Actually, I'm mixed up. Her book came out already, and what she's thinking is, she has this book tour coming up, and she's leaving tomorrow on a plane for Los Angeles, or maybe San Francisco, I forget which, and she's been trying to pretend it's not happening, the book or the tour or any of it. She's sitting in this sky-blue vintage Thunderbird of a chair and staring up at that big fucking hole in her brain, and what she's thinking is that she didn't even know she had anything left to give, but she's giving it up now, she's giving it all up, she's pouring it into that two-centimeter hole, and that night she cancels everything, she eats the plane ticket and digs herself a two-hundred-centimeter hole in the middle of her living room that goes all the way to Wuxi, where her ancestors were scholars for a thousand years, all those brains one after another, strung out in a line like paper lanterns across the sky, and then seven million centimeters away, in Wuhan, people start getting sick, and suddenly it's like somebody blew a hole in the entire world, the whole big China brain of the world, and TMS is done, the clinic goes quiet, she hears nothing from them, nothing, not so much as a postcard, and then everything just fucking stops.

It's OK, brain. We're OK.

The stupid end to this stupid story is that the magnets didn't help because what we didn't know then is that I am bipolar. Evidence for the success of transcranial magnetic stimulation in bipolar patients is partial at best, since excitation of the prefrontal cortex, like antidepressants, can trigger hypomania. A patient is considered to have bipolar II disorder when their psychiatric history includes at least one hypomanic episode lasting four days or longer, as well as at least one depressive episode lasting two weeks or longer, often much longer. The symptoms of depression are common knowledge: low mood, little pleasure or interest in doing things, lying on the couch like your entire body is an anvil, crying a lot. Hypomania, by contrast, is like mania without the psychosis. Symptoms include excessive goal-oriented activity, racing thoughts, not shutting up, and euphoria. That's me: up and down, positive and negative. You know, like a magnet.

Now my psychiatrist has me on lithium, a mood stabilizer, like she's shipped me back home to a sanatorium in the Alps. It means I can't take ibuprofen anymore; nonsteroidal inflammatory drugs can make it harder for your body to pass lithium, potentially leading to toxic levels of the metal in your blood. And lithium really is a metal: unlike most drugs, lithium carbonate occurs in nature. They discovered it at an alkaline lake in Tibet in the eighties, and later in a little town called Kings Mountain in North Carolina, not far from where I grew up. But most of the world's supply of lithium carbonate is synthesized from brine water in Chile and Argentina by people who know how to do that sort of thing. Then they sell it to other people, and those people use it to make batteries and heat-resistant glass, and to make tile mortar set faster, and to make fireworks red, and to keep china from cracking when you glaze it.

Brain, how's your chemistry? My chemistry teacher was young and handsome in a wiry way, and he wore his dirty blond hair short. He had sunglasses on his forehead and tenth-grade girls wrapped around his finger. He probably liked music, I don't know. He was a decent chemistry teacher too, though sometimes he would start working a problem on the whiteboard and get lost in his own hieroglyphs. Which, right—lithium carbonate. The molecule is simple: two lithium ions and one carbonate ion, consisting of one carbon atom and three oxygens. If you want, you can synthesize lithium carbonate through what's known as a salt metathesis reaction. You just take lithium chloride from a salt flat in Chile, a salt of equal parts lithium and chlorine, and you treat it with another salt, sodium carbonate, also called soda ash, which you probably got from a mine in Wyoming. In the reaction that follows, the sodium ions will give up their carbonate ion and receive the chlorine, leaving the lithium ions free to bond with the carbonate. Now you've got two new salts: NaCl, which you may recognize as table salt, and Li_2CO_3, the lithium salt of carbonate.

And you know what, brain? Maybe I just wasn't getting enough salt.

KAITLYN GREENIDGE

What She Would Always and Should Always Be Doing

FROM BuzzFeed

THE FIRST ROLE I was cast in was a rock. I was two, the youngest in our neighborhood, and so in our block-wide productions I was given the part best suited for my abilities. I don't remember playing the actual role, only the review—that I could never stay still, the one skill the part required.

The neighborhood plays were conceived of and written by my older sister. She has always only ever wanted to be a writer, and she pursued that dream with a steadfastness that meant she was a playwright by her early twenties. It was always a given that my sister would fulfill her dream—I only ever saw her persevering, never any struggle. When she was in college and I was in middle school, she staged her first productions, and I remember going to them with the supreme sense of the inevitable: that this was what she would always and should always be doing.

I had the same fierce desire to write, but not the certainty. It seemed that making a living out of your words and imagination was too good to be true—a fabulous existence that would always be just out of reach. I read widely about writers' lives, and they all, to a person, seemed to revel in pain and alienation. As someone who had had enough of that before the age of fourteen, I wasn't sure I wanted to sign up for a job where people judged the depth of your excellence by how deeply you had suffered. I had accepted that my childhood and adolescence would be full of suffering, but I was not prepared to have it continue into the self-willed space of adulthood.

The first play my sister had produced outside of college was staged in the same space where I had done children's theater—an old abandoned middle school that our town was half-heartedly attempting to turn into an arts space. In fifth grade, I had acted there, in my last year of unselfconsciousness. I had gamely played the part of a saloon girl in a spaghetti western parody that the children's theater put on. My best friend and I were both cast, and I remember the best part about being in the play was that I got to wear a blush-colored dress with puffed sleeves—what I considered to be the height of beauty and sophistication then.

My sister's play came my sophomore year of high school. In the intervening years between that elementary school production and my sister's, though, I had grown a kind of artistic consciousness, or at least a vague understanding that how I saw myself and my own body in the world differed drastically from how everyone else saw it. Nowadays, I have the words for what I was experiencing: misogynoir; fatphobia; colorism. But then, it was only the distinct feeling of wishing to disappear, because the body I inhabited suddenly seemed to draw commentary from anyone and everyone around me.

I had never, before, given much thought to my body—it was merely something that moved me around. But in sixth grade, I began to gain weight, and in seventh, a not very good psychiatrist put me on a high dose of an antidepressant that caused me to gain even more in a short period of time. Suddenly, my body did not make sense to the people I saw every day, even some of the people who claimed to love me. I remember going to get my hair braided at my cousin's house and her saying, as I settled onto the pillow she'd placed on the floor so she could reach my head, "You wear dresses that short? I'm scared of *you*." Before that moment, it had not occurred to me what length my dress was, but I instantly understood—I had grown too fat for the skirt to go past my knees, and the extra inch of skin above them was somehow a threat. My body was a topic of conversation to all, the understanding being that it was fundamentally *wrong*, a problem to be solved, one that could be figured out if I just thought about it long enough.

It took a long time for my ambitions to catch up with my body. Like all adolescents, I was still making and remaking myself. In middle school, I still thought that maybe I would be an actor. My mother dutifully signed me up for more children's theater workshops, which eventually resulted, in eighth grade, in being invited to audition for the role of Dorothy in a regional production of *The Wizard of Oz*. I remember the audition very well—being instructed to pretend to sneak from one end of the stage to the other and furtively pick up a book. Halfway across the stage, miming the movements of discretion, I suddenly felt more in my body than I ever had, and with a shock I realized how embarrassing this all was. My movements were not natural but in the wholesale quotation marks of someone who was deeply self-conscious. I was not good at this. I was a terrible actor.

With this new self-consciousness came a silencing that extended into my daily life, a literal one. At home, I was still vicious and sharp-tongued—I still earned my childhood nickname of Surly. But in public, I could rarely speak. It felt, at the time, as if I had swallowed a large, round, smooth stone from the bottom of a clear cool river, and the rock sat at the bottom of my throat, preventing any sound from coming out. I often longed to speak—I wanted to speak—but I could not get a sound around that stone, no matter how hard I tried. Perhaps the most disorienting thing about the mutism was that few people seemed to notice it. In my small private high school, where I was one of very few Black students, it was easier for everyone around me if I didn't speak. The few times I was able to push out sentences in class, I remember them usually being met with a long, awkward silence before the conversation continued, and another student, ten minutes later, repeated what I had just said as if my words were their own. Being mute was a kind of burning indignation, one that I tried to fight against every day, but very few people outside my family expected me to have a voice at all.

A few years after this revelation, the spring of my sophomore year, my sister had her first production. It was a semiautobiographical piece about a single mother and her daughter and the discussions they have over a series of car rides. My sister had written one of the daughters as a preteen, and they were having trouble finding an actor to play her, so somehow, either the director or the producer volunteered me for the part.

It was a supremely disorienting experience for me, a person whose whole life was beginning to be defined by dissociation, to inhabit my sister's imagined version of me for a paying audience. The role was needling and bratty, a classic younger sister, an archetype that came with that designation; she had a few good one-liners. My sister had written the role to be charming, and because she is a good writer, it worked. Audiences liked it. I remember only applause.

The play had a short run—three days, I think—and on the final day of production, the director approached my sister to ask her if I might want to act in another production. This woman's friend was mounting a production of Ed Bullins's satire of Blaxploitation, *Dr. Geechee and the Blood Junkies,* a play which most of the Black actors in Boston were unofficially boycotting. The play is a kind of allegory for the crack epidemic—a long-form exploration of the metaphor of addict as violent zombie. It takes elements of *Shaft* and parodies of nineties media like Court TV and movie announcements to form a pastiche of criticism of mainstream media representations of addiction and race. This is a very generous read of the play. It was a production that found great humor in the idea of a Southern sheriff fighting a vampire—that was the whole joke. The director was a white man in his sixties. His stage manager was a Latina woman in her early twenties. The rest of the cast seemed impossibly grown-up but, looking back, they were all probably in their mid to late twenties as well. The director was scrambling to fill roles—the actor playing the part I was offered had walked off set and refused to participate. I was the youngest cast member, still in high school, and I was offered the part not because I was good but because I was young enough not to ask any questions.

As a fifteen-year-old and in violent, silent internal revolt of everything around me, I told myself that I hated Boston, that I wanted to leave the city and the state as soon as I was able. I knew that when I did, it would have to be of my own volition—my mother was a single parent, only a few years out of grad school herself, and even if she had had the funds to bankroll an escape, her principles would never allow her to do so. With such a huge desire to escape, the only way out seemed to be college in another state. But I was not, for a long time, a good student. A chronic procrastinator, it never really occurred to me to finish my homework on a regular basis. My sophomore year I had turned things around and begun to get A's, but I was keenly aware that when I applied to schools I would have a string of terrible semesters to explain. I was also interminably shy and hated to do activities, so I was on the lookout for extracurriculars that could fool an admissions board into thinking I was a team player.

So it was partly my own cravenness that led me to agree to do the play, despite knowing about the boycott, but it was also the adults in the production—mostly white—who spoke of the boycott as a frivolous thing, a case of Black artists being too sensitive and not understanding *nuance*, that thing that everyone calls for whenever anyone calls something, rightly, racist. In my memory, Bullins only came to a few rehearsals, and I only knew him as a great and respected writer, which is what everyone told me. Wikipedia did not exist then, so I had no way to know about the abuse allegations brought against him by his former wife, the womanist poet Pat Parker, who once said that she "was scared to death of him." I only knew that these older artists had deemed it silly, anti-artist, almost, to question the work we were putting on. I did not know yet that I could question why these white producers and white director were so eager to put on this particular play.

Because the cast was already deep into rehearsals, they had all hyperbonded, in that way only actors can, weeks before I arrived. The part the woman had found too demeaning to play was that of a sex worker who gets bitten by the star blood junkie and then goes into a writhing transformation onstage, a grotesque parody of an orgasm that ends in the character becoming a zombie herself. I don't remember if I read for the part before I played it, if I even read the script—I must have, but I did not register what it would ask of me. For this part, I had to first enter the stage in a skimpy costume, then proposition the lead actor. From there, he'd indicate that he would pay me for sex, reach over, pull me into an embrace, and sink his teeth into my neck.

I had never even held hands with another person, let alone kissed anybody, and I was acutely aware that this was the most physical contact I had ever received from someone who was not in my family or a doctor. It was mortifying. To compound the humiliation, the costumer gave up on trying to find an outfit for me and told me I should dress myself. This was in the mid-nineties, when plus-size fashion was either large, shapeless sacks or overalls. Back then, I mostly wore overalls. I knew what I was supposed to wear to suggest that I was a streetwalking zombie, but I also knew that no store sold those types of clothes in my size.

And on top of all this—I was still not fully living in my body, then. I hovered above it most days, wounded by its continuous mortifications. And though I was able to speak in my initial interview with the director, I was not able to keep up the facade with anyone else. I slunk into rehearsals and sat on the bleacher seats and stayed quiet, hoping none of these people would ever notice me.

The production was to be held in a Unitarian church in town— a big, drafty building with a color-blocked mural on the front dedicated to racial unity. We rehearsed at night, in the middle of a Boston winter, so the church was always dark and drafty; I remember mostly the hazy lighting, the wind whistling through the eaves, how the whole wooden structure groaned in the cold. Even though I had been warned that others found the play offensive, I still wished, after my first conversation with the director, to be part of it. I had told myself that if I got this role, I would be able to be a more interesting, less strange and damaged version of myself. In my head, I made up an elaborate fantasy of what else would fall into place in my life if I got the role—I'd bump into my crush on my way to and from the theater, and he would find my double life as an actor with artists so much older than me so alluring and we would quickly start dating and everyone would finally begin to recognize me as the artist I knew I could be. I told this story to myself over and over again so many times that I began to almost think it was real, and it was a disappointment each evening when I arrived for the start of rehearsal and I didn't see the boy I liked—though I knew he didn't live anywhere near the theater and in fact I probably would never see him at all. In that fantasy, though, I was able to go back to take control of some sort of role-playing, since the one I had on the stage had gotten away from me.

Every time the lead actor grabbed me by the shoulders and made to bite my neck, I flinched and froze and my whole body went stiff. I tried to will myself not to. I tried to think myself out of that response, but my stubborn body wouldn't listen. But I couldn't help it—he made me want to recoil into myself, and that was all I could convey onstage.

The director was getting increasingly frustrated. First, he sent the stage manager over to talk with me. I had wished on so many occasions that she would be my friend, but I thought of her as so much older than me, and I saw the omnipresent clipboard she carried as a sign of her own supreme competence. Her body would never betray her, I told myself. It was probably perfectly in line with her mind. She took me to a dark corner of the church and tried to give me some advice. "Just relax," she said. "Get used to the cast. Hang out with people. Talk with people. It will be fine."

At that point in my life, the concept of relaxation was a foreign one. I was so silent outside of my house that most people chose to read muted panic as tranquil calm. At home, no one ever *relaxed*. Ease was a state to be distrusted, repose was rigorously questioned. If ever I was to stop moving, not actively go about the house tidying or reading or some other virtuous activity, my mother would ask, "Are you depressed?" Which, it was clear I was, but any desire to stop and wallow in it was pathologized. The key was to be depressed but keep it moving—perhaps the motion would carry you to a calmer state.

So when she said "relax," I did not know how to respond. Eventually, they called over one of the actors to give me deep breathing lessons. We stood in the church secretary's office, which had become a kind of hangout spot for the cast. Here, I would usually spend my breaks doing my homework, listening to the other actors boast to one another about how hard they had partied the weekend before. I was a very sheltered teenager, if you have not already gathered, and so I took these feeble brags at face value.

The actor who gave me the breathing lessons played the town sheriff. He was scrawny and wiry, with ruffled hair, and was considerably less intimidating than the lead, who was tall and broad and movie star handsome—Denzel Washington as a local. The actor who played the sheriff, in contrast, gave off more of a Steve Zahn vibe. The sheriff had me stand in front of him, while all around us the cast gossiped and lounged and ran lines. "Put your shoulders back," he said. "Plant your feet on the floor. Breathe in very deeply, now out. Close your eyes."

It was another kind of humiliation, to practice breathing in front of an audience. But I willed myself to do it—I closed my eyes and expanded my chest and let out one big whoosh. For a moment, the change in oxygen levels left my brain feeling thin and plastic, a pleasant feeling. Then I opened my eyes and noticed that the sheriff had been staring at my breasts moving the whole time.

He was embarrassed to be caught and quickly turned his eyes away. We didn't talk about what happened, and I certainly didn't tell anybody about it. Back then, it was something to be shrugged off, another penalty of girlhood, and to tell someone about it would put me into the same category as the woman whose role I had taken over—too outspoken, too *sensitive,* a word that I took as a slur. I did not want to be sensitive, because to be sensitive suggested a weakness, an irrationality that had been subtly conveyed to me about all those actors who had said no before me.

I did not make the connection, then, that to be an artist, to be a writer, means that on some level you must remain sensitive to the world, to the parts of it that everyone else tells you it's normal to respond to with a deadening. I did not know that sensitivity was necessary—I thought it was only being messy. And I did not know that sensitivity requires a base-level knowledge of your self and its own reactions that I was incapable of cultivating.

The role I had been asked to play required, after the lead bit my neck, for me to become a monster onstage. For weeks, I wasn't able to do it—the director would cue me to scream, to start my transformation, and I could only come out with the feeblest of squawks. But after the breathing lesson, I could do it. I erupted into a series of whoops, loud and insistent, guttural cries that I paused to echo in the theater even as I slunk backstage. At the time, I did not make the connection between all my suppressed rage and alienation and my ability to make that sound. I only was relieved that my body was finally doing something right, something that I actively wanted it to do, for once. After we opened, every night, the audience cheered at my exit—the scream was played for laughs. I wish I could say that I felt free in the screams, or that afterward I found my voice, or that they were a source of catharsis. But it would take many more years before I learned how to scream for myself, not for a performance to please others.

I think, looking back, I wanted to act because I did not know myself at all. I thought to be an artist, you had to know yourself with the same kind of rigid control used to memorize a multiplication table or a series of lines. I did not know that self-knowledge is an expansive thing, ever-changing, its fluidity part of its power. That it can only be cultivated through periods of rest and reflection, and that my body is my partner in my quest toward self-knowledge, not my opponent. But those lessons were years away.

My Gentile Region

FROM *The New Yorker*

ON AUGUST 24, 2020, as I attempted the first pee of the morning, I felt a tightness on the underside of my penis. A tiny hair had formed a tourniquet around a skin bridge on the genital. I was not in immediate pain, but I knew that something irrevocable had happened, as if time itself had caught up to me with an abacus in hand, demanding a full accounting.

My penis was shaped by the Cold War and God's covenant with Abraham. My father, born in a small village outside Leningrad in 1938, had been circumcised. By the time of my birth, in 1972, Jewish children were generally not circumcised in the Soviet Union, part of a long-standing campaign against religion. Seven years later, soon after our arrival in the United States, my father fell under the influence of some "Chabadniks," Hasidic followers of the Lubavitcher Rebbe, who were going door to door telling Soviet Jews in Brooklyn and Queens that they had to circumcise their boys. The surgery was performed under general anesthesia at Coney Island Hospital, the Chabadniks singing and praying joyfully in an adjoining room, and resulted in an immediate infection as well as painful urination that lasted until I was nine.

Most poorly performed circumcisions stem from two misjudgments on the part of the circumciser: either too much or too little foreskin is removed. In my case, it was too little (and, one might add, given that I was seven years old instead of the eight days prescribed by the Torah, too late). After the infection had subsided, the shaft of my penis was crowded by a skyline of redundant foreskin that included, on the underside, a thick attachment of skin stretching from the head to the shaft of the genital, a result of improper healing that is called a skin bridge. A small gap could be seen between this skin bridge and the penis proper. In texture and appearance, the bridge reminded me of the Polly-O mozzarella string cheese that got packed in the lunchboxes of my generation. It produced no pain on its own after the infection had died down and the two years of difficult urination were over, but the strangeness of my penile appearance—and the manner in which it was brought about—became lodged in my consciousness. In my novel *Absurdistan,* which was written in the mid-2000s, when I was in my early thirties, the hero, Misha Vainberg, is also circumcised under Hasidic auspices and under pressure from his religion-obsessed father. "Eighteen is too old for cutting the dick," Misha begs the Chabadniks who have driven him to a Brooklyn hospital, but he is told by one of them that "Abraham was ninety-nine when he performed the bris with his own hands!"

I had long used humor to articulate the trauma of non-neonatal circumcision, the forcible removal of a part of me that had been intended by nature as a nexus of pleasure. But, looking down at the hair that had wrapped itself around my penile skin bridge in the shape of a gift bow on the morning of August 24, 2020, I knew that my luck had run out and that the forty-year interregnum between the brute pain of the initial procedure and whatever would happen next was over.

I mention luck because lucky is exactly how I felt in the preceding weeks and months and years. Lucky and guilty, I should say. For the past decade, I had spent the better part of every year in the mid–Hudson Valley, and I was there with my family at the dawn of the pandemic, a safe hundred miles from the growing calamity in the city. Since my wife and I had a child, seven years ago, I had committed myself to living longer, to walking for two hours a day and swimming at least a mile in the pool on our property. Once a sickly child (asthma), I now felt stronger both through exercise and through the panoply of designer drugs with names like metformin that were supposed to catapult me past the usual circumscribed life expectancy of a post-Soviet male. I had halved my alcohol consumption to two drinks per day or fewer. My involvement in several television projects had frequently taken me to Los Angeles. Phrases like "talk soon" and "let me circle back" dripped off the tongue with the smooth consistency of the chia parfait that now constituted the entirety of my breakfast.

As the pandemic surged and my television projects died, as they mostly do, I celebrated being with my family and conducted masked grocery runs to local villages. Some of my favorite people lived nearby and together we hosted weekly barbecues, where I watched my son pitter-patter along the deck while learning his first Weird Al Yankovic songs, an American boy lost amid a diorama of safety and plenty. The novel I had started writing, set in a country house just like my own, was proceeding at a quick pace. The main characters were nearly all immigrants, but unlike those in my previous works they had mostly escaped their backgrounds. The immigrant children of my fiction had taken charge of their lives, as I had mine. But only fools and Americans think they can outrun the past.

My problems can be traced back to chapter 17 of Genesis. God tells the ninety-nine-year-old Abram that he will be the father of many nations, super fruitful, and that his kids will be the sole owners and operators of the land of Canaan; that his ninety-year-old wife, Sarai (soon to be Sarah), will bear him an Isaac (or Itzhak— "He who will laugh"); and that henceforth he will be called Abraham. There's only one small catch: "Every male among you shall be circumcised."

Perhaps the best-known proponent of circumcision is Maimonides, the medieval Sephardic Jewish philosopher and Torah scholar who lived within the Islamic communities of Egypt and Morocco. "The bodily injury caused to that organ is exactly that which is desired," Maimonides wrote. "There is no doubt that circumcision weakens the power of sexual excitement, and sometimes lessens the natural enjoyment." A friend from Jewish day school, David J. Fine, who is now himself a rabbi, recently quipped, "Maimonides didn't have too much sex. He worked very long hours."

The reduction of sexual excitement remained a theme in Jewish commentary on circumcision, but it also took on a strange self-effacing aspect. Some Jewish scholars thought that uncircumcised men would prove too irresistible for Jewish women, and that men without a foreskin would not be led into constant temptation. "It is hard for a woman with whom an uncircumcised man has had sexual intercourse to separate from him," Maimonides wrote,

praising the circumcised Abraham for his chastity. In a comprehensive volume on the subject, *Why Aren't Jewish Women Circumcised?*, the Harvard professor Shaye J. D. Cohen quotes a medieval
rabbi, Isaac ben Yedaiah, at length in a section titled "Envy of the
Gentile Foreskin":

> A man foreskinned in the flesh desires to lie with a
> beautiful-looking woman. . . . She too will court the man who
> is foreskinned in the flesh and lie against his breast with great
> passion, for he thrusts inside her a long time because of the
> foreskin, which is a barrier against ejaculation in intercourse.
> Thus she feels pleasure and reaches an orgasm first. When a
> foreskinned man sleeps with her and then resolves to return
> to his home, she brazenly grasps him, holding on to his geni-
> tals, and says to him, "Come back, make love to me."

Therefore, circumcision denies pleasure to both women and
men. And, according to this logic, Cohen explains, "the woman
will become sexually frustrated and will lose interest in sex, allowing the man to devote his spiritual and physical energies to the
contemplation of God and other noble pursuits"—among them
the study of the Torah.

European Christians considered Jews effeminate owing to their
circumcisions, deeming them a studious, unathletic, hemorrhoidal
people unable to gallop through Palestine bedecked in armor and
spearing unbelievers. In fact, the Israelites almost certainly inherited the custom from the Egyptians, who, according to the British scholar Rebecca Steinfeld, saw the procedure as a masculine
test of strength. The oldest reference, she observes, is found in an
Egyptian tomb, built around 2400 BCE. Two young noblemen are
shown having their genitals cut by temple priests. An inscription
reads "Hold him and do not allow him to faint."

The tradition has continued in the Middle East to the present
day. In Israel, circumcision fever truly broke the thermometer in
the 1990s, as waves of Jews arrived from the detritus of the former
Soviet Union. According to *Haaretz,* doctors competed to see how
many immigrants they could circumcise in a day, while, not to be
outdone, one of Israel's ultra-Orthodox burial societies managed
to circumcise the corpses of recent arrivals who had died in the
Holy Land.

Alex Moshkin, a comparative-literature professor at Koç University, in Istanbul, moved to Israel from Stavropol, in southern Russia. "Many fathers themselves did not do the procedure," Moshkin told me. "They kind of pushed their kids to do it. The older people were, like, 'I don't think I need this.'"

The newly arrived immigrants were also pressured by ultrareligious Jews and by Israeli society in general. As Moshkin observed, "These rabbis—many of whom didn't speak the language of the immigrants—often spoke on religious matters or the need to shed one's Russian skin in favor of a new Israeli identity and a new Israeli name." The immigrants felt that they needed to change, he said, "in order to belong to the Israeli collective." The motivation of families in America was not altogether different. We all wanted to belong.

The hair knot around my skin bridge could not be prized loose using tweezers, and any attempts to dislodge it with my fingers only tightened it around the string of superfluous skin. My wife's research led to one remedy: Nair. For days, we applied the hair-removal lotion with calligraphic precision. The knotted hair appeared smaller in diameter, but it remained wrapped around the bridge. In fact, it was now digging into the skin, releasing what looked like a stream of pus. I noticed this during my long swims, especially while doing the breaststroke; not pain, exactly, but a sharp ping of discomfort as the underside of the penis came into contact with my swim trunks.

Several days later, I sought medical attention in a neighboring village. Because of the pandemic, a pleasant middle-aged woman was performing triage outside the doors of the urgent-care facility. When I tried to explain my predicament to her, she said, "Oh, honey, it must hurt so bad to have an ingrown hair in your gentile region." If only that region had stayed gentile. The local urgent-care doctor tried his hand with some forceps but was clearly not an expert at removing tiny hairs wrapped around extraneous pieces of penile skin. I would have to go to the city to seek a specialist.

My primary-care doctor recommended a urologist on the Upper East Side. Like many of the urologists I would subsequently meet, he was middle-aged, Jewish, and possessed of an easy humor. Let's call him Dr. Funnyman. In fact, the first thing I noticed when I went to see him was a Jewish-humor anthology on his desk. He asked me if I was famous, and I did my customary blush and said no, I certainly didn't think of myself that way. "You're not Dr. Shteynshlyuger, the urologist?" he asked. When I informed him that I was Gary Shteyngart, the novelist, he told me he had never heard of me but loved the work of Michael Chabon.

Dr. Funnyman took out a pair of forceps and in a matter of seconds had cut the hair tourniquet from the skin bridge. "I'm amazing!" he said. I was overcome with gratitude and relief. I took a photo of the offending hair to memorialize my liberation. Dr. Funnyman told me that the skin bridge had been strangled by the hair to such an extent that it would probably soon separate into two pieces hanging off the penis. If this happened, I could come back and he would give me local anesthesia and remove them with cauterization, a relatively simple procedure that he had performed before. That night, I drank vodka with friends on the Lower East Side, and when I got home to my apartment in the city I locked myself in the bathroom for an hour and wept without quite knowing why.

Within forty-eight hours, the skin bridge had broken into two parts, "a minimal stump distally with a larger stump proximally," according to the doctor's notes, the latter of which was an unsightly piece of skin flapping in the summer wind. I have always imagined that beyond its pleasurable utility the penis must be an incomprehensible thing to most heterosexual women, like a walrus wearing a cape that shows up every once in a while to perform a quick round of gardening. Neither my past lovers nor my wife had remarked on the condition of my phallus, but now my genital was truly unbound, as it had always been in my imagination, its freakishness undeniable. It was time to return to the city for my second circumcision of a lifetime, an unlikely double mitzvah, or good deed.

On September 8, 2020, my wife drove me to a pharmacy on Second Avenue, where Dr. Funnyman had left a scrip for Valium. Buzzed and dissociated, I floated into his office and put on a gown. The doctor, the nurse, and I were all wearing masks as a precaution against COVID, which reminded me of being seven again and having a mask placed on my face and being told to count in reverse in a language I barely knew as the general anesthesia took hold. I remembered the colors around me changing into a medley of greens and yellows as the world pulled away, like the impossible sensation of entering a tunnel backward. I remembered being scared even as I lost consciousness and needing my mother even more than I usually did. When I woke, I would be given the name of Abraham's son Itzhak (a name I never used once I had made my exodus from Jewish day school), but on this day in 2020 I hoped to remain Gary. This is a minor procedure, I told myself.

My gown was lifted and a metal grounding pad was attached to my left thigh with a bandage. Dr. Funnyman said that this would keep me from being electrocuted while I was being cauterized. That sentence did not inspire confidence. I grabbed the nurse's hand as lidocaine was injected into the shaft of my penis, and she gave me a squeeze ball to pulverize instead. (Later, Dr. Funnyman laughed and said I had been "a lightweight." He also explained that he was joking about the electrocution.) I could not see what happened next or, mercifully, feel very much, although according to the notes "the distal stump was simply fulgurated using a pinpoint Bovie. The proximal end was resected and then fulgurated giving an excellent cosmetic result." To "fulgurate," in medical terms, is to destroy by means of the heat from an electrical current. From my supine perspective, I saw and smelled smoke, pieces of my penis being burned away. After it was over, I examined the result. The skin bridge was no more, which, speaking "cosmetically," was positive. But parts of the remaining redundant foreskin were inflamed and, along with the termini of the erstwhile skin bridge, covered in what looked like a dense layer of Eastern European soot. Dr. Funnyman told me I would be able to resume normal activities soon, but in the meantime parts of my genital would swell and "look funny" for a week.

Four days later, when I was back in the Hudson Valley, my wife and I hosted a barbecue, and I found myself recounting the event. Two close friends who live upstate have cancer, and I hit the comedy notes of the story, as if trying to emphasize its ludicrous nature compared with what they were suffering, but also perhaps to show that I now also understood something about physical pain. In any case, my prognosis was a quick and complete recovery, and I imagined the skin-bridge excision as a brief interlude in a future work of fashionable autofiction.

The afflicted area improved slowly, but peeing was now painful. A part of the redundant foreskin that had always resembled two flaps was becoming more swollen. Two weeks after the surgery, as I was finishing an hour-long walk, it felt as if hot clothespins had been attached to the areas where the skin bridge had been excised and were pulling ever downward. Whenever any clothing came into contact with the affected area, a Klaxon of pain would sound across my central nervous system.

I wrote to Dr. Funnyman, who replied that, given my initial soreness, he was not surprised that it was taking me longer to heal than expected. "For slow learners like yourself, this could take six weeks," he wrote. I assumed he meant "slow healers" instead of "slow learners," but I came away with the feeling that the fault was somehow in my body and its inability to "learn" how to respond to a minor genital bonfire. In a later email, the doctor surmised that "there's something about your skin chemistry that's just different from the average bear." I took umbrage until my wife explained Yogi Bear to me. Perhaps the doctor was right. Something within me was wrong. I was not a very average or fast-learning bear.

My condition began to take over my daily life, like a game of Twister but with each wrong move resulting in a jolt of groin pain. To get out of my car without the affected organ scraping unduly against my underwear, I began to propel myself from the seat in one quick motion, until one day I hit my head hard on the doorframe, and spent weeks nursing a headache. Eventually, I quit driving. Lifting grocery bags became impossible. Sitting on a hard chair excruciating. Drying my groin with a towel unbearable. Wearing jeans unbelievable (only sweatpants would do). Playing hide-and-seek with my son out of the question. Even sleeping required a fort of pillows placed in strategic locations to keep my penis airborne through the night. I had been advised to use numbing lidocaine jelly, and to wear soothing Xeroform gauze held in place by an improvised bandage. My wife, upon seeing the shaft of my organ covered in bandage and gauze, sadly compared it to the Elizabethan collar worn by dogs (not that I was in danger of licking myself). Erections became dangerous, and at night I turned away from my wife so that I would not smell the deliciousness of her hair. I began to wonder: Was this the rest of my life?

I decided to expand my medical horizons. My primary doctor recommended a specialist in "minor outpatient urological procedures" whom I will call Dr. Neuroma. I visited the doctor's aerie in the medicinal slab of the Weill Cornell tower on York Avenue. The doctor, younger than Funnyman but not as funny, could not give a full examination, because touching either of the termini of the former skin bridge produced intolerable pain. He ventured an opinion. In all likelihood, I was suffering from a penile neuroma. Some readers may be familiar with Morton's neuroma, a highly painful malady that often manifests itself between the toes and may make walking difficult. This was that but in the penis. "A tiny nerve gets swollen," the doctor said. "A nerve was snapped or cut during the surgery, and the proximal end is angry or inflamed or trying to reach for the other end, but there's no other end to receive it and that may be felt as pain." In this interpretation, my nerves were a bunch of ragtag troops stranded on a remote island who had not been informed by general staff that the war was over.

The doctor left for what felt like twenty minutes to answer a pressing text message. When he returned, he said that my problem was a rare outcome, "one chance in a hundred, bad luck for you and bad luck for the doctor." He also told me that he expected I would get about "eighty percent better" and would learn to live with the rest of the pain. In the meantime, I should "keep it moist and lubricated down there," and take gabapentin, a drug that was primarily used as an anti-seizure medication but that could also reduce nerve pain. I walked out of the hospital building into a surprisingly hot October day with the softly spoken but uncontestable words of the doctor ringing in my ears. "Penile neuroma." "Bad luck for you." "Live with the pain."

My primary-care physician had recommended another doctor, whom I will call Dr. Cortisone. After the razzle-dazzle of Cornell, this doctor's office felt more familiar in a urological context, smaller and lower ceilinged, its walls festooned with quotes from Maimonides and a waiting room populated with older Rothian Jews huddled over copies of the *Post* while waging a final battle with their prostates. The doctor examined my penis and pronounced it wonderful. He even thought the initial Lubavitcher-inspired circumcision had been done with care and did not speak ill of the clumps of redundant and now inflamed foreskin. Dr. Cortisone told me I did not have a neuroma. He recommended three hot baths per day and instructed me to apply a dab of 1 percent cortisone cream to the stumps thrice a day to reduce inflammation. Additionally, he thought the anticonvulsant drug gabapentin was too strong to be deployed this early. "This is a minor issue that will heal given enough time," he said. I was not a chronic-groin-pain patient hobbled for life. The key was to forget the pain and move on.

Back home, I stripped off my Elizabethan collar and applied the first dabs of cortisone. My penis stung, but with a sense of joy. Everything was going to get better. And yet Dr. Neuroma was a highly respected Cornellian urologist, and when not responding to text messages he conveyed an air of deep institutional knowledge. So was it a neuroma or not? Would I heal up to 80 percent and no more, or would I get to live a normal life? Why did everyone have a completely different approach to the issue? And what was the issue?

Dr. Neuroma had told me that, when it came to the male genital, MRIs and other modern tools were "low yield," and that any further surgery might only make matters worse. When I talked to my friend Mary Karr, the poet and memoirist, she was surprised by how few diagnostic tools were available for the penis. "Why can't they slap it between two pieces of glass?" she asked. "As fond as people are of dick, that I can't believe." She was right. It startled me how little literacy my otherwise literate male friends had about the organ. When I mentioned the glans, some responded with a version of "You mean the mushroom part?"

Things got worse. The cortisone had dried out the affected areas, and my pain was easing to some degree, but my wounds were now covered with long unsightly scabs. Dr. Cortisone thought this was a sign of progress and assured me that the scabs would fall off during one of the long hot baths. "You're ninety-five percent of the way there," he told me. Not completely convinced by the doctor's excitement, I took some photos of my penis and sent them to my primary-care doctor. "That's just horrible!" he cried. He told me to return to the city and seek further care.

After consulting with a dermatologist and receiving yet another prescription for lidocaine, I visited a highly recommended and very handsome surgeon who happened to work down the street from the dermatologist. He was a good listener and did not dismiss my concerns. Dr. Handsome agreed with my primary doctor. The scabs were a problem and their very presence kept me from healing. He made an analogy between my penis and the hot molten magma building within a volcano. (Dr. Handsome doesn't remember this, but I recall at least one of us drawing a volcano on a pad.) "If you want," he said, "I can get rid of the scabs with just some Q-tips and some saline solution." True to his word, he removed the thick scabs very gently and with a minimum of pain. For the first time since the initial surgery, I felt that I was being cared for and looked after. Is this it? I thought. Is this my liberation? "In seven to ten days," the doctor said, "the new skin will grow in and I expect you'll feel great."

In seven to ten days, I was in the worst pain of my life. There were some improvements. My penis was no longer covered with scabs, and yet walking for more than ten minutes was impossible. I was losing my mind. I had finally tried gabapentin, but it brought about a mild psychosis during which I wasn't sure what was real and what was not. The penis is an outcropping of privilege in the male of the species, but it is also a pleasure palace constantly sending signals to the brain. Having pain in the region amounts to a never-ending genital tinnitus. It is impossible to think of anything else.

I've always had a rational fear of dying, but when I imagined a life without being able to walk or swim or have sex or travel or do anything without pain or an Elizabethan collar, I wondered what it would be like to kill myself. I looked out the window and onto the fresh snow gathered below and considered the coldness of its eternal compress. Shortly thereafter, I read a BBC article about Alex Hardy, a British man who had committed suicide in 2017 after being circumcised in Canada as a young adult. He did not share his travails with anyone after his operation, but in a long farewell note to his mother he wrote that "these ever-present stimulated sensations from clothing friction are torture within themselves; they have not subsided/normalized from years of exposure. . . . Imagine what would happen to an eyeball if the eyelid was amputated?" That analogy perfectly articulated my own experience.

Male circumcision is an important part of Islam—two-thirds of circumcised men are Muslim—as well as Judaism, though I can speak with a modicum of knowledge only of the faith in which I was brought up. My friend David Fine, the rabbi, has a progressive outlook on many issues, but he is staunch on this subject. He tells me that a man need not be circumcised to be Jewish; in the matrilineal tradition of the religion, a boy born to a Jewish mother is automatically Jewish, and yet, to Fine, circumcision means that "we are God's partners in creation."

The Talmud specifies that, if a child's older brothers die of complications from the procedure, the child should be spared circumcision. In *Why Aren't Jewish Women Circumcised?*, Shaye Cohen, quoting Rabbenu Tam, the well-known twelfth-century Talmudist, writes that even "a man who was left uncircumcised out of 'fear of the pain of circumcision' . . . is not to be considered an apostate since his 'heart is directed at heaven.'" If adult men may be excused from the procedure because of their fear, what are we to say of an infant about to experience what is likely the greatest pain of his young life? Or of a seven-year-old who wants only to please his father?

The Jewish religion generally seeks to ameliorate unnecessary suffering among its faithful. And, outside orthodoxy, large swaths of the Torah are subject to interpretation. Is a practice born of ancient Egyptian feats of endurance indispensable enough for us to continue cutting one of the most sensitive parts of the male anatomy, where any miscalculation may lead to tragedy?

Yet, even for highly assimilated Jews, circumcision, according to Diane Wolf, a sociologist at the University of California at Davis, "is really the last ritual to go." In such families, she singles out fathers as the main drivers of the practice. "What is the connection there, between masculinity and circumcision?" she asked me. When it came to her own son, she opted for the brit-shalom naming ceremony (a version of which, sometimes called the brit bat, is also performed for girls). When her son asked her why he wasn't circumcised, she told him, "You are a Jew in your head and your heart, not your penis."

The question of whom circumcision is for becomes even more fraught for Soviet Jews in North America and Israel. Sasha Senderovich, who teaches at the University of Washington, and was born in the Russian city of Ufa, said of the post-Soviet foreskin, "It could be seen as a Jewish bodily mark all its own—a mark, for example, of a circumcision that could not have been performed because it might have invited the unwanted attention of suspicious neighbors or the state." For Senderovich, "the uncircumcised Jewish penis is not a problem that needs to be fixed."

In the nineteenth century, circumcision expanded beyond a religious custom. The squeamish Victorians believed that the procedure would lead to better hygiene (and discourage masturbation).

American physicians reasoned that Jews had far fewer sexually transmitted diseases such as syphilis because of their missing foreskins. In truth, Jews may have suffered from lower rates of these diseases by having less sex outside their communities. Today, some doctors support circumcision because certain studies show that it may lower the risk of HIV transmission and infant urinary-tract infections.

On the other side of the ledger, though, two out of every million boys circumcised in the United States die from the procedure, according to the American Academy of Family Physicians; other studies place the death toll higher. Estimates of complications vary from around 0.2 percent of surgeries to as much as 10 percent. Most are relatively minor, but some have resulted in amputation of the glans or the entire organ. Among ultra-Orthodox Jewish communities, the centuries-old practice of the mohel, or ritual circumciser, suctioning the blood from the penis by mouth has resulted in several infants being infected with herpes; in 2011, a boy died. The belief that babies don't fully experience pain during circumcision because their central nervous systems aren't developed has been shown to be false. A 1997 circumcision study at the University of Alberta ended enrollment early because doctors found the procedure too traumatic for babies who were not anesthetized, while even a form of injected anesthetic, the dorsal penile nerve block, did not eliminate all pain.

Many people around the world, from parents to legislators, are reconsidering the practice. The parliaments of both Denmark and Iceland have debated banning the procedure, and the proportion of infant boys circumcised in the United States between 1979 and 2010 dropped from 65 percent to 58, according to the CDC. It is possible to envision a near future in which the majority of male American infants begin their lives with their genitalia intact.

Outside the snow-glazed window of my New York apartment, the pandemic was raging and the president had declared that he had won an election he had just lost. As a former citizen of a failed superpower, I was always looking for signs of irrevocable collapse, ready to whisk my family to the airport and then to whichever half-decent country would take us (Ireland, by that point). But how would I propel myself to the airport in my Elizabethan penis collar? How would I leave behind the nearly dozen doctors (and one excellent hypnotist) who were now taking an active interest in my situation?

My seven-year-old son knew that something was wrong. During our brief walks in the country, one of my hands held on to his little one, while the other hunted through the pocket of my sweatpants, trying to keep my collar in place. He made me a daily menu where I could mark off which dishes I wanted for lunch and dinner. I was the child now, dependent on my son's and my wife's hugs and soothing words.

On the advice of my psychologist, I began to keep a journal tracking my pain level on a scale of 0 to 5. Peeing was the most painful (I could now urinate only sitting down). The relatively pain-free moments almost always accompanied the presence of family and friends:

11:00 [a.m.] pain level at about 3
12:02 [p.m.] after talking to tony bass [my psychologist] and paul [my friend Paul La Farge]: down to 1.5
12:05 after pee back to 3 right away
12:15 hot shower down to 2
12:20 down to 1 happier thinking of family
By 1:30 back up to 3
2:30 pee then shower, down to 2
2:50 lidocaine cream up to 3 depressed
3:15 down to 2 working in bed underwear off, feeling sad
3:29 finished writing for the day feeling panicky
3:40 pee 3 put on bandage going for walk
4:15 walk 3 but a little happier to be outside
4:46 return home after 50 min walk about a 3
5:20 after bath and about 20 minutes 1 or even .5
6:30 dinner sitting in chair 1–2. Happy time with family mind not in pain
6:45 after pee back to 3 [my son's] first episode of the Simpsons
8:20 down to 2 after hot shower
9:14 up to 3 lidocaine cream applied
9:35 still pain taking Ativan to sleep
2:54 [a.m.] wake up to pee. Painful 3 or 4

"I miss you," my wife said, despite the close quarters in which we lived. "For the first time in the fifteen years that I've known you, your humor is gone."

I told her that I felt like an "unperson." She asked me why. It was not an easy question to answer. As an adult, prior to the hair in my "gentile region," I had not been wrapped up in my penis and its affairs in the way of some men I have known. In fact, I suggested to my wife that I would be fine with getting rid of it to stop the pain. She was not enthusiastic. But the idea of "unpersonhood" stuck with me. Back in New York, I walked through the lobby of my building and into the city with the nub of a secret, a hand in my sweatpants holding up the bandage that was, in turn, holding up a part of me that was now entirely foreign to me, like an angry animal that would not retract its claws. My psychologist recommended that I revisit Gogol's masterpiece "The Nose," in which a proboscis escapes the body of a minor St. Petersburg official to carry on a life of its own. "You are mistaken, my dear sir," the nose says when its owner confronts it at a prayer service and demands that it return to his face. "I exist in my own right."

In my memoir *Little Failure*, I had written about having a hole cut in my underwear by my mother so that my infected penis could breathe the murky Queens air. Soon after the operation, relatives came to visit me in my sickbed and take a gander at my broken boyhood. Now other memories returned as well. Even after I healed from the initial circumcision, I despised the remains of my penis so much that on the rare occasion I was alone in my family's apartment I would stand in front of the mirror with my genital tucked between my legs, marveling at the purity of myself without the wrecked mountain roads that crisscrossed my organ's underside. Back then, I could barely speak English, and the children in Jewish day school made fun of me both for being Russian—a "Commie"—and for being poor on a government-cheese order of magnitude. Recently, I learned that the biblical penalty for not being circumcised is *karet*, which means being cut off from one's community. As a seven-year-old, I had been duly circumcised in a miserable hospital, and still I was subjected to my classmates' playground version of *karet*, having been both cut and cut off.

The months passed. I got better, I got worse, I got better. I had seen so many doctors that my urine was now infected with klebsiella, a bacteria commonly found in hospital settings. A nurse who was present during an examination of my genitalia fainted on the spot, which did not improve my hopes for recovery or my self-esteem.

My wife introduced me to a friend and college classmate of hers, the plastic surgeon Olivia Hutchinson. Dr. Hutchinson and one of her partners examined me and told me that my nerve trauma would take a while to heal, that the nerves were now embedded within fibrous scar tissue, and that the collagen fibers were still settling after the cauterization. Despite the pain it caused, I was instructed to "palpate," or massage, the inflamed and fibrous lower stub of the former skin bridge, in order to loosen some of the scar tissue and to allow the traumatized nerves to grow straight. This was sometimes agonizing, but it really helped. Dr. Hutchinson showed me how to tend to the tiny wounds that collected lint, bandage material, and dead skin.

Each visit to Dr. Hutchinson lessened my anxiety, until I came to believe that kindness must constitute at least a third of a doctor's repertoire. While she focused on the physical aspect of my pain, she did not discount the psychological part of it. Another doctor, a urologist at NYU Langone, made a similar observation: "If you stubbed your toe in 1999, you'll forget about it. This is a traumatic event your mind can't let go."

The final breakthrough came after a visit with Dr. Robert Moldwin, the director of the Pelvic Pain Center at Northwell Health, in the village of Lake Success, on Long Island. Dr. Moldwin prescribed an ingenious compound cream containing amitriptyline, a tricyclic antidepressant. He helped me further understand the mind-body connection: "First, there's a significant organic component to the pain, and patients start to feel helpless, they catastrophize it. Chronic pain carries a high likelihood that the patient will dwell on it. The pain can then become embedded in the spinal column, in the brain." As spring settled over the East Coast and masks started to come off, I found that, while the cream helped ease the genital pain, it still, at times, reminded me of the unfortunate young British man Alex Hardy's formulation of an eyeball with the eyelid amputated.

What am I left with in the end? I hope I will continue to get better, though I doubt I will ever be completely right again. I may have to slather my genital with ointments for the rest of my life. There are new associated complications from the various medications, and the treatment of my post-traumatic stress will continue. Even with excellent insurance, I have spent many thousands of dollars for medical care and will continue to spend more.

While discussing the topic with my friends, I came across four instances of pain and disfigurement as a result of late circumcisions or of surgeries to correct botched childhood circumcisions. In the Philippines. In Canada. In Portland. In a neighboring village.

The man who lives near me, a forty-eight-year-old musician, is the son of Italian farmers who moved to the US. They did not speak English, yet were somehow persuaded by American doctors to have their son circumcised, a procedure rarely done in Italy. He remembered, as I did, a period of difficult urination. "I was screaming," he said, "but the masculine Italian response was just to laugh about it." A second surgery was performed to correct the first when he was around six years old. He told me that the psychological effects of both surgeries have been lasting: "It's affected my sexual performance and my experiences around partnering and creating bonds with people."

We will never know the full extent of such stories, because men are not supposed to talk about these things. We must either laugh it off or be stoic about what happened "down there," like the Egyptian nobles of 2400 BCE.

On January 5, at the epicenter of my time of troubles, and, soon, my nation's, I took a walk down a road leading past red barns and other frigid structures that frame the winter landscape of our country home. I could smell leaves rotting in the snowbanks and found it strange that they had survived this long. A loud wailing wall of wind had built itself up around me and I shivered in my sweatpants as one hand held up the bandage around me. I was listening to a podcast called *Time to Say Goodbye*, and its format, three Asian Americans trashing neoliberalism, reminded me of my friends back in the city, many of whom I had not seen in almost a year because of the pandemic and my condition. Their voices made me less lonely, and behind me our house shivered in the distance, a place of love and care. It was just after four, but the sun was setting, and in its descent it punched its rays through the thick clouds of our latitude, as it sometimes does on the covers of evangelical brochures. As a militant agnostic, I believe there are things one just can't know, layers of endlessness that wash up against our brief earthbound corporeality. The moon is typically gendered as female, but the sun is all over the place: the male Ra to the ancient Egyptians, the goddess Amaterasu in Japanese mythology. The sun was retreating to make room for the winter night, but I clung to the last bits of warmth. Despite what I held in my hand, I could not assign gender to the setting orb. I felt that, if anything, the Sun was beyond gender, and, in Their divinity and mercy, They would not want me or my brothers to feel this much pain.

JESUS QUINTERO

Anatomy of a Botched Assimilation

FROM *Your Impossible Voice*

IN 1986 WE moved from Linda, California, where I went to Cedar Lane School with all the migrant children, to the neighboring town of Olivehurst, where I would go to school with the whites. During the Great Depression, the poorest of the US— Oklahomans—left their dust bowl to get into this bowl: the concave bowl being California's Central Valley north of Sacramento, and the rim being the mountains. Olivehurst was full of poor white people, and then we came. We were pioneers, one of the first Mexican families to call this Okie place home.

Like them, we were hillbillies. My parents came from the Mexican hills, los cerros, San Jose De Vargas, a third-world village. Pigs roaming the only dirt road, three-walled houses, a cauldron of food stewing outside under mesquite embers. Without a school at the ranch (the last person who attempted to educate the town had been shot), my father had the equivalent of a first-grade education. My mother, part of the community's regal elite, bordered on the equivalent of a third grader's comprehension, almost brave enough to read out loud when no one was nearby. Between them, they had the think-tank capacity of an American fifth-grade education, dependent on the adages of los misterios to explain what were nothing more than concepts found in basic science books. Anything that wasn't understood was a miracle.

Like the Okies, we were attempting to assimilate and transfer our rancho burdens (la pobreza, los problemas) and exchange them for a series of unfortunate events: work, new neighborhoods, and adolescent rites of American passage, along with those volatile variables that mysteriously appeared without warning, an ominous premonition, our own Okie-Trash Santo.

La pobreza's laws of physics created a parallax: that which was closer to us seemed to crumble more quickly than the plane at a distance. The old-world San Jose de Vargas ethos had taken root in our version of El Norte, expediting entropy. In our little world, we were stuck in our own vortex, a black hole that sucked the life out of everything. Our home on Ardmore Street was sagging, as though the foundation was crumbling under the collective weight, the gravity of my family's history. It had blisters, the cheap paint bursting from the heat. It was the unforgiving sun: the paradox of both giving life and stripping it away. At least ours wasn't as bad as the surrounding Okie homes that always looked like they had been struck by tornadoes. They had redneck industrial, abstract sculptures piled and displayed in their front yard, side of the house, even the roof, the randomness of objects working in conjunction: a gutted mattress filled with bicycle handlebars. Ruptured standing stereo speakers on top like a Koons bunny. Two tires as eyes and grill grate. Maybe part of a boat. Maybe a camper would appear next week, one that would never get disassembled for parts. And maybe a long-haired man would live in it, always shirtless with a dog chain as a necklace. And maybe he would then bring along the first car that would collect cobwebs, and it would eventually be used as an artifact for a sociology case study of the nonworking class. Since the academics never showed up, however, it would slowly transform into a pawnshop, starting off with a broken baby stroller and ending with a weight bench, weights on top of the roof. Always, always, a busted TV and some couch, where we used to imagine watching a TV show, playing a game of charades, making sure that nails, glass, or screws didn't poke through our bare feet.

Monopoly money strewn like confetti. Fake money everywhere. Pieces of games.

And bottles. Endless bottles of cheap aluminum beer, Old Milwaukee, in a Hefty garbage bag, waiting to be taken to be recycled, but not until they were bleached white by the sun. Our game was crunching them with our feet. Some father would offer us a drink as we got thirsty. Some shirtless kid with dirty Popsicle remains on her chest would wander over, hair of a discarded doll, wiry and thick like a Brillo pad, look at me already with the universal countenance of a beggar. She'd take a sip as if from a baby's bottle.

These were my friends. These were my neighbors. These colorful white people who treated me as their adopted child. This was my life. This was home. Dirty Mexican, *Beaner*. This wasn't my own invective, hurled at myself. It was them, los Okies, who reminded me that I was dirt. They inculcated in me an indelible, profound sense of worthlessness, but they were just as vulnerable. The color of these white people was an off-white, tinged with the same color of poverty as my parents, mixed with equal parts despair, an eggshell white. Maybe they were delicate and fragile like eggs, one bad drop away from cracking. Like us. Their door was always open. I didn't even have to knock.

Unlike them, my parents were never home, always leaving early to work in the Yuba County fields. As farm laborers, peach pickers, they were always the first to be at work, el campo, and always the last to get home, la casa—leaving with the car's lights on, 4:30 a.m., and coming back with them on, 8:30 p.m. They had no concept of nine to five. My parents' penance was five to nine, a migrant's dyslexic working hours.

I didn't want my parents to know that something was tragically wrong, when they had come into this country for this opportunity—school. They had no idea what was going on with me personally or academically. They could never imagine, but I was still worried about humiliating them, especially since my father placed such an emphasis on being a "Quintero," which had great value and honor for him, though it had lost its currency in the cultural exchange rate. Nobody knew how to spell it, let alone say it. Since their English was broken—no, shattered—and they only spoke a country Spanish, I could get away with mistranslating for them the urgent school calls filled with academic, institutional jargon. All the letters that piled up in the mailbox. They were too tired after work to look inside it, and, besides, they could barely peek inside the envelopes: it was just a reminder that they barely knew how to read.

I did what any good first-generation immigrant kid would do. I protected them by lying, using some cultural white lies that eventually began to spill into my own reality. I was much more an imaginary version of myself than the one that inhabited my body, struggling with what was what, keeping up with the tangled yarn I wove to keep them and myself at bay from the inevitable.

I was one of the only Beaners in a damn near all-white school, Yuba Gardens (the grounds being nothing but asphalt). In 1986, it was the worst place to live in the USA, and I was the worst student. My parents couldn't afford the artifacts to segue me into this new world: the clothes. I used my older brother's T-shirts, which hung below my knees. I wore the *same* pair of highwater pants from last year, every day—the only one I had. This made me part FOB, part wetback, part rural 'Merican with dirty fingernails.

Two years later, I was in danger of flunking out of eighth grade, having to repeat it. As a student of life and in school, I was constantly in trouble—stealing mi ama's car, a beige 1979 Plymouth Duster, so I could drive my little sister to school, using a couch cushion so I could see over the hood; stealing some acid we had concocted in science class so I could spill it onto a GT BMX bike frame, just because; and, of course, climbing up to the school's ceiling to turn off the power supply during a school dance, back when record players were used.

The great thing about trouble was that it provided me with an immediate intrinsic worth. Being an accidental delinquent made me feel alive enough to be seen as though I mattered: I spent more time in the front office than in class, more time cutting school than attending it. The few times I was there, it was mostly after school, doing time in detention, or doing some form of "community service." Yuba Gardens didn't have the resources necessary to deal with problem kids such as myself. It didn't have the funding to hire a bilingual counselor to deal with teenage, cross-cultural transgressions, so they provided me with the next best thing. In a last-ditch effort to get me out of there, an alternative to help me catch up on academic credits, the senior staff created a makeshift after-school program, providing me with an internship in order to make me cognizant of my bad choices. They paired me with a hard, avuncular figure, the only Latino "faculty" member at the school, who just happened to be a janitor; it was the academic equivalent of scared straight.

He was the first Mexican I knew who didn't work in the fields, in el campo, el sol. Santos could have been a former inmate who held his last fiber of dignity close to his chest. As far as I knew, no one ever questioned the polarities between us, our shared references. We, too, were the same and not: citizens of the underground.

Like me, Santos worked with what he had, and it wasn't much: How much was I worth, anyway? What was my value? Weirder still, what was his?

"Follow me," said Santos. "Why didn't you go to school today?"

"I did," I lied.

"You shouldn't cut." He smacked my hand. His hands were scarred by bleach, knuckles swollen by fights gone by like they could bulge right out of his skin.

He opened his closet, filled with industrial supplies. "Here," he said, exhaling to make up for his loss of words. "Take it." He handed me a mop, staring me dead in the eyes. When I attempted to take it, he held on to it, so I had to yank it; he still wouldn't budge, forcing me to pull on it like a lever, but I was scrawny and small, a runty human Chihuahua. "What's your problem," he barked, throwing the mop down on the hallway floor.

"Problem?" I lied. "What are you talking about?"

He guffawed in disbelief.

Since all the students were gone, the thwack of the stick echoed. "Pick it up." He placed his hands on his hips, tapped his foot. "Are you listening?" Santos slowly sucked on his toothpick, one wooden fiber, a splinter at a time, until it disappeared. He spoke through the side of his mouth. "Huh? Why don't you listen, eh?"

"Yeah," I replied, despondent. I bent over to pick up the mop, held on to my pants since I didn't have a belt. "I'm listening . . . yeah."

I looked over my back, trying to read his next move.

"What'd I say, huh." He disappeared into the closet, bent over. "Repeat it," he said, his voice now dampened by the tight acoustics of his office. "Eh?!"

I weighed my options: what was the right answer? What hidden lesson, if any, was there within the statement: *the mop, the required force to pull a lever, repeat.* What idiomatic intent, what rhetoric within his statement could be gleaned to reveal the true meaning not just of my life, but all life in general? I heard a bucket spill over, and my feet were immediately soaked in water.

"You idiot," he yelled. He'd deliberately kicked over the bucket of dirty mop water. "Pick it up!" The water spilled in the shape of a cartoon hand, then morphed into tree branches in winter.

I failed. I must have taken too long to formulate an adequate response, lost in these janitorial, Rorschach inkblots, finding beauty and possibilities in the mess and spills of life. Sometimes I would repeat what he had said, but that's not what he had intended, not *literally*. Life was a form of tricky punishment, hidden trapdoors that were triggered and motivated by some boiler room of internalized oppression. Like in the classroom, there were lessons outside of the class that I couldn't quite understand.

"Andale. Vamos . . . leggo." Santos was heading toward the classrooms and hurried his steps, supplies in each hand, towels and rags looped around his belt. As he walked over his man-made puddle, his work boots left an imprint, that ubiquitous stamp that a Mexican animal was there: the small crucifixes, crosses down the spine of the sole, and the rays for traction along the periphery of the boot, reminding me of La Virgen de Guadalupe.

I quickly mopped the spill away and followed Santos, making sure that I walked exactly on his footsteps, just like I followed my father's in the peach orchards, those familiar indentations on the earth's soil, the same design: a worker animal's paws with purposeful strides, steps almost a gallop to quickly get to their measly economic destination.

Santos had the stroll that indicated that he'd been in prison: his overblown chest puffed out as though it was the only humanity left inside of him, attempting to walk his two pectoral muscles like people walk their dogs. His forearms had some pastiche of prison art: the prison guard tower running the length of his forearm, clocks, a chola with the sombrero. His hands were in a permanent "C" like Lego characters, engineered specifically to fit the following accessories: the broom, the mop, the plunger.

Santos opened the door to my math class, slid the doorstop in place—the rags on his side forever moving, a Newton's cradle of ghetto physics. "Listen: get to work since you, you know . . ." He hid behind his eighties aviators, head tilted up at a forty-five-degree angle. He flexed his nostrils: ". . . Never mind. Just, you know, make it fast."

He nodded his head to indicate, "Come in," fidgeting with the key. *Get to work. Do it.* Although I was functionally illiterate, I knew the body language of my people, mostly indicating various stages of work, subtle commands to maintain energy, not waste time talking, the threat of small banter robbing precious work time.

I attempted to walk past him, but his girth blocked the entrance. "Listen . . ." He puffed his chest as though taking a hit. "You know what you have to do, right."

He exhaled long and hard. I nodded my head and saw my reflection in his shades. He lifted them up and placed his hand on my shoulder, seeing eye to eye. I looked away. He squatted down, got to my level: "I need this place gleaming, do you understand? Look at me."

I was taught to look at people's eyes, but I wasn't taught the power of maintaining a gaze long enough to register an understanding. I looked at Santos and nodded. There was this hard juggling act of not talking back to your elders and getting your ass kicked for ignoring them. I thought it was another lesson. There was always punishment. I was always wrong, a pendejo. I braced myself.

"I'll see you soon, okay?" He patted my shoulder, gently.

"Okay," I said, looking down at my damp shoes. "See you soon."

"Chuy," he said. "Chuyito." His voice became soft. It was unusual given that his voice normally came out like ragged, rusty shanks, in the font of tattooed pinto letters with sharp edges. "No. Really. I'll see you soon." Santos had this unpredictable vato way in which he would vacillate from being an endearing person, speaking in the diminutive as though speaking to his abuelita, and then, midsentence, finish in fury or malintent, changing the color of his face and tone of voice, red and dark. This always kept me on my toes.

I feared him. Which meant that I respected him. A lot.

"Do you understand?" He tilted his head to take a look at my face at another angle to see if it registered. "See you soon, know what I mean."

He placed his shades back down, pushed them up to the bridge of his nose, and shook his head in disappointment. He got out of the doorway to let me in to my assignment, this classroom that needed to be picked up, and he disappeared. His numerous keys chiming with each manic stride.

"See you soon," I said. He didn't look back, like I hadn't said anything, like I wasn't even there.

In eighth grade, I was in trouble so much that I had my routine down. I turned half of the desks on their backs, their bellies exposed. There was a sound to hearing their backs crash against the tile, the screeching of their heels in resistance before succumbing to the blunt force beyond their control—*sass*—a sound of power and dominance. I associated loud sounds with hard work, especially with a deep, steady breath accompanying it.

If cleaning were a subject, I would have been in honors. With the same immigrant intensity and speed, I used the Bepco freeze spray on the bottom of the desks, all lined up in rows like trees and vegetables. Once they were removed with a clean swipe from the joint scraper, I was rewarded by the fruits of my labor, the smell of mint from a Wrigley's, grape from Big League Chew, watermelon from Hubba Bubba. I picked each one off the ground, that synthetic produce. Trash. Next . . .

I was being groomed as a form of cheap labor. By that point, it was automatic, something that I'd try to unlearn: the classroom was my own mini-orchard that needed my manual labor: desk cleaning, mopping, board erasing, erasers that needed to have the chalk pounded out of them—these words and ideas that in the end became nothing but dust—the emptying of garbage bags. Detention was supposed to be about humiliation, but my life had been a constant barrage of culturally awkward situations; it was my default setting. It was home, a home that made me feel safe.

Within five minutes, I was already sweating, the well-earned marker of a hard Mexican worker. This urgency I learned from my parents, the physical precedent set: seeing mi apa work, chingandole en el sol (bravo) reminded me of those old films in kindergarten that provided the viewer with twelve frames a second, and every so often the film would skip, missing a couple of frames, and the subject or character would magically reappear elsewhere within the continuum of the film, a quantum leap, breaking the sound barrier of work. He was irascible, an always on-edge man who could easily summon the peerless anger of a second-class citizen with a third-world past. He channeled that into his work: one second my dad was on the ladder—the next he was by the bin, dumping his peaches from his costal, his burlap sack. This was my first taste of magical realism, the illusion and trickery of seeing him defy the laws of physics, economics, and human limitations. I was supposed to transfer that example and apply it to my academics, but there was a disconnect, except if maybe I could pack books in a box, get them ready for shipment?

I worked so hard that I had enough time to shimmy Mrs. Brokaw's

desk open and modify the grade book and the attendance sheet. I
picked the lock, went into the desk, and simply retrieved the in-
structor's official green pamphlet. Using my finger, I quickly found
my name, and began changing o's into 8's on assignments, started
to place a checkmark where there wasn't one, making it seem like
I had been in school when I hadn't been. When I was altering my
records, it felt like the clock's second hand clicked. I could hear
the electricity humming within the school walls. My heart pounded
hard, pounding against the inside of my chest as though I had a fist
inside, working its Catholic magic. *Por mi culpa. Por mi culpa. Por mi
gran culpa.*

It was always me against the clock, needing to work fast enough
to get home before my parents did, back from working in the
fields, smelling like sun and earth. The pounding of their steps to
dislodge the last traces of dust, announcing that they were home.

What motivated me with cleaning, not studying, was my father's clarion call, repeating my last name under my breath . . .
soy Quintero . . . soy Quintero . . . soy Quintero . . . and then, in
one fell swoop, when he was depressed, "I am nothing . . . Yo soy
nada." Without ever having the privilege of taking a reading class,
not even the time to read a book, his vocabulary was limited, never
working in nuance or subtly, always expressing himself in binaries.

After I cleaned the room, my attendance, and grades, I looked
for Santos.

It was time for the next assignment, or was today garbage day?

There was a good chance that we could hit my science class.
There was plenty of cleaning I needed to do there, and I was even
getting paid to fix some other student's problem. I was just getting
warmed up.

"Santos!" I yelled, and my voice echoed throughout the vacant
school. "Where are you?!"

Normally, Santos had a small Walkman, listening to some cas-
sette tape, oldies, whistling in that Mexican way used to pace yourself, some cadence to measure the revolutions of the shoulder
blade to buff out tough stains in tight circles. If he wasn't cleaning,
he was easy to identify by the dangling of his many keys, so there
was no other option but to hear him. Even with clothes, this invisible man made sure he was heard.

"San . . ." I clasped my hands to make a bullhorn ". . . tos!" I
blushed in shame when I realized that the voice that shot back at

me with a thick Mexican accent was mine. Students used to laugh at my limited English, a set of refrigerator poetry bought at a flea market with missing articles, antecedents. Subjects and verbs rarely agreed since they were catapulted by my tongue, and I was always taught that agreeing was a form of weakness. There was always tension, drama, inside my house, inside of school, even inside of my fucking mouth.

"Hey!" A stray piece of paper was hurled across the hall by the wind, and I was afraid that I was being watched by Santos. There were always these unspoken pop quizzes that he'd use to shape me up, always psychological. This absence could have been intended, his attempt to teach me another lesson that I had yet to find the meaning of, some profound moral to rectify my inner turmoil. *Perhaps he's hiding and gauging how I will respond, if I'm motivated and independent enough to show some initiative?* These constant, unexpected situations were simulators meant to show me what a fuckup I was, opting for some unreachable choice that managed to evade me. It wouldn't be too long before it wasn't fight or flight: I would simply freeze.

I quickly lapped the school, hoping to catch an open door, a sign he was inside, still on the premises, but all of the doors were closed and locked. Out of breath, I made my way home, and that's when I noticed that his truck, always the last vehicle on the lot, was gone; the lot was empty.

It was time to go home and clean up, make la casa glisten as though slathered in manteca.

Our Mexican house was different from its neighbors yet not: the chain-link fence, the perimeter of our front yard, drooped in some areas as though made of rope that had lost its tension. Because of this, the chain-link would detach itself from parts of the beam, protruding outward as though somebody had blasted it to make an escape. Ivy clung and suffocated parts of the fence, weighing it down, serving less as a botanical curtain for privacy and more as a guard to hide the bald, thinning yard. It was mostly packed dirt, etched with earthworm indentations, their own highway. They escaped by cracking the earth's surface and burrowing deep into the earth's marrow.

Clearly, we had one of the best houses on the block, I was thinking, even though the driveway was gravel that never seemed to do its job of leveling itself, always succumbing to the perpetual hole it attempted to fill, and that's when I saw it . . . there . . . this anomaly that was out of its environment: a jewel of a lowrider truck that sparkled with life, metallic paint in a pattern shining in a constellation from its own galaxy. The color was a candy, root-beer brown, and it had the same sheen and transparent effect of a sucked Jolly Rancher.

Santos was there, right there at my house, there in our home. Our place.

Parked next to it was my father's truck: it always had a layer of orchard dust, mud sprayed and dried on its fenders. The parts that used to be red were now a dull pink from the sun, the vibrant color oxidized into a flat, muted dull that was now transitioning toward gray. There were so many times it had run out of gas because gas cost so much. It hurt my father seeing his hard-earned money disappear as he pumped, the numbers spinning as though it were years he was sacrificing instead of currency.

That truck always smelled of leftovers, food on the verge of spoiling, el lonche that my mother prepared, often at 3:45 in the morning, transforming into the smell of death. What? *Mi apa?* Home? Now? What—4:15 p.m.?

My father hated being there. Home was for the weak, as was rest, especially just sitting down like a pinche huevon; my dad quickly built a venerable reputation, always the hardest worker, always sought after. He worked like he was always late for something, which was often his next job.

He was the oldest child in Mexico, learned how to work when he was five, using his father's jacket to retrieve the cattle, the sleeves from the coat dragging to the ground behind him. He was born to work, especially since he was made out of pragmatism, a biological tractor, an accessory to cultivate the land, not quite intended to fully develop as much as put in work on the physical end, and that's it. In El Norte, among the pickers (peaches, prunes, olives, tomatoes, lo que sea), he was hunched over in a perpetual state, running and working in a panicked frenzy, part convulsion, part chiriporquias; my family and I were puppets being handled by someone with muscular dystrophy, a synchronized seizure operated by the delicate, indistinguishable line between survival and poverty.

The door was always open, since running the swamp cooler during the day was a waste of money. I felt like leaving, going over to my friend's house, and hiding out. Perhaps running away was an option. While I was weighing and contemplating my next move, Santos appeared in the doorway, he seemed to be leaving, but he saw me, his silver shades still on.

"About time," he yelled from the porch. He rolled himself on the heels of his foot, his thumbs locked around the belt buckle sans his rags. "What took you so long?!" He was right below that Okie redneck woodwork purchased at the Yuba Sutter Fair, a *Los Quintero* sign.

My mother came out with a flyswatter, telling me, "Que dice? Watchusay?" My father peeked over Santos's shoulder and hit his fist against his palm.

When I got inside, they were already sitting down, conference mode. To compensate for the small space, the living room was stuffed with excessively huge furniture. Our eighties vinyl sofas were creased like used brown-paper bags. The buttons had been removed, exposing the white stuffing that resembled wisps of smoke. To combat the decay and guide the eye beyond the deteriorating furniture, mi ama crocheted long doilies out of yellow yarn, three of them each on the backs of the sofas; on the coffee table were three (the biggest always at the center, flanked by smaller ones at the side). They were webs spun to redirect the eye, these geometrical kitsch adornments with the symmetry of a disease that afflicted the poor, kept spreading over time, eventually infecting the whole damn house.

"Como están?" Santos offered social niceties. Then to me, "Sit down."

I ignored him; flippant by nature, partly resigned to the events that would unfold, my body was already going into shock, numbing itself. My ears started to flush red. I wanted to self-destruct, vanish, and splatter. Adrenaline coursed and I felt like I needed to go boneless like a dishrag.

"Hey!" My dad barked at me in a way that only an immigrant from another country can, that old-world, Pavlovian command. "Sit down. Sientate."

I would need leverage, need to be in the position to take off should the situation escalate. I already had a leg up since the front door was always open to cool off the house, but it always brought in a swarm of flies. There was the constant tapping from them crashing against the window, trying to escape.

"Sit down, mijo. Please." My mother insisted, so I made space on the side table, right by the door, gently placing aside the fragile porcelain figurines. The micro ballerinas were one of her prized possessions. "Por favor."

I trusted her. I sat down while I held and twirled the delicate ballerina.

"Gracias," she said, using the flyswatter as a fan.

She looked out for the flies that buzzed overhead but were hard to spot. She traced the flies with her eyes to telegraph the trajectory, swatting away with the flyswatter, swinging, missing. Swinging. Splatter. Her shirt was transparent with the day's sweat, revealing a wifebeater underneath. She smelled of armpit, dark lines of dirt caked onto the creases of her neck. She was, as usual, in the periphery, there and not, always an extra. Hard physical labor made her exhausted, lifeless, a little pale.

Somehow, she always mustered enough energy to never let us go hungry. Always washed the dirty laundry that turned into mud in the washing machine, using a dash of gasoline to get off the tough stains. Cleanliness was akin to godliness, and who else was closer to God than all of us, the dirtiest people of them all—them Mexicans; them themless . . .

Santos clapped his hands. "All right? Do you know why we're here?"

"No," I lied.

"Well," Santos shot back. "Why are you here?"

It was more of an existential question, and my capacity to imagine was as limited as my father's English. I shrugged my shoulders. Played dumb.

"What's wrong with you? Guess?" They always ended the talk with rhetorical questions, expecting me to have profound answers to abstract social questions that required thorough, incisive responses, an understanding of philosophy, history, sociology, and especially psychology.

"School?" I offered, looking down at the porcelain figurine, twirling it with my fingers so it could spin.

"Yes," said Santos. "And what about it? Huh? What do you think?"

"Think about . . . ," I replied, looking at the treasure in my hand, ". . . what?"

He threw his hands in the air.

To survive, I had learned how to tune out, walk through life with my internal mute button, gathering pieces here and there, my Mexican, Chicano mind just not quick enough—yet—to process information while in panic mode. It was my own closed caption with the Spanish version, a translation of a word that may have been "off."

Santos brushed me off, pulled up his pants a bit, and placed his shades inside his shirt pocket. He took the bottom of his shirt to wipe down his sweaty forehead.

"Look. Let me tell you why we're here, okay?" He looked toward my father and began gesticulating, attempting to use his own form of sign language to express to my father what he had just expressed to me. "Aqui!" he offered. "Nosotros." He made a circle with his index finger, stirring a big pot, to indicate all the people who were present. "Todos." He brought his arms together to make a hoop. He may as well have been using Morse code.

Mi apa, like the obedient student that he never had the opportunity to become, leaned onto the edge of his La-Z-Boy, half *come again* and half *I'm listening*, the body language of being at attention. He pinched his face in the universal sign of confusion, "Gwat?!" He shrugged his shoulders in the air a bit.

"Listen . . . ," Santos tried again. He looked up at the ceiling as if to retrieve the few Spanish words at his disposal . . . dusty, unused, clearly weathered. He blinked but nothing came out.

He frowned and gave up. "He's not doing very well. Your son." He pointed at me. "Him."

My father's facial expression remained the same, as if the words weren't intended for him. Nothing registered, but he looked concerned, eyes fixed. His hair was still matted to his forehead from the day's sweat, stiff by the salt. "Que dice?"

". . . Your dad deaf?!" Santos was getting annoyed, perhaps it's why he'd been leaving in the first place. It pained me that he spoke to my father in the same disrespectful way that he, at times, had done to me.

My mom got up and was attempting to swat away a fly that was trying to land on my father, who stood still, unfamiliar with the cues and formalities of a professional, serious interaction. He was a street mime on pause, waiting to be turned on by work, only work.

"How do you say that, what I just said?" said Santos. He scooted back onto the sofa, a little resigned. He took out a box of toothpicks and placed one in his mouth. "I need your help."

I ignored him. Sweat was running down the side of my face.

"Chuy," he whispered. "Please?"

I stayed motionless, mimicking my father. If I close my eyes, they won't see me. If I stand still, this scene won't play out, just a frozen frame.

"Hey." My mom came over by me. "Watch out. Mijo. A fly?"

They buzzed and hovered like buzzards, they tapped on the window, so many of them that the window vibrated. Mi ama went over and splattered several. She closed the door and I heard the fresh pot of beans boiling. The windows began to steam.

"You? You speak Spanish?" my dad pleaded with Santos.

Santos nearly pinched his fingers together, held them up in the air. "Muy poquito."

My father looked away. Rams lock horns; poor people lock eyes to gain respect. Looking away indicates a form of submission, being meek and subservient. Santos, this other, had enough gravitas to make this other, my dad, avert the gaze that attempted to dehumanize an object, push him further within his descending inferiority complex.

"Are you ready?" Santos said. "You speak Spanish, right?"

"Sí," my mom responded. "My son? He good? He good English speak."

"Tell him that you are the worst. Ready? Just translate it? Te va decir en español," Santos told my dad. And, briefly, my father's face relaxed. "Go ahead. Tell them in Spanish. You're a piece of shit . . ."

I was always interpreting for them in those days, which meant seeing white people speak to me in a broken way as well. I had to interpret, *piece* together these dirty bits: *Say you, to them, me no understand mucho Espanish.* And they'd look at me the same way they'd look when talking to a toddler, attempting to transmit what they were saying much more with their eyes, the enunciation and intonation of words.

I got up and faced my father. I was weighing my options: How do I tell my father that I am a piece of shit. Worse still, a Mexican, but I couldn't tell him that. He often reminded me of the shame of his dark skin, how he wished he could be whiter like his wife, my mother.

"I'm worthless," I whispered. Some translations are meant to be lost in translation.

My dad looked at me with eyes of concern and anticipation. He had this innocent look of constant awe, of fireworks in the sky. It was his immigrant way of indicating that he was processing, registering the world and sounds around him, although he couldn't decipher anything.

"What?! Speak louder. And tuck in your T-shirt," he spat. "You are embarrassing us."

"I'm no good. I'm a bad student," I replied in a regular volume.

Santos interrupted and fed off my momentum, despite my watery eyes, my quivering voice.

"Tell him that you are going to be in the worst classes in high school. You're going to be in bonehead classes," he said in a caring, empathetic voice, hard but firm. "That's if! and a **good** *if,* if you pass."

"¿El? My son? He no good? No bueno?" my dad shot back, starting to button up his work shirt.

They may as well have been speaking in Nahuatl.

Me? The worst? Santos nodded his head, slowly, like it wasn't even a point of dispute, just a slow, steady affirmation that hammered itself with each nod.

"He no good school? School? It no good?" said my father. My father attempted to rearrange his broken Spanish into a mosaic, twisting and spinning his words like a kaleidoscope, trying to find the difference between a pronoun and noun.

"No." Santos shook his head in exaggeration; he took a deep breath and offered, "Escuela no bueno."

My father looked relieved. "Oh."

Santos had accidentally laid blame on the school, suggested its institutional offering was restricted, deficient.

"Muy malo," Santos said and made the emphasis as though a response to a terrible dish. "Bad, you know? Malo."

My father got up. He finally understood. I could tell he was fighting the urge to stand up and beat me into agave pulp. He caught himself and sat back down, grabbed the edges of his armrest and readjusted his weight. To calm himself down, he was picking away the cotton from the cracks of his La-Z-Boy.

"What's wrong with you?" my dad spat. "What are you thinking?"

"Why? Why he no goods?" my mother said.

"Look." Santos got up and retrieved a folded paper from his back pocket. He unfolded with care, looking down at it, chewing on his toothpick. "Here. Give it to your dad." He handed me a document. "It's your report card."

Santos looked at mi apa. "Grados?" offered Santos with uncertainty, a contestant on *Wheel of Fortune*.

My hands shook, I looked at the canary-yellow sheet, my heart cracking my ribs open with fear. My temples throbbed, and my shirt started to stick to my back. The beans cooking in the kitchen were making our house a sweat lodge.

"F's," he repeated. "Muchos."

I wanted to quickly transform the F's into B's with a mechanical pencil.

My dad got up and yanked it out of my hands. He squinted at it, read the subjects out loud but with a Spanish twist: Matematics, D; Ingles, F; Ciencias, F . . .

He stopped halfway and then swallowed, handing it back to Santos.

"It's yours," Santos said.

My father threw it on the ground.

"Tell them what else you did? Do they know what's going on?"

God. Dios mio.

What had I done? I'd been spinning a yarn of lines, no, infrared lasers, and I had trapped myself in a corner.

What else had I done? There were so many things? I was a Native American story doll with heads protruding everywhere around me, telling and convincing myself of tales that contradicted each other.

Silence: the buzzing. The pot's lid hitting against the rim from the pressure building inside.

I shrugged.

"Bah," my dad responded, never once thinking that local, rural, Mexican colloquial village conjectures had their own restrictions and boundaries. *"Bah,"* he said louder, this time with his head up, not talking to the ground.

"What is that," Santos offered, ". . . your dad's a billy goat?"

Santos read a list of my crimes to my father, but what stuck out to me first was the word *deficient.* I wanted to interrupt him and recuse myself. No: why was he talking about "the fish net" (defi-cient?), but then this other word popped up: *truancy*. I thought the truth was crazy, part true and part lunacy. It must be so true, coupled with an adverb, ly, a high degree, confirming the verac-ity of the account. I accidentally constructed my own etymology and planted seeds to root words that would never come to frui-tion.

"But," my father would say. "Why can't he act like the white people? This is a white school. It's the best."

In Linda, my classmates had been the children of other migrants who picked the fields clean, anything that popped out of Califor-nia's skin. We were all on that skin together, living brown aphids— pests, a locust wrath. We were both harvested and dropped there, picked by the world and its mysteries for our labor.

Santos just continued, oblivious to whether we understood or not. He continued from some script that he'd memorized, some academic Miranda rights: demerits, credit deficiencies, matricula-tions. How could we be American if we didn't understand *that* En-glish? We were puzzled like my cousins who had just arrived from Mexico, seeing us and our place for the first time, uncertain how to proceed, attempting to process while being too preoccupied by any thread of possible danger.

When Santos left, he shook my father's hand, scratched by tree branches, peach fuzz, and juice dried up as micro stains.

Before he left, he bent over and offered me a toothpick.

"Gracias," I said.

The door shut behind him, and I heard the lowrider start and disappear.

"Come with me, cabron!" yelled my dad. "Andale, pendejo. Let's go out to the back."

I stood there, frozen, looking at the poster of La Santa de la Guarda, the whitest thing—a saint guarding the whitest children crossing a dangerous bridge. It was affixed onto our seventies wood paneling, even though it was the late eighties.

We were stuck in the past.

Stuck in the old ways: here and there.

Of course, we once had a goat in the backyard. My little sister had become so attached to it, feeding it thorny weeds, snuggling up to its snout as she gently combed its goatee, using her fingers as a comb, stroking it until its eyes shut. *Of course,* at one point we did have chickens, a rooster that could not wake up before us, crowing to an empty house. *Of course,* there were other animals that were also "others." *Of course,* there once was a nameless, anonymous pig in our garage. We had our own private petting zoo.

All those animals had been slaughtered in our backyard; I don't think any of them had legal papers. Of course.

On the day of the slaughter, my little sister was told to take a bath while we all tried to corner the scared goat, which evaded us. Unbeknownst to us, La Santa Muerte had visited it on the day of its death to warn it of its fate. It managed to find the holes as we attempted to corral it within this enclosed Mexican, human fence that became tighter and tighter. The local compadre with a knife, dead center, instructed us, wanting us to hold it still once we wrestled it down, but it knew it was going to die. It magically leaped over us, headed for the road toward freedom, but my father threw a direct hit with an axe, right on the neck. It fell on its side, mid-stride, still in the air, the nameless creature's legs still running like a dreaming, sleeping dog.

In that old way, that unbridled ingenuity and resourcefulness, our pet was hung from its hind legs—on our rusting swing set—bleeding out, all the blood rushing to its slit throat, exposing its blindingly white spine.

"Go get your bicycle pump, mijo," instructed mi apa.

When I returned, the goat was already off the swing set, on the ground, and my father made a slit on one of its ankles. He inserted the tip of the air hose and encouraged me to pump away. As I did, the skin freed itself from the skin. The black hide with white patches puffed up like a balloon about to burst.

Like a chivo into a casco . . . not like a lamb to a slaughter.

My grandfather once took one of our chickens without any warning or indication, kind of like an old rancho reflex of survival: hungry = animal = death. He grabbed it by its neck, swung it over his head like a cowboy's rope, over and over again like he was qualifying for the Mexican hammer throw in the Olympics. He showed me the neck and face like a sock resting across his cracked palm. He asked me if I wanted to keep it.

Like a chicken in a Mexican backyard . . . no, never like a lamb led to a slaughter.

Running: like a chicken with its head cut off: that stream of blood bending to the force of the speed, an antenna of an RC car.

But nothing had bled like the pig. Chavelo straddled it, pulled back on its neck like a camel clutch and slit, immediately filling the garage with a pink mist, a terrible gender reveal gone wrong. It convulsed and squealed, haunting the whole house. My tio took the tail end of La Muerte's black robe and attempted to cover my eyes with it, but I still heard the gunshot when they were tired of the noise. It still smelled like the lab of death: gunsmoke—sulfur—and the unmistakable smell of pools of blood: iron, copper, zinc, fat . . .

Like a pig heading toward a Mexican quinceañera . . .

Not once. Not ever, never ever being a lamb led to a slaughter.

Before any party, a life has to be transformed into death before the celebration even begins.

"Do you know what sacrifice is?" my dad yelled at me, pushing me toward the back end of the yard. I tripped over my mother's roses. "You have no idea!"

My dad howled with the primal pain of all of our ancestors before words were even born.

Between fits of rage, he paused to gather himself. "One," he panted, catching his breath, his hair no longer stiff, electrified and alive. "One," he held up his finger. "You were born here, idiot." He was walking closer to me and I was now cornered. "Two: you speak the fucking language." I could now smell his dried lungs, the smell of a dehydrated, taxed human being. "Three: you are legal. You have papers." That was it. What else could one need?

He picked me up by my oversized shirt, lifted me a little, and threw me to the ground. The collar was now stretched. I didn't know if I should get back up or stay down. I opted for down, knowing it's easier to use my knees as shields to block the blows.

"And . . . you have school, you idiot. Do you know what an honor it is—an honor, my God—to be here?" He pointed at the ground with both fingers. "Huh?"

My father wasn't familiar with API scores, property taxes, a school full of white teachers. Even before I got there, they had already failed me with those degrading looks.

"Yes," I said, to make him stop, guessing what he expected me to say. I was always wrong, throwing wild punches at the world.

"You don't know anything! You don't know what I've been through."

The scarcity of his emotion and experience, his poverty was penetrating us through our pores. He kicked me. I felt his industrial boot crash against my femur. I heard people laughing and giggling.

"We are with the best people. The whites?" he continued. "We moved away from the Mexicans, see?"

He spun around with his hands out to demonstrate the environment before us, his attempt to offer me the world. My Okie neighbors were peeking through the holes of the wooden fence, our mini border, enjoying the show. I heard someone say, "What the fuck are them sayin'?"

"Do you want to be like me? A fucking wetback picker?"

Sometimes the Okies would clean up their backyards by throwing their unwanted junk over into our yard. It wasn't surprising to find some unexpected odds and ends magically appear on our side. As my father lectured, I marveled at a broken game that I hadn't yet acknowledged, perhaps a recently discarded arrival. Milton Bradley's Operation.

It was missing the pincers.

"Why can't you be like them, huh? The white people?" My father pointed at one that he caught out of the corner of his eye.

"Fuck off!" wailed the Okie, taking a drag off a cigarette.

No response: above me nothing more than a thought cloud filled with an ellipse, searching, struggling, needing these words that were so alien to me. I wanted to say that they were born speaking the language, and I wanted to tell him that they were no better than us.

"Sí, papa . . . sí," I begged him.

"Don't be like me. I'm nothing." He started sobbing in that third-world way, a profound lament that told the wilderness to have mercy on an injured prey. The last strategy for survival. "Soy nada, cabron."

Operation: all of the pieces were missing and the metal edges rusted. Ants crawled in and out of where the nose used to be—the red bulb was shattered. I thought that maybe I could salvage it, but what could I use for the missing pieces? What could fill the space inside the Bread Box? Mi ama's yarn could possibly replace and substitute for the rubber band. That's when I saw a glistening, ruby-red jellybean stuffed into the butterflies in the stomach. The ants started to crawl up my fingers.

"Are you listening?!" My dad attempted to penetrate my skull. "Cabezon! Think! Think!" He pointed his gnarled index finger onto his temple, ready to shoot. His nails always had blood blistered underneath. I think; therefore I am, but thoughts are constructed by the patchwork of syllables and phonics working in conjunction, these arbitrary sounds that had failed to render this reality, myself included.

I laughed instead at my unusual relationship with Operation, attempting to focus on the white cartoon patient needing help, that red jellybean inside, the trail of ants marching in unison, seeking substance from the insides, the most unlikely of places.

How does humor shield you against the world? How does it deflect what you don't want invaded? What is still raw within you that only humor and a wry, sardonic wit can defend you against?

My father got upset that I giggled. He pulled me up by the scalp of my hair, perhaps having the muscle memory from when he picked onions. It felt like he was attempting to rip my roots out. The force had me wailing in pain, and I thought about the chicken, running, even after it was decapitated.

My hollow body became ready to be stuffed with knowledge.

"You are such a fucking mess!" he said. He demanded, "Get out!"

I cried, massaging my scalp, which was already forming welts from the pull. My father started pulling out his own hair from his sides with a lethal ferocity, attempting to split himself in half, coming up only with tufts of hair. It was his way of apologizing, country empathy—these conservative values from a primal past. Family First.

Of course. *Of course . . .*

I didn't know what he meant: leave the house? Leave the town? Leave my people? Get out?!

We had just gotten to Olivehurst, which was better than our starter home; we hadn't even gotten started.

"Kick his fucking ass!" an Okie said after swigging some schnapps. He got up on the fence to get a better view. "Beat his ass. What are you waiting for, Beaner?!"

My father paused, shocked. He shot me the eyes meaning *help,* the ones that I'd become accustomed to read as a substitute for words he didn't have.

There still isn't a word that describes crying and laughing at the same time.

That's what I did before I tried blacking out by holding my breath, already expecting to be misinterpreted for what I'd done.

ELIAS RODRIQUES

Mother Country

FROM *Virginia Quarterly Review*

AFTER MOVING TO California, in 2010, it seemed as if Mom would spend the rest of her life there. She never complained about the weather, as she had in New York. Though I had never known her to be an especially active person, in California she went hiking nearly every weekend, and even became a docent in an open-space preserve high in the hills. And after years of working for temp agencies that shuttled her from city to city, she now worked full-time as a civil servant in the Alameda County Department of Agriculture. (As far as I could tell, the job consisted mostly of telling people that they could not legally grow weed in their apartment; they had to do so in a field.) Most importantly, her employer contributed to her retirement. It seemed, for the first time in her life, that she would not have to work until the day she died.

In California, with her children finally grown, Mom could now pursue the dreams she'd put on hold when she had my older brother, her first child, at twenty-three. She joined a trans South Asian poetry collective, though she was neither trans nor a poet. She stockpiled oil paints and turned stray sheets of paper into canvases, mostly for paintings of silhouettes resembling her younger self, me, or my brother. She also constructed woodblocks, stamps, and art books. It seemed as if she would continue her weekend artisanship until retirement, at which point she could spend her days in front of an easel on a ridge, with late sunlight casting a golden hue on the canvas.

But something changed in Barack Obama's second term. Mom complained more often about microaggressions at work and in public, about white people whom she barely knew claiming to be good friends, and about white Californians who paraded their progressivism while inadvertently uttering antiblack sentiments in the same breath. They had bumper stickers that said Black Lives Matter, in her account, while advocating for racist housing policies that displaced people of color in Oakland and San Francisco. "California liberalism," she once wrote me in an email, hides "super conservatism" underneath a veneer of political correctness. She spoke of her neighbor, a British expat who told her the only Jamaicans he'd ever met were British bus drivers who smiled a lot. She sent me several emails each week about politics. The subject of one read, "Bwoy! Colonialism is a bitch." Another read, "Wow! U kno that fdr was a real fukka?" She sent these critical emails from her government address. I asked her to stop, fearing it would cost her her job. She said she didn't care.

After Donald Trump's election, Mom grew even more vocal about her anger. But she also began to talk about something else: home. She called to share long-forgotten stories, often told in one breath, about growing up on a coffee farm in New Monklands, Jamaica. Did I know that, after Grandma moved to the States and left them with her stepfather, she and her sister spent many Friday nights in muck, turning over rocks and catching *janga* (crayfish) to cook on an open fire for dinner, while their stepfather drank at the rum bar? No, I hadn't heard that one. What about the time her sister, Auntie Peaches, named and befriended a goat that the family later slaughtered and served for dinner—had I heard about her bawling at dinner? That one was new to me too. Did she ever tell me about how Grandma had warned her not to hug the newborn chicks, but when she saw them in the coop they were too cute to resist, and so she picked one up and drew it close and squeezed until she felt something wet on her feet, suddenly realizing that she'd popped the chick like a balloon, its innards tumbling out? That story I did know, since she shared it every Christmas dinner.

Mom's art also turned to stories of home. She began researching our ancestry, reaching as far back as Barrett Mclean, who was born in 1828. She compiled a family tree into a hundred-page-long art book full of woodblock prints, photocopied birth certificates, and Jamaican nursery rhymes. She sent the book to me, she said, so that I would not be confused when she spoke about our family history (and, perhaps, so that I would not forget our ancestors).

She also made a shorter book replete with handmade stamps and stories of her sliding down a grassy hill, past yellow-tipped birds and spotted cows. She sent that book to Auntie Peaches, who responded with stories of catching lizards and digging for potatoes. Her research forged winding paths through several of the islands' regions, through family name changes and two centuries, all of it leading to her childhood. It was as if history ended on a farm in a remote corner of the island.

None of her stories was happy. They blended the everyday traumas of farm children with histories of enslavement (on the Black side of our family) and indenture (on the Indian side of our family), layered over with the uncertainty of a country taking its first steps after independence. Even if she rarely spoke of life after she left the farm, I knew that her own childhood was cut short when she and Auntie Peaches were sent to live with a relative of one of Grandma's friends, who beat them. The optimism of Jamaican independence, meanwhile, as David Scott has memorably written, now looks tragic from the contemporary perspective. The burgeoning nation's dreams of economic equality were undermined by widespread poverty, and the visions of safety that came with nationhood were replaced with a murder rate that rose to the world's highest in the late 2000s. The future—both hers and the country's—cast a dark pall on Mom's tales of fishing in the Morant River. But these qualms about what came after those years were my problem. When she spoke about her youth, her words flowed quickly. She seemed transported to a place beyond reproach.

So it wasn't a surprise when she started talking about returning. I thought the decision was risky, if not irresponsible. In California, she had work; if she left, how would she feed herself or pay her rent? But whenever I raised this concern, she said she would figure it out, and told me to stop fretting.

These conversations often reminded me of the times she'd tell me, "Boy, you a boy and you no man yet." Besides, she'd say, she'd moved without work before: Since 1992, she had lived in no fewer than six places in two different countries, including three states in America. Her itinerancy made me wonder what she was looking for. Most of her complaints about the places we lived were about the racism and sexism she experienced. She may have thought she would find freedom from antiblackness, if not freedom from misogyny, in a majority-Black country like Jamaica. That seemed unlikely, but I tried to let go of my anxieties; no matter how much I worried, she would do as she pleased. Beyond that, when she spoke about home, she reveled in the idea of wading in rivers and sharing mountain landscapes with animals, which never happened on her hikes in California. So maybe it was the natural world that lured her back. There may also have been something else she wanted to recover—the deeper stability in belonging to and understanding a people and a terrain. I can't say for certain. But I wanted her to find a place where she felt like she could live the rest of her life in comfort. So, despite my fear that she would run out of money, I did my best to trust her.

Mom planned to stay at the home of one of her best friends when we lived in Jamaica, Auntie H, a former senior lecturer at the University of the West Indies who had moved to Canada after her daughter grew up. Auntie H owned a home in Silver Sands, a gated resort community in Trelawny, a parish on the north side of the island named for the eighteenth-century British governor of Jamaica, William Trelawny. The parish contains much of the Cockpit Country, an interior mountainous region that was home to the Leeward Maroons, a group of largely Black people who fled slavery, created new settlements away from British slaveholders' surveillance, and fought several wars against the British. The parish was also home to almost one hundred sugar plantations that fed into the triangular trade, wherein enslaved Africans were brought to the colonies to cultivate sugar and other goods sold in Europe, the profits from which were then used to purchase more enslaved people. The tension in this history—slavery in Jamaica was defined by high death rates, yet marronage in the region has made it a beacon of hope in academic Black studies—intrigued Mom. She wanted to visit anyone and any place that could teach her about Trelawny.

The pandemic changed her plans. Jamaica's response to COVID-19 kept infections and deaths low: by December, only 258 of the island's nearly three million people had succumbed to the disease, about 6,500 fewer than comparably sized Chicago. But the country's success had required heightened restrictions. As a result, Mom was not sure when she would be able to enter the country, and even if she did, the government's (understandable, commendable) regulations ensured that she wouldn't go rafting with a guide, or tour Maroon land or visit historical archives. In light of all this, I assumed Mom would postpone her plans indefinitely. But in the summer of 2020, she put in her two weeks' notice, renewed her passport, and bought a plane ticket. On September 13, she got tested for COVID; two days later, she was tested again. Both tests came back negative. She boarded her flight to Jamaica on the seventeenth.

What she found was predictable, yet it still surprised her. After landing in Montego Bay, she waited in customs with a mask on. When she finally approached the officer, she handed him her passport. "Rodriques," he remarked, "big name, that." He told her to quarantine for two weeks and instructed her to download an app that would track her location and her COVID status. She hired a car east to Trelawny. As she traveled, she saw a red-and-white helicopter stationed on a flat plane of bright-green grass, its propellers cutting a sharp line against the pale-blue sky. To its right, just beyond two lushly canopied trees and a line of dark-green bushes, a sandy-colored roof peeked out. Day one, she wrote to me, and she knew she could never live here again. The helicopter was how wealthy people traveled, while their gardeners and other laborers maintained the property. She asked how much I thought they paid their employees. I wondered what the exchange rate was but didn't bother to look it up. The question made her point clearly enough.

Shortly thereafter, Mom arrived at the house alone. Auntie H was recovering from eye surgery, which made it hard to travel, and the pandemic had largely closed Canada's borders. Nonetheless, she graciously let Mom stay at her place rent-free. Mom and I didn't have the kind of relationship where I could have asked what the absence felt like and received an answer other than, "I'm fine." Still, I assume showing up without her friend, knowing that she would have to self-isolate for two weeks, came with the quiet pang that accompanies seeing the emptiness of a home one is leaving for the last time, that it may have even come with fear. Whatever she felt, she was not unaccompanied for long. Just hours after she got in, a health officer showed up to ensure she was indeed quarantining, and staying put.

Then she heard the news from a passerby: Something had happened to D. K. Duncan, a politician born to relative poverty in 1940 who had risen through the ranks to become the minister of

National Mobilization and Human Resource Development under the socialist-leaning prime minister, Michael Manley, in 1977. As his son, Keith, said of his work, he was a champion of poor Black Jamaicans and equal rights in one of Jamaica's most radical periods, helping to usher in nationalized health care, paid maternity leave, and more. And, as Mom learned, he had died at the age of eighty from complications related to COVID-19. His passing must have felt like an unnecessary reminder that the midcentury's anticolonial fervor and the 1970s' radical dreams were both long gone.

In Trelawny, Mom was surprised by the heat. Having spent the last decade in the Bay Area, she was used to less humidity and breezes blowing even on ninety-degree days, the heat never lasting past dusk. Jamaica, on the other hand, was an oven that had been preheating since March. When she awoke around five thirty in the morning, the thermometer often read ninety-two degrees, and when she went to bed around eight thirty at night, it was still above ninety. Bound inside, she left the doors open to let salty breezes enter with the sound of the distant sea. Mosquitoes pockmarked her body with bites. The occasional cat wandered in. (She also saw mouse droppings, but the cats didn't seem to help.) Once, while she was in the living room, she heard shredding and tearing somewhere else in the house. She followed the sound to the kitchen, and there saw a mongoose—a long, tan, ferretlike creature—trying to get into her garbage. Upon seeing her, it scurried out. I assume Mom envied its freedom.

Unable to leave, Mom found life more expensive and cumbersome than she'd expected. She paid a taxi driver to buy her groceries, and he understandably hiked up the prices to account for his labor. She bought produce from an older man who passed by the property twice a week. His sweet potatoes, she said, were reasonably priced, but the fruits were expensive. (I suspect they were worth the cost; since leaving Jamaica, I have not had a single mango that compares to those on the island, nor have I been able to find good breadfruit or any fresh ackee.) All the while, the local health officer called every few days to ensure that she had not broken quarantine. She hadn't, but that was getting harder to do as the days wore on.

Still, she found ways to pass the time. She read. She made a makeshift greenhouse by covering planters with plastic bags. She bird-watched from the backyard. She sent me a blue ink drawing—mostly contours, with the occasional curve to mark a feather—of a heron standing by a pool, sketched into the title page of *Modern Nature: The Journals of Derek Jarman, 1989–1990*. "You should hear the night herons," she texted. She thought they lived on the roof and came down in the evening to look at their reflections in the pool. It was dangerous to be around when they descended. They guarded their territory—the pool—viciously.

She also sent a phone recording of birdsong. Over a staticky rustling, perhaps waves storming the shore or the wind jostling leafy branches, a bird emitted cries in twos, its trilling voice softening, then cutting through the air again. In time, another, faraway bird responded. I hoped they provided some solace and, if not a vision of days to come, a reminder that, somewhere, living things communed. I wondered if she would remain attentive to their songs once she could leave the house or if she would tune them out, relegating them to background noise.

Finally, at the end of September, her quarantine ended. She had long been looking forward to this day, when she could go to the grocery store to stock up on whatever was available at market prices, but the fridge had broken. She could only buy nonperishables as she waited on the mechanics to receive the part to fix it. They had been waiting for several days already, and it looked like it would take several more. "Welcome to the 3rd world," she texted. She didn't know when she would have a fridge again.

A few weeks after that first encounter, another mongoose wandered into the house. This time, when Mom walked into the kitchen, the animal stayed put. She didn't know what to do. She couldn't pick it up; mongooses are, essentially, land otters in that they appear to be cute but are in fact apex predators with very sharp teeth. No matter what noise she made, it didn't budge. Eventually, she backed away, went to the next room, and emailed me asking how to get a mongoose out of the house.

I had no idea. If I were on the island, I would have come over, though I was just as likely to get hurt as she was. With a sea between us, I couldn't do anything. Even more alarming, she was emailing while the animal was still there. Part of me was afraid that she wasn't taking the threat seriously; our family had a long history of foolhardiness in the face of danger. (Once, when the police locked down my septuagenarian grandmother's block in Flatbush and positioned snipers on roofs for a raid, Grandma snuck around to the back entrance to get into her building.) I suggested Mom call animal control. She didn't respond.

When she awoke, there were no new mouse droppings. She suspected the mongoose had killed the mice. By the afternoon, it sounded as if she had begun to grow fond of it. "Same way it find its way in," she wrote, "it can find its way out." At this point, I grew even more worried. Not only had she gone to sleep with a predator in the home, but now it seemed that she was considering living with it. I told her she had to get rid of it; mongooses were dangerous. She responded that she knew mongooses were dangerous; they killed her chickens in New Monklands. But she had not seen the mongoose since. It must have left. If it had while the doors were closed, that meant there was a hole in the house somewhere. The mongoose was gone for now, but others might come back. What if they didn't let Mom go so easily?

The ludicrousness of a near-sixty-year-old woman not mongoose-proofing her home so frustrated me that I couldn't help but complain to my friends that she was being unreasonable, to which they often responded that the animal might not be so bad. One said we were encroaching on its home; it was just reclaiming its territory. She was well within her rights to kick it out, I argued, and the more I spoke about it, the more I raised my voice, the more I began to suspect that my passion was motivated in part by uncertainty: I knew my mother and the mongoose couldn't cohabitate, but I didn't know who had the stronger claim to Auntie H's house. Neither of us—neither the mongoose nor my family—were native to the land: The British brought our ancestors from Africa and India through slavery and indenture, and they brought the mongooses from India to hunt rats. Given the mongoose's overpopulation, it was likely that animal control would kill it. I started to pity the thing.

Thankfully, the mongoose had disappeared. I thought about how Mom considered any intention of fully separating oneself from nature—through a home, for instance—likely to fail. One could never really keep the mongooses or the mosquitoes or the cats or the birds out, not completely. Even if she wasn't paying attention, even if she did not notice, the birds kept singing.

*

Though the animals of the island would not leave her alone, she was isolated from the people she loved, and it took some effort to conjure them. At one point, she began painting an abstract landscape of yellow dunes bordering the sea, a roughly shaded blue sky. Where the sky met the shore, two silhouetted boys sprouted from the sand, their bodies emerging at about the waist. One of them had a few facial features drawn in, a few lines to suggest a shirt, standing half a head taller than the other. He reminded me of my brother. The other boy, shaded in red, had no features or shirt. I suspected he was me, and that the painting reflected Mom's sense that she didn't quite know me. That was my fault. After I left for college, I threw myself into my job, nightlife, and friends, all while missing her calls and neglecting to return them. While she came to know my brother, who lived with her as an adult, she knew little of the adult I had become.

The distance didn't make it easier for us to communicate. Two weeks after the mongoose incident, Mom asked when I was coming to visit. It would be good for my writing career, she said, to train my eye on the landscape. She could have said that she wanted to see me, but instead she justified our reunion with the carrot of professional success. Even during my teenage years, I made it clear that school was my first priority, using homework and the prospect of leaving poverty, going to college and getting the hell out of Florida, in order to be left alone. Unsurprisingly, my response to her question about when I would visit Jamaica avoided sincerity. I wrote that I wasn't sure if I could come. I didn't want to quarantine, and we didn't know what the COVID rates would be. Even though it was possible to fly and not contract the disease, the thought of traveling felt irresponsible. I didn't want to be the cause of an outbreak in Jamaica, and I certainly didn't want to kill my mother. But not visiting made me worry about our relationship, especially on her birthday, when she turned fifty-nine without anyone to celebrate with. I tried reaching her through WhatsApp, but she didn't answer. I tried again with no luck. I texted, waited, stressed. Finally, after what seemed like a painfully long time, she texted back, using someone else's Wi-Fi to let me know that the internet in her house was out. She was waiting on the repairmen, but it was Friday, and they wouldn't be back to work until Monday, earliest. I never reached her on the phone that day. Now that she was on the other side of a border, which made calling her on my cell difficult, and where fears of spreading a disease prohibited me from traveling there, she seemed even farther away than she was when she was in California, even if Jamaica was miles closer.

Separated from her friends and family, Mom dove into the history of the region's people. At one point, she sent me a picture of Rum Jetty, a six-bedroom beachfront home in Silver Sands. It had once been a warehouse for the sugar and rum cultivated by enslaved people there. Her picture framed the home as if approached from the ocean: a long, squat, cement rectangle topped by a series of pyramids, austere and imposing. The house was a part of Jamaica's history of slavery, Mom wrote, as was the jetty for which the compound was named, a spit of concrete with a veranda at its end. "I feel those spirits when I walk out there," she wrote, "and the warehouse turned resort house makes me sad every time I look at it."

What spirits followed Mom as she wandered the island she once called home? What did she feel now that she was a tourist standing above the sea her ancestors crossed by way of the Middle Passage? She was not in the picture itself, but I couldn't help but see her walking down that jetty, barely more visible than the spirits themselves, almost translucent, sure to fade enough to match the luster of ghosts bobbing on the tide like sea-foam.

In late fall, Mom emailed: "I belong." She had been waiting for the early October rains of her childhood, at the foot of the Blue Mountains, the ones she said blanketed the sky every year on her birthday. In the States, whenever it failed to rain on that day, she would say she felt out of place. The same seemed to be true of her birthday that year in Jamaica. "Town gets rain," Mom wrote. "Montego bay gets rain. St. Thomas and Portland but apparently, not Trelawny." But then, just a few days later, at 5:30 a.m., water poured from the sky. By the time she emailed me late that afternoon, it still had not stopped. The rain had finally come, bringing her home.

That rain was different than the ones of her youth. Hurricane season, which officially runs from June to November, with the stronger storms mostly coming toward the end, was the busiest on record in 2020, with thirty named storms (the previous high was twenty-eight in 2005, the year Katrina ravaged New Orleans).

The shower that Mom wrote about came as a precursor to Tropical Storm Zeta, which hit the region after three weeks of precipitation. The storms damaged dozens of roads, flooded riverbanks, triggered landslides, to say nothing of the estimated $18 million in infrastructural damages and $13 million in agricultural losses. The following week, Tropical Storm Eta wreaked yet more havoc.

When Mom reached out again, she said little about the rain. I'd read the news, and assumed the aftermath was too painful to talk about, so I didn't push. But I remembered what she did during hurricanes in Florida, when I was younger, as storms blanketed our windows, blurring a perpetual dusk. She read and painted in the gray light of each day; she watched the palm trees stretch and bend in the wind. Maybe she did the same during storms in Jamaica, and maybe she and many Jamaicans who remained unhurt by the rain—who escaped the flooding and landslides and had space to think beyond their own survival—wondered what future awaited the island in the face of ever-worsening assaults from the weather.

I avoided beginning with violence in this story about Mom's return to Jamaica in part to make room for some other vision of the island. The overwhelming association between the country and murder can cast too long a shadow to let anything else grow. "It is an old cliché of anthropological area studies," Deborah Thomas wrote at the beginning of *Exceptional Violence*, "[that] if one wants to study violence, one goes to Jamaica." But violence often comes regardless of one's choice.

In early November, after the rain, Mom caught a cab to Montego Bay. Along the way, she saw cops stopping motorists. They were just making money off people with cars, Mom said, ticketing instead of taxing. The driver, who was also Black, responded that Black people were the ones giving trouble, getting themselves pulled over. Frustrated, Mom described the ways racial profiling worked in the States. When she relayed the story, I recalled the time my friend and I were pulled over, suspected of having robbed a nearby Cheesecake Factory. Mom was in the back seat. When we talked about this incident later, she asked where my friend and I learned to sit so still. To her it seemed almost genetically inherited, the way our hands rested on our knees or the dash, looking straight ahead, never making eye contact with the officer, as if the slightest movement could get us killed. She may have recalled that night—or any of the other nights she feared that her sons might be gunned down—as she insisted to the driver that all cops, everywhere, were violent and racist. "If you find your head in a lion's mouth," the driver responded, "you take your time to get it out."

Mom agreed, though she disagreed over who was to blame. She didn't like cops, she wrote me, but she knew who had a gun, a badge, and who was backed by the powers of the state. So she kept her distance. Should she cross paths with the police, she was always aware that they could kill her. "So that is what my taxi guy was saying," she wrote. "He plans to live to see another day, like the cops or not." She planned to do the same.

Shortly thereafter, she went to the supermarket in town so she could stock up on all the goods she'd run out of while stuck inside. There, she saw a taxi van with the back door open. The driver was helping a passenger on the other side of the vehicle. A young man, mid-twenties by Mom's estimation, saw a backpack sticking out of the open back door, and snatched and slung it across his shoulders. He tried to walk away nonchalantly, but someone told the driver, who, though closer to middle-aged, was "well spry." He spotted the thief, ran after him, grabbed ahold of the bag. They wrestled for control. The younger man spun and contorted his limbs until he slipped out of the straps like an eel escaping a bare-handed fisher.

The confrontation, however, was not over. The driver ran back to his taxi and grabbed a metal bat. Weapon in hand, the driver ran after the thief, swung, and hit him on his rear. Passersby lambasted the young man: How did he let himself get beat up by someone so old? Frustrated with their jeering, he put his hands up and swung at the driver and failed to make any serious contact. The driver swung even harder, beating him with that metal bat all over. Mom feared the driver might hit the boy in the head. A metal bat, even without much room for a full swing, could certainly do plenty of damage. She had just planned to go to the store. She had not intended to witness a murder.

One of the onlookers said they should get the police. We don't need the police for this, someone said. Somehow, the scuffle ended, the jeering stopped, and the crowd dispersed. The driver kept the luggage and the young man hadn't been killed. He disappeared, as did she, knowing better than to linger at the scene of a fight. She couldn't help but wonder if he'd actually made it home.

I asked Mom how she felt after witnessing it all. She repeated the story, as though there was nothing to think but that it had happened. What she saw was what she thought. The violence was a fact of life. I wondered how it colored her sense of this place she called home. Perhaps her resignation to the assault came from a sense that the island was a far cry from the place she grew up in. Having left in 1999, she missed the country's most violent years, statistically, though she continued reading the *Gleaner* and remained aware of the prevalence of violence, including the year that Jamaica topped the world's murder rates at sixty-one per one hundred thousand. By the time she returned in 2020, the annual murder rate rarely dipped below forty. Perhaps she just saw the violence that day as part of the new Jamaica.

Then again, Mom never harbored any naïve ideas about Jamaica being a peaceful place. Her biological father had killed someone with a knife in self-defense; her stepfather had hit and killed a bicyclist while driving. When she was young, she was viciously beaten by caretakers, and robbers had held up her and her mother, at gunpoint, in their own home. When we lived there briefly in the 1990s, our home was broken into twice. And she lived through enough political riots to know the sight of Jamaica Defense Force tanks rolling down the streets of Kingston (an image that constitutes one of my own earliest memories). One of the reasons she often gave when asked why she left was that things were getting too wild on the island, a claim met with nods and murmurs of agreement from Jamaicans of her generation. Statistics suggest that violence got worse over time; nonetheless, these Jamaicans seem to have the sense that it had always been dangerous. Maybe Mom saw the driver beating that young man as the cost of being home.

As far as Mom was concerned, the omnipresence of violence was not that different from her experience of the States. When she was a teen in America, her own mother had been mugged and shoved, leading to a lifelong knee injury. In her twenties, her younger brother had been found with a bullet in his head in an abandoned warehouse in Philadelphia. When we lived in Florida, she feared my interactions with cops and self-identified rednecks could turn lethal. Now that she was home in Jamaica, reading the news about the States, she talked about the two countries as though they were the same. In the days leading up to the 2020 presidential election, she warned me to stay inside, fearing political riots would sweep the country. She emailed to note that the Carter Center—the "center just for countries with despots," in her account—was monitoring the US election as it had the Jamaican elections in 1997 and 2002. It was impossible to escape the specter of violence, she suggested, the fear of having the weapon turned on her.

Migration has never been a simple means of finding safety for most of the Jamaicans I have known, many of whom followed relatives to cities in the US, Canada, and the UK, where they found poverty, to say nothing of health disparities and unfulfilled ambitions. This didn't stop them from moving, searching, and hoping. Mom had been disappointed by moves before, but she still kept seeking a life free from violence and inequality, a life filled with birdsong and wandering cats, the steady clapping of waves on the shore and the sensation of spirits all around her, rain that announced her birthday without prophesying destruction, and a history that spoke to her. Retirement in California was a fantasy more mine than hers; she knew well the ways of the world, the difficulty of getting a fridge fixed in Jamaica, the fear of being held up at gunpoint, a son drifting away into professional American dreaming. For now, she's searching for some other, better life than the one she has found. I don't know what that will look like or where she'll find it, but I trust that she'll recognize it when she does.

At the Bend of the Road

FROM *Guernica*

MISSING: HAVE YOU SEEN THIS PILGRIM?

The flyers are pasted to dusty windowpanes in roadside cafés, stapled to skinny utility poles along fields, pinned on the overloaded corkboards of pilgrim hostels. It is July 2015. Three months ago, along the Camino de Santiago, a Christian pilgrimage trail through Spain, France, Italy, and Portugal that is increasingly popular with secular walkers and international travelers, a woman disappeared. Her name is Denise Thiem. She is a forty-one-year-old Asian American woman from Arizona. In the picture on the flyer, her face is framed by jet-black hair. She sticks out her tongue as she rests on a stone bench, a turquoise backpack nestled at her feet like a patient dog, waiting to get up and go.

Nine hundred kilometers of road, a horizontal line drawn across the Iberian Peninsula, is a long way to walk. In the desert-like mezeta, the stretch between Burgos and Léon seems to consist of nothing but interminable wheat fields; there is little for eyes to rest on but the wavelets of heat distorting the horizon, the occasional utility pole, the flyers. I look away from the missing woman. No, I have not seen her, and my first instinct is to unsee her. Instead, I listen to the winds rustling through the wheat, like waves rippling an inland sea. This flyer cannot, must not, intrude on this landscape, of golden grass rising to the skyline, abandoned mud houses with shattered windows. Before I saw the flyer, the mezeta had the parched romanticism of an old western movie set. Now it begins to thrum with something sinister.

I put the flyer out of my head and pick up my pace, heading

toward a village where blocky red buildings line the main street,
where the cheap metal chairs left out in the sun will sear red marks
into my thighs. I unbuckle my backpack, its blue fabric soaked
through with sweat, and order a calamari sandwich, defrosted
squid rings on a baguette slathered with mayo. I check my phone's
battery. Then I hoist my backpack onto my aching shoulders again,
and pause to watch a herd of goats being shaved on the outskirts
of town. The animals writhe and groan weakly among mounds of
wool, disconcerted, but not altogether disturbed. The other goats
just watch, waiting their turn.

I imagine innocent explanations for Denise's disappearance.
Perhaps she's gotten lost, or had a spiritual epiphany that dictated
she should unplug, fall off the map. Perhaps she just wanted some
time to herself. I myself am a loner pilgrim, and proud of it. I
don't stop at churches for communal masses, or start the day's trek
with a pack of new friends, like many others do. Being a pilgrim, to
me, has come to mean a one-on-one relationship with the road, a
private contemplation of its beauty and its difficulty. I walk in solitude. Later in the day, I may drink a cold beer with other pilgrims,
trading news of albergues with plentiful cots, but every morning
I set off on my own. I can stop for a tortilla or a coffee whenever
I like, speed down a hill as fast as I want, call an end to the day
at whatever medieval village I choose, dress my feet wounds however I please. One afternoon, sitting on some concrete steps, I rip
out an entire toenail that had blackened and begun to smell foul,
like something that had died in its bed. No one bears witness. I
can handle it all, all on my own. But every time I see Denise on
the flyers, I feel something pierce the carapace of perfect solitude.
Something that makes me turn and look over my shoulder. Something like fear.

In the book I am listening to while walking, women are being
killed.

I'd heard that Roberto Bolaño's 2666 was difficult to stomach,
but downloaded the book because of its sheer length—thirty-nine
hours. Enough to fill a few days of walking. I love Bolaño, and
had looked forward to letting his hefty tome slowly dissolve into
my brain, accompanying me as the relentless sun beat down on
scorched fields, saving me from stretches of boredom.

Set mostly in the town of Santa Teresa in the Sonoran Desert, a thinly fictionalized version of Ciudad Juárez, 2666 contains an infamous section detailing the murders of women, hundreds of pages that read like a Mad Lib of police records. The victims are factory workers, waitresses, prostitutes, schoolgirls, neighbors. "In this city they killed little girls," a television psychic cries at one point. Bodies keep being found. Bolaño lists the facts of each crime clinically, unflinchingly, leaving the reader a mix of desensitized and dazed. I listen to this as I walk along highways sprawling out of cities, along rural paths coiled around patchworks of fields. The women whose horrid deaths bloom in myriad ways against my eardrums feel far from these country trails and pastel dawns, yet sharpen my sense that I am alone, vulnerable, exposed.

The guidebooks, most of which are written by men, do not mention the way some older pilgrims' hands like to brush up against young women's buttocks, how they might come too close to your bunk bed with their Tempranillo-soaked breath. I wake one morning to the chatter of two nervous women pilgrims, who discuss whether they might take the bus through an area where men parked in white vans had reportedly harassed pilgrims. I plug in 2666 and start the day's walk. As I listen to the litany of crimes afflicting the Sonoran Desert, I dig a nail into one of my bedbug bites, to ease the nagging tickle under my skin.

When I enter Astorga, the city where Denise Thiem was last seen, the sky is overcast, and every gray stone paving the ancient city is heavy with menace. Flyers of Denise are everywhere here, pleading, inescapable. I lie in my pilgrim hostel cot, pinned down by anxiety like granite. I no longer think of innocent explanations for how Denise could have gone missing, where she might be. The next day I would wake and set out on the path she walked the day she disappeared. The same yellow arrows pointing down a country road, the spiky shrubbery, the rocky hills. At which bend of the road had things gone wrong?

I do something I'd never done on the Camino: I ask Nan, an Argentinian woman who I'd seen on the path many times and who is also walking alone, if we can walk the next stretch together. She replies: Of course. We meander out of Astorga and she tells me about her beach shack on the Argentine coast. She gives me a pack of Argentinian Marlboros that I'll keep and smoke for years, long after they've gone stale, whenever I need to steel myself. That night, we reach our destination without incident. The next day, I start walking alone again. I'll see Nan in other hostels, wave to her when I pass her at a bocadillo stand, miss the diversion of her companionship—but I can't lose the freedom of choosing my own rhythm, of feeling unrestrained by anyone else's footsteps.

A few months later, in a farmhouse not far from the path Nan and I walked, Denise's remains are found. She'd been lured in by a farmer, then murdered. One gruesome detail stands out from the news reports: her hands had been dismembered and separated from her body, and were never found. I wonder if Denise had still been alive that day Nan and I passed by. That day with Nan, I'd walked with my chest constricted by more than my backpack straps, thinking of Denise, breathless from the tightness in my lungs. In that moment, she felt close, so close that I could have been her: both of us Asian American women with jet-black hair and turquoise backpacks. From a distance behind, on the trail, we must have looked indistinguishable.

In 2666, a male detective and a female asylum director go on a date and discuss phobias. He sips a beer, she whiskey. Gynophobia, fear of women, afflicts men and is extremely widespread, the director remarks. "It can't be that bad," the detective protests. Then there's optophobia, the director says, which is fear of opening the eyes, and, "in a figurative sense, that's an answer to what you just said about gynophobia." She goes on: "But the worst phobias, in my opinion, are pantophobia, which is fear of everything, and phobophobia, fear of fear itself. If you had to suffer from one of the two, which would you choose?"

The fear of fear itself, the detective answers.

"Think carefully," the director cautions. "If you're afraid of your own fears, you are forced to live in constant contemplation of them."

After that summer of walking, I find that what I most yearn for is not the serene fields, but the pain. The soreness that settles in after the hamstrings have been stretched to their limit, the tenderness of the foot's worn-out sole against the gravel's dull probe, the screaming knee, the blood-filled abscess deep under meaty calluses. Early on during that Camino, before I threw out the ill-fitting hiking boots that congealed my socks with pus and blood, I'd met a Norwegian oil executive who was suffering from a poison-ivy-induced leg rash. "I have Aspirin 1000 in my backpack," he whispered theatrically as we limped along side by side. We paused beside the path and each popped a thousand-milligram tablet into our mouths, and the next hour was like flying, all pains and aches gone. But we were sheepish: the pilgrimage is, after all, supposed to be about withstanding pain, a blisterous, grueling journey toward the remains of a martyred saint. In the end, I tapered off the painkillers. The pilgrimage had transformed my relationship with pain, taught me to walk with it and through it. Perhaps, I thought, it could teach me the same thing about fear.

When I thought of Denise, I told myself, *This is paranoia.* She was one woman out of the tens of thousands who make the trek and safely reach the Santiago cathedral every year. Maybe, to prove my fear a folly, I should walk the pilgrimage again. It was just like how I believed the answer to a fear of flying was to get on more planes. I turn to the odds for comfort: I repeat to myself that plane crashes are exceedingly rare, I check crime statistics in my neighborhood, I determine that the chances of being mugged between the subway exit and my front door are equivalent to being struck by lightning. And there is a simple anesthetic for paranoid fear: not being alone. Every child knows that the monster under the bed never comes out when someone else is in the room.

The next year, I enlist my then-boyfriend to accompany me on another Camino, through the Basque country's turquoise coves and pine forests, through the pastures of Cantabria and the rugged mountains of Asturias and into the Celtic gloom of Galicia. I never once worry: he is by my side and gregarious, and we always catch up to friends we've met along the way and drink one-euro glasses of Verdejo together in ancient plazas. When we see the occasional lone female pilgrim, a weighted silhouette in the fields beyond, I feel a pinch. That utterly solitary, utterly vulnerable, utterly free woman was once me.

Then, four years later, during the pandemic summer, I fly on a one-way ticket to Europe to see my family. I have made plans with a dear friend, B, who lives in the UK, to meet in Lisbon and walk the Portuguese route of the Camino together, this time cutting through the Iberian Peninsula vertically. I'd asked B to join me because we were both on the cusp of big life changes, had left our

long-term relationships and packed up the rental apartments we
last called home. She is a hiker too, and has always been interested
in a pilgrimage.

Two is good. Two is safer. Still, I have nightmares about Denise,
about empty fields and men lurking in bushes. I am consumed
by thoughts of remote locales where, were anything to happen,
there would be no witnesses. I share my worries with B over phone
calls. She says we could carry pepper spray if it would make me
feel better. I acquiesce half-heartedly, embarrassed. When had I
become such a fearful person? Where is the girl who walked across
Spain alone in her Teva sandals, who stopped for ColaCao chocolate milk at cafes along the way, who watched the sun rise over hills
dotted with olive groves in perfect, magnetic solitude?

In Lisbon, I turn twenty-seven alone. Before B flies in to join
me, I rent a small apartment overlooking the Rossio train station.
In the mornings, I watch the doors of the station disgorge com-
muters who diffuse into the streets and up the steep staircases.
Perched on the threshold of a new journey, I feel excited, but still
anxious. Late at night, after picking up takeout of grilled octopus
and eating the tentacle alone in my apartment while watching yet
another MTV rerun, the clinks and chatter of the cafe on the little
plaza below drift in my balcony's open doors. In previous years,
these sounds would have beckoned me downstairs; I would have
sat alone in the middle of it all, enveloped by the buzz and the
smoke, content if no one talked to me, secretly pleased if someone
did. But now I stay inside and drink alone. I pull up Amazon on
my laptop and type in "pepper spray." I scroll through the options,
my eyes drifting to the estimated delivery dates—it can arrive on
time. But then I close the window. Every night I do this and the
delivery window shrinks. My mouse hovers over "order," but I can't
go through with it. I can't envision actually carrying a weapon on
my body, a physical testament to my fear that would weigh down
every step.

Then B arrives, and there is no more time for Amazon deliver-
ies. I thought I might feel relief, but instead I find myself on Wiki-
How: "How to Make Pepper Spray." I eye the piri-piri hot sauce
on my counter. No, that would be ridiculous. B and I eat at a little
restaurant up a cobblestone street not far from the apartment. Before going to sleep, I ask B with feigned casualness whether she
happens to have brought any weapons. B has always been so ma-

ternal, so well prepared. "No," she says, "but I have this Swiss Army knife." It is the same small red tool she had used to cut up apple slices in our dorm when we were sixteen. "Okay," I say, laughing uneasily, embarrassed again. "That will do." That will do, I tell myself.

In 2666, a university professor with a seventeen-year-old daughter calls a colleague to confess he is a nervous wreck. His daughter likes to go out to the movies, he explains. "Don't worry so much," his colleague says. "All you have to do is be careful; there is no point giving in to paranoia."

I remember what my mother told me when I was a little girl: don't show your fear, because those who can smell it will come for you.

The next morning, B and I strap on our backpacks. We take a picture in the mirror of the apartment before we set out: we are radiant.

We have planned a long walking day of thirty-five kilometers, ending at a horse farm in Vila Franca de Xira. We retrieve our credentials from the Sé Cathedral, and begin walking out of Lisbon, following the yellow arrows that define the Camino. We are giddy with freedom; our backpacks are heavy, but that's all we have to carry. Our life possessions are locked away on other continents: hers in a storage locker, mine in a friend's basement. We buy bread, cheese, and chouriço at a supermarket and eat in the shadows of an elevated highway. B cuts fat slices of chouriço with her Swiss Army knife and hands them to me, red oil dripping into the soil beneath us.

The fields we walk along are sometimes flanked by low bamboo bushes strewn with trash and toilet paper. In the late afternoon, B walks ahead to take a phone call. She is only a short distance ahead of me, but I momentarily lose sight of her as she walks across a little wooden bridge.

Right as I am about to cross the bridge, a man emerges from the bamboo bushes. He is wearing a blue face mask. I pass him quickly, darting around the bend. B is sitting on a stone platform behind the tall green stalks, still on the phone with her friend. "There's a man behind us," I tell her. He is right there, coming around the bend, and we stand aside so he can pass us. The plane never actually crashes, I tell myself. The monster isn't under the bed. He will walk past us.

But the man heads straight for me. He locks me in a choke hold, his arm hot and tight around my neck. My brain registers this with a mix of disbelief and finality, and the first thought that crosses my mind is: "It's come."

He shows us a small black knife with a pointy double-edged blade, a stabbing knife, which he brings to my neck. He does not ask for money, but barks at B: "Get down on the ground!" His English is mangled. When B fails to comply, he repeats the command. "No," I say, and he tells me to shut up. He starts dragging me off the path and toward the bushes. This is when I know: I'd rather fight and die than let it happen. I scream at the top of my lungs, then bite into the flesh of his arm.

He tries to force me down to the ground. I stumble to my knees. My backpack is incredibly heavy. I wrestled in high school, and muscle memory returns: no matter what, just don't get pinned. Several times, I succeed in half getting up, just for him to push me down again. I feel hopeless. I keep screaming.

Then B is by my side, holding the little Swiss Army knife, coming at the man. I rear up again. The choke hold loosens and the man takes a step backward and B screams for me to run. I stumble away. The attacker is still standing across from B, but something has shifted, he is backing away. Then B starts running toward me, yelling that she is hurt, and that is when I register the blood on her hand and legs. She lifts her wrist, which is leaking blood and has duct tape around it. The attacker stabbed her, and then, bewilderingly, panicked at the gushing blood, put duct tape on her wound, and told her to run.

Farther along the road, we wave to two passing cars for help, but they do not stop for us. There is a repair garage nearby, and its workers help us call the police and an ambulance while B administers first aid to her wound: the incision missed her main artery by millimeters. The policeman takes a few cursory notes, then asks for B's passport and where we are staying that night. We never hear from him again.

At the hospital, hours later, B's wrist wound is sutured. After the surgical procedure, the medics have told us, they can do nothing more to help. We are on our own. No more police, ambulances, authorities. What had happened had happened, and this is it. We call a taxi to take us from the hospital to the horse farm.

The owners of the horse farm learn about our situation from the taxi driver in a gesture-heavy game of telephone. They are sympathetic. They show us the majestic stallions they keep on the ranch, and their many dogs—Portuguese guard dogs and a ragtag crew of old Labradors and rescue mutts. "There's no use going to the police," the husband says. "In this country there is an epidemic of domestic violence, of killings of women, and the police don't care unless the women are dead. But don't worry. Here, you are safe."

The detectives of *2666* set out to resolve the crimes. In between they drink mezcal and eat greasy breakfasts and tell interminable sexist jokes: *Women are like laws; they were made to be broken.* At one point, a policeman who killed his girlfriend is arrested in the middle of a poker match; as soon as he is wheeled away, the card game resumes.

A young recruit called Lalo Cura observes the corruption and ineptitude of the authorities. When Lalo Cura takes out a tape measure at a crime scene, his colleagues scoff. They think he is crazy to even bother. After all, La Locura means madness.

The next day is gloomy and rainy, and we walk to the town supermarket for food. I notice every man watching us. Movement on the street, glimpsed in my peripheral vision, triggers fight-or-flight responses that flood my body with adrenaline. We still have the attacker's backpack strap, which I'd ripped off during the struggle, and the bloodied duct tape. That night, we talk to our hosts about contacting the police. The husband insists it is useless. The wife is also pessimistic, but says she understands why it is important to us, and that it is important for her, as well.

We drive to the station at 8:30 p.m., and our hosts talk to a policeman standing guard. When he hears the description of the attacker, he tells our host that a schoolgirl was attacked just a few hours earlier by a man fitting a similar description. He says it is important we come in and give our account, but adds: "The policemen are eating dinner. You understand—dinner shouldn't be interrupted at the end of a workday. Come back at 10 p.m."

We go to a small familial restaurant across the street to wait, where the husband chain-smokes and eats a plate of meat pounded thin and swimming in oil. I eat nothing. At 10 p.m., we return to the station and spend another hour in the waiting area, watching the chief sit idly in his glass office. Finally he waves us in. He types out our passport information, fathers' names, mothers' names, and addresses for the record. Only B has been stabbed, he says, so I can count as a witness, but not a victim. In the end, we take a picture of the police report. It is careless and full of inaccuracies. When we offer the strap and the duct tape, the chief laughs and waves them away.

At the ranch that night, an enormous Portuguese dog stands guard outside our door, and when I come out to the cement yard under the inky sky, he leans his heavy head against my leg. The horses, their pelts shining and their majestic muscles twitching, strain their necks outside the stable, and I caress their warm muzzles. It feels like those animals are all that keep me tethered to the ground.

It is impossible, of course, to keep walking. The next day we leave Vila Franca for Lisbon. We are two anonymous girls with heavy backpacks on a train, and what happened to us is a pebble thrown into an ocean, quickly engulfed and irrelevant. In our Airbnb, B retreats to her room and I go into overdrive, posting on a prominent pilgrim forum about our experience, searching for clues about past attacks. I find one, then two, then three. Buried threads where women pilgrims talk about that very same stretch of the route, the first day out of Lisbon. One woman was beaten and robbed. Another sexually assaulted at knifepoint. Another raped and tortured and left to die. The last woman sees my posting and offers to connect. She is a Dutch woman named Yolan. She'd been attacked right by the elevated highway where we had eaten our lunch. On the phone, she tells me and B about what she'd survived. She says she still feels the pain of her wounds, as they'd permanently damaged internal organs. She says that the Portuguese government still owes her the meager reparations the court had ordered.

These were only the stories of the ones who posted, who were written about in the local tabloids, who lived to tell the tale. The

real number of victims must be much higher, a nightmare out of
2666. But for future women who will walk this path alone, there
is no warning, no awareness of the danger of this stretch, no database, no collective mechanism for action. It took being attacked
and surviving to know what to dig for.

In 2666, the medical examiners are kept busy—some of the
women's corpses bear similar marks, possibly indicating a single
culprit. Some victims are seen getting into the same black Pere-
grino car before they disappear. Bolaño sprinkles in red herrings,
suggesting an emergent puzzle to solve. But when one purported
serial killer is locked up, and women keep dying, the patterns start
to seem beside the point.

Yolan and I compare notes on our attackers: they are not the
same man.

B and I stay in Lisbon for one more week. When we aren't dealing
with bureaucracy, we take our bodies to markets and restaurants.
We stare at the plates of grilled seafood in front of us, at the narrow lanes and string lights, and think: Is it possible to feel okay?
We take walks to a park perched high on a hill, Jardim da Estrela,
with its regal Banyan trees and shady gardens. One day a figure
runs toward us on a semi-secluded path, a dark arrow, and B and I
both freeze with white-hot fear, the blood drained from our faces,
ready to fight. The figure zooms by. He's just a young boy running,
chasing his friends, playing.

Our bodies eat our wounds. B's gash becomes a thin white scar
along her wrist. My light bruising fades quickly. The more lasting damage is a persistent, low-level paranoia. I am most afraid, I
think, not that this man will reappear, but that from now on I will
live in this state, forever slowed down and shut in.

Yolan didn't stay shut in. She returned to the Camino years after her attack. *To prove to myself I could walk again,* she says. She
sends us pictures of herself holding hiking poles, standing before
dizzyingly verdant mountains.

Once more, I cannot hold the gaze of the woman in the pic-
tures. *I can't walk the Camino again,* I think. *Not like that. I just can't.*
I would keep myself safe by confining my body, by shoving my

turquoise backpack under my bed, by forgetting solitary dawns on rural trails—by opting to stay inside altogether, even if it meant forgoing what made me feel most alive.

But it cannot last. Back in the UK, I fall first in love, then into a deep depression, and I lie horizontal in a rental apartment on London's Brick Lane, leaking tears into pillows as another call to prayer rings from a mosque and dissipates into the gray clouds. The winter months roll by like fog. Sometimes I decide to get out of bed. Many times I fail. Some days I succeed.

I take tentative steps. I often think of Denise Thiem. I sometimes think of the man, the smell of his sweaty, warm skin against my neck. Some days he is everywhere. Some days he is nowhere, and I go a little farther along the roads I wander down, but never too far.

Just a few months later, Sarah Everard is kidnapped and murdered on her way home, across the Thames from where I'd lived. Women circulate a screenshot: "Tell me when you get home safe." An exhausting message: a woman walking is always in danger.

I listen to 2666 again. The women killed in the book—and in real life—came to the city to earn a living. They are women who take the bus and walk to work, who go out at night for a drink. They are venturing out, deciding where their bodies can be. And with movement comes risk—of exposure, of violence. A risk that, I finally understand, travels with me, and that I carry with every step. It is risk that, just like pain, I must coexist with.

That year, I walk twenty-five hundred miles. Before and after the attack, on city streets, suburban trails. Far from the yellow arrows and shell signage of the Camino, my legs do what my brain cannot. Just like I carried my body months ago, it now carries me.

My steps today are heavier—I slow down more often, to survey my surroundings, to catch my breath. I cannot imagine catching up to the girl who once unhesitantly sped ahead to chase solitude, with her jet-black hair and a turquoise backpack, sandal soles worn thin by changing topography. But that's the nature of pilgrimages: reaching a destination a thousand miles away is unimaginable. Still, I can see her, walking tall and alone, up where the road bends.

ERIKA J. SIMPSON

If You Ever Find Yourself

FROM *The Audacity*

IF YOU EVER find yourself piss poor and struggling to survive in a world obsessed with money, I'll teach you what I've had to know from birth. If you are young and your mother has no boundaries and no friends she trusts, like mine, she'll tell you up front everything that's going wrong. Which is either the best choice or the worst, but you can decide that stuff in retrospect.

1. The only things that matter, and the order of their importance, are food and rent. Don't pay no bill before you've eaten. Because how you look sitting around with all the lights on but nothing to eat? You can ignore any gas, electric, or water bills that come in a white envelope. Those are nudges. Once you get a red letter or a final notice, call Customer Service.

My mama said the best phone representatives were women who had Southern accents thicker than ours. Those are the ones you tell your story to when you need an extension on the bills. As a single mother, she sure didn't have money, but she always had her story. I'd sit sheepish beside her while the voice on the house phone rattled off three-digit numbers we owed. Mama's face would frown up like she could be seen, and she'd tell them how her mother died a couple months ago, and how her husband left her with two babies, and how she couldn't get a steady job. The operator would let her put twenty dollars down and we'd live to heat the house another day.

It's interesting because the real first rule of being broke is not to let anyone know you're broke. But a good sob story has value in it if you gain favor instead of sympathy from telling it. A favor being a waived bill or a free meal, because remember: you've got to eat sooner than you've got to pay the rent.

2. There are a few embarrassing ways to get food when you don't have any money. If your mother is a devoted Christian—which you will not be, as you can see that God isn't real if devout Christians suffer as much as your family does—**you can ask the church for a food donation box.** You'll learn quickly though that the bounty isn't plentiful enough to endure the heavenly sisters swarming around your raggedy apartment.

Whenever we asked for help from the church, Mama would clean the tables and sweep the floors and tell me to look hungry but not starved. Appreciative but not desperate. The church ladies loved to gossip. Everyone knew that from the extra hour they spent whispering in the parking lot after the sermon. The sisters insisted on dropping the box of food off inside. They'd lightly touch the counters with a prayer hand and strut around the kitchen like the Make-A-Wish Foundation for bringing canned peas, ramen noodles, and powdered milk. Mama knew a description of our place would pass through the congregation afterward. But you do what you gotta do to eat. They never even brought snacks. Just nonperishables and prayer.

The worst part is that afterward, you have to come to church at least two more Sundays in a row looking thankful. Extra points if you give a testimony and pass out while you're clapping and screaming *Thank you, Jesus! Thank you holy saints for blessing us!* While the congregation get to shouting *Amen! Amen!*

You'll still be broke on Monday morning.

Another way to eat is with **reverse Robin Hooding,** in which you challenge the poor to give to the poor if they're working for the rich. This trick works best at places with cafeteria-style serving. You'll be used to sharing your mother's shame, but this one feels particularly embarrassing. This is the one where you've got to look like a child starving in Africa on command, and you pray no one's behind you in line.

I stood like a sad prop as my mama asked the cashier at JJ's to slide a hot plate of fish and greens to us for free. She had him pile the to-go plate up nice and big with fried okra, creamy mac and cheese, and an extra catfish filet before admitting we had no money to pay for it. *My babies haven't eaten all day,* she pleaded. I didn't look at my older sister and she didn't look at me. We were both pretending we didn't know each other and that we didn't exist. The cashier didn't look at Mama as he slid her the plate. And we lived to eat another meal.

When you can't take sporadic food any longer, or the feeling that everyone at church knows your business, or the look in a teenage cashier's eyes when they realize you have absolutely nothing, you can **take the bus down to the family aid office and apply for food stamps.** Food stamps are the most stable and humiliating option. Nowadays they give out plastic debit cards with a picture of your state on the front so you remember who's footing the bill. But back in the day, the caseworkers would hand you what looked like Monopoly money: bright Easter-colored food vouchers representing ones, fives, tens, and twenties. Oranges and pinks loud enough to be heard. Bright enough to tell everybody in line behind you that you on government aid and your daddy left your mama for a white woman and now your mama can't even support herself or the babies she laid down to have. If you need money for more than food and don't wanna carry around play-play money, you could do like Mama and flip it.

Mama could sell fifty dollars' worth of food stamps for twenty-five dollars' worth of real cash to teachers she subbed with, her post office lady friends, or sisters from church. It was a beautiful hustle. We got to have money to spend on bus fare and replacement clothes, and they got to have food stamps without *having* food stamps. Nobody wanted to be the black family on welfare.

3. Conceal what's real. Parade your poverty only for people who can help, never for those who will judge you like the church ladies. If you're ever broke during grade school, you'll learn that your mama's worried about rent while your peers are worried about designer clothes.

Kids at my school flashed Sean Jean and Baby Phat paired with fresh Timberland boots. The seventh-grade boys would clutch their belt buckles like they worked somewhere. Like they didn't just beg their mamas in the mall over summer. Name brands show your peers that your mama isn't worried about the rent. My mama told me the truth, *we ain't got it like that.* So I got regular clothes from T.J. Maxx and Walmart.

4. Statement pieces are for the rich. Buy *staples* **you can wear a few times without being noticed.** A good pair of jeans and a nice pair of khakis. A black shirt, a white shirt, and one with a collar.

Mama said to always keep your jacket and your shoes nice, since that's what catches people's eyes first, though we rarely had money to replace my sneakers before the soles started talking. Lay low. If you don't have anything, don't flaunt anything. I'd seen baby negroes tear a girl apart because the stitching on her FUBU dress looked off. They'd surrounded another boy like a pack of hyenas over his shoes. They howled up at the tile ceilings, cackling with their tongues hanging out until he crumpled within himself. *Boy I thought them were Air Force Ones! He rockin' Skechers!!* If you can't afford the real thing don't even bother with something resembling. That's all you'll look like, something resembling. Stick to plain black sneakers from Walmart.

You can talk your way out of paying bills and con your way into some food stamps. You can hide that you're poor in public as long as you can shower, but you can't hide an eviction.

If it's the first of the month, and you can't afford the rent, you can call the landlord and let them know you need more time. Asking is better than silence, unless you've been late on the rent before. Don't panic yet. **5. The money isn't** *due, due* **until the fifth of the month.** If you really don't have it—and this will get a little awkward with daily notices and letters—but if you really don't have them people's money, you have at least two full months to try to raise it. **6. They can't legally evict a nonpaying tenant by force until the third month.**

Mama did well teaching public school until she challenged the principal's morals. He told her to bump grades for a few failing white kids whose parents had donated money. He threatened to fire her if she didn't comply. She told that white man *mother fuck you.* He iced her out of the school system like a mafia lord. The last check withered away into nothing after food, partial rent, clothes, car payments, partial bills, and credit card debt. Despite Mama's best efforts on the phone with the property owner, even praying in tongues real loud every time he mentioned how much she owed, we had to pack our faded furniture and go in month three.

We moved from the apartments with the shiny new appliances and front-facing balconies and into ones with the fake entrance gates that always hung pathetically open. Where the units themselves masked endless roaches, scattering across the counters and from under the trash can no matter how much we cleaned. Substitute teaching jobs came fewer and farther between for Mama and soon her credit score couldn't even get us the dirty brick flat level apartments on the cloudy part of town.

Once my aunts and uncles got tired of Mama calling for Western Union money wires and the child support checks from the father I never met dried up, evictions came one after the other.

7. If you're more than three months behind on rent in an apartment building, make sure someone is always home. Because as soon as the office manager peeps you heading to the grocery store, they'll violently throw your things into the street. They'll throw your clothes out still on the hangers, the whole dresser with panties leaking out the drawers, books, pots, and photo albums right onto the sidewalk, right in front of where you park your car every day so everybody knows the stuff is yours. The worst part of this eviction isn't the neighbors knowing how broke your family is but that the very same neighbors will take your furniture if you aren't back fast enough. TV sets and coffee tables disappear the quickest. You'll never see who takes your stuff cuz you're banished from the complex now. You'll probably have to change schools again too, depending on how far away the next apartment complex is. Another perk of laying low at school is that you don't have to miss anybody or explain why your family has to up and leave.

Whenever we got evicted, we'd rent a U-Haul if Mama could afford it or just stuff our sentimentals and clothes into the back seat and try to find somewhere to stay before the eviction hit Mama's credit report. I'd sit quietly in the back seat with boxes piled up around me, and on my lap. I'd try not to let Mama see me crying over lost Goosebumps books or Barbie dolls. That's just how it goes. We stayed in rotating apartments in three-month intervals and then seedy rent-by-the-week motels after Mama's credit report started hissing with venom.

The roadside motels were slimy-looking haunts with stiff comforters on the beds and lamp lighting that gave everything a yellow teeth stain kinda vibe. A good tip for living in a motel because your mama hasn't found a good job yet is to leave twenty minutes earlier on school mornings and walk over to the bus stop in the fancy apartments down the street. Mama said if people thought we weren't doing so well, The State could take me away from her. So remember not to tell anybody our business. Keep up appearances. Conceal.

There were other families staying in those motels, but somehow we never knew faces or names. Nobody looked anybody in the face at six thirty in the morning. Mamas waved goodbye to kids. We ran across the parking lot like roaches scattering out, heading toward a bus stop that doesn't make a comment on our lives.

8. Avoid motels if you can. Motels are the easiest to get evicted from. You have to secure the thirty-five-dollar daily fee to keep the door clicking open, which sounds cheap, but totals more than a house after a month.

This kind of eviction, the motel eviction, is way worse because they lock your stuff *inside* when you don't pay. Or at least your key card stops unlocking the door, and they won't let you back in unless you pay within twenty-four hours. Mama says the manager let the maids divvy up your stuff amongst themselves.

One Sunday, when we got back from begging the Lord for money at church, our motel door wouldn't open. We knew we were out. I wailed for my favorite teddy bear, the last good item I had left after several evictions. Mama rushed me into the front office for the clerk to see. *You'd let a baby cry over a few dollars?* She convinced him to let us in for just a moment, and I stood moaning and yanking on my pigtails beside the manager while Mama filled up three big garbage bags with our things. She handed me the brown plush teddy in front of him so he could focus on her baby smiling and not how we were getting our stuff without paying. I didn't feel like a baby anymore. But I definitely felt helpless all the time.

If you ever find yourself with a credit score too low to say out loud, and with a mountain of debt too high, be careful. **9. The poorer you get, the bigger you dream. Mostly because the more debt you collect, the more it will take a miracle to climb out of it.**

My mama dreamed big. Mama started using the money substituting to try and open her own business. She wanted to use her PhD to help people, offer therapy and life coaching as if we hadn't just moved into a motel indefinitely. I felt stuck in my mother's struggle story. I started strategizing on how I could break the cycle of poverty with the lessons she taught me.

One benefit of living in hotels was that you have access to cable television. While Mama was running after education like it would save her life, I was paying attention to pop culture. The only black folk I saw making money were on TV! I watched Raven-Symoné flashing her little dimples on *Hangin' with Mr. Cooper*. On TBS they played *The Lost World: Jurassic Park* all the time. Mama said TBS stood for *throwaway bullshit* but I loved that one because Jeff Goldblum had a black daughter and they didn't even have to explain it too much.

If all them degrees weren't making her any money, then Hollywood could. I became obsessed with the idea that I would be famous. I knew we didn't have any move-to-LA risk-it-all money cuz we were already risking it all for Mama's business dreams. PBS had a show called *Zoom* and they had a lil black girl up there singing and dancing and doing arts and crafts with the other kids. They said it featured *kids like me* so I knew they probably weren't talking about no little girl who stays in a hotel room and sleeps on the floor inside a Rugrats sleeping bag. What I did know was the kids on *Zoom* looked local, and so I searched flyers hanging on telephone poles and the bulletin boards for folks looking for talent.

Most of them advertised babysitters and cheap lawyers for hire, but I found a good one hanging up in the Office Depot for a show called *All That* on Nickelodeon. Mama was trying to figure out how to print off copies of a trifold brochure for her business at the public printers. She'd probably use money that could go toward our rent, but for once I wasn't calculating the funds. This show was comedy-based and looking for kids age seven to twelve with loads of personality, which was about all I had to my name. If Mama could use every resource we had to achieve her big dream, I was allowed to dream too. She agreed to take me for an audition.

The producer told us to meet him at the public library in the heart of Atlanta. Mama had me wear the khaki pants I wore to school and a hot pink shirt. She braided the top of my hair and then curled the back, and we both hoped I looked like an "everyday kid." The man greeted us right out front, an older white man dressed in jeans and a khaki vest like we were going on safari or something. He had a big camera hung around his neck and a tripod flung over his shoulder. He shook Mama's hand, and she smiled at him with her best red lipstick on. He told us he had reserved one of the quiet reading rooms in the library and that I was his last kid of the day. He told my mother to wait outside while we filmed. That made me nervous. In eight years of my life, I had never been alone with an adult man. Never hugged my father. Never prayed one-on-one with the pastor. All men felt dangerous to me. I figured I had never been touched or gone missing, and it was probably because Mama never had a man around me.

Mama nodded reassuringly and left me to film in our quiet place. The man set the camera up and pointed it at me. He said there were no lines, just scenarios, and he wanted to film me talking to the camera about an assortment of things. He told me to say my name and after I said it loud and clear I added, *are all my friends ready to play?* He ate it up. I gave him a blockbuster kid performance, holding up books and talking about reading on rainy days, dramatically pouting before grinning big. I asked the camera lens if it knew what gravity was and started bouncing up and down on a "sugar rush."

The producer loved everything I did. He popped his head out the room door for Mama to come in, telling her she had a little star on her hands. I'd done it. He told us he'd call us back with a wiggle of his eyebrows and left, hugging his camera to his chest. My hopes were up.

Here's another lesson Mama taught me, a riskier one, which I try not to add to the list. **10. Check now, cash later.** Every now and then we could write a check to get groceries. She told me that checks didn't get cashed right away, so we had time to put money in the bank to cover the food. Especially if you write it on a Friday and let the weekend stretch the time. I knew good and well her bank account was so negative it couldn't be saved, but I didn't say anything when she asked to pay in check.

After my audition, Mama took me to the late-night movie to celebrate. I knew we were lingering around near a Western Union for my uncle to wire over this week's motel money when he got off work, but I enjoyed the show nonetheless. We saw Will Smith in *Wild Wild West* and afterward sat on the curb outside the theater eating leftover popcorn and discussing it. Mama said it felt like a TBS kinda movie.

She never told me that she wrote a really bad check once. She had to drive us from North Carolina to Atlanta after my father left us. She wrote a check for the full amount of a brand-new Buick and drove us off in the middle of the night like thieves. Mama gave the car away five years later to a man and his wife for three thousand dollars cash.

A cop with puffy pink fists clutching his belt buckle walked up to us. He told my mother it was kind of late to be out with a child.

She agreed with him entirely. He asked for her ID. We sat waiting in silence while he walked over to his parked vehicle to run it. Mama whispered *father God in the name of Jesus* under her breath. The cop came back and said it looked like she had written a bad check several years ago. Mama tried to tell him our story. How she was all alone out here with a young child to raise and choppy income. The cop said there was a warrant out for her arrest, and he'd have to take her in.

Our popcorn spilled on the ground when he handcuffed her. He made me ride downtown in a separate car, like she would kill me if we rode together. Mama went to jail for a full year.

If you ever find yourself sitting on a bench in the hallway of a police station, waiting for a verdict on what will be done with you after your mama is put in jail, you will remember that your mother said being taken into foster care is awful. She has told you how hard it can be for families to be reunited. She told you that you will be unloved and used for a check. You tried not to think about the child support that your mother receives and how it's almost the same thing. Because you do feel loved. More than anything, you feel loved. When your mother is at her absolute poorest, you will realize that all you really own is love. But once she is behind bars, and your sister is tucked safely away at college, you start wondering what your options are. **11. The cops will call your aunt and uncles to see who wants to raise you before they throw you into the system.**

My aunt drove from Greensboro, North Carolina, to Decatur, Georgia, to get me from the precinct. She did not pay my mother's bail, but she did claim me. She whispered into the phone on the officer's desk that at least she knew my mama had somewhere to sleep. We drove to North Carolina straightaway. I fell asleep in the dark stretch of trees and highway and woke up in another reality.

What no one tells you, on all the nights that you're praying to your mother's God for a house or new clothes, or to feel normal, is that those things won't feel normal straightaway once you have them.

My aunt set me up in the guest room, and I asked her quickly, smartly, *who all sleep in here?* I had never been to her house for more than a few hours of a Thanksgiving or family reunion. When we visited, we always slept at Grandma's house, all three of us in one bed, Mama and her two little girls. Not that different from the hotel rooms we got accustomed to, where it was Mama to one bed and me and sister to the other.

My aunt told me that my cousin had his own room, and the oldest had moved out, so I could stay alone in this one. The bed was big and empty. My aunt was not rich by any means. She lived cautiously, saved, married a military man. And by the time she had to claim me, she was dealing with my cousin's mental disabilities and trying to free herself from an abusive marriage. Mama's phone calls for money had been only a minor annoyance in her life before I arrived. Something to talk about amongst the other siblings, a weary wire transfer if only to make sure her nieces were fed. Now I was seated at her table. Nine years old and feral.

The year spent with my aunt while my mother was in jail was the most pastel-colored of my childhood. For the first month there I couldn't shake the feeling that I would be put out. The bright colors and stable living did nothing for my happiness. It felt like something I was observing. From my point of view, my aunt's life was perfect. Every night she would open the fridge, pull out fresh meat and vegetables and cook something! The stuff was readily available in there. Tuesdays were spaghetti night and Wednesdays were piano lessons. Insane to me. Extracurricular Activities. Just doing stuff after school to do it. My aunt took us to *Hercules on Ice* one weekend! We sat in the fifth row—with popcorn from the actual concession stand—watching Hercules and Megara skating right in front of us.

12. Middle class feels like the one percent when you're stuck below the poverty line.
My aunt had a living room and she had a den, another thing I had never heard of before, with two big bookshelves full of colorful VHS tapes, and I loved to watch one every night. I connected with Orphan Annie. I wondered if she for real felt comfortable with Daddy Warbucks or if she missed the orphanage sometimes. Between Annie and the Little Princess, I felt like the wrong kind of orphan. How could I disappear into a comfortable suburban life when my mother still had nothing?

13. There will be reminders that you do not belong when you least expect it. You may be safe for a while with a family member, or on a dear friend's couch, and for a moment you will feel like you've escaped the quicksand that is poverty. But you haven't yet.

You have found another Band-Aid, like the hotel rooms. There will be days where your Band-Aid will be ripped away. Like Easter Sunday.

My aunt made me wear the yellowest dress I had seen in my life. She was adamant about Easter. We were going to JCPenney before church to have pictures taken. A family portrait. She was trying to make me feel more like a daughter than a niece since I'd overheard her conversations on the phone. Pictures were proof, and Auntie wanted some.

The whole way over I thought about my mother. Her last letter said that she'd be out in a month or two. She said she would send for me as soon as everything was ready. I wasn't sure what everything was, or how she could get it ready, or if she knew I was taking family portraits with her sister. The photographer asked "the parents" to sit and we filled in around them. While he took photos, I thought of the audition I had at the library. I wondered if the man had tried to call my mother. If he had sent me a ticket to Hollywood, now collecting dust in her PO box. I wondered if I could have rescued us or if he was just some man with my pictures on his camera.

The photographer told us to move in tighter, and I placed my hand on my aunt's shoulder. Family is family after all. Maybe it was time I leaned into themed outfits, portrait studios, amusement parks, and dinner at the table. Maybe I could be normal. I tried to smile as big as my aunt and really mean it.

The photographer commented on how pretty Auntie's daughters were. Her spitting image. She laughed, and hugged me close to her side. "Well, this is my niece here. I ain't had but two so far."

I tried not to flinch at the clarification. And yet.

The photographer says cheerfully, casually, carelessly, "Then let's get a couple pics of just the main family!"

Auntie gives me a tight smile. Uncle readjusts in his stool. My older cousin takes the softest step forward to where I am standing and I slither away. I watch in my hand-me-down dress from behind a clothing rack as they take pictures that look more normal. A husband, a wife, and two kids. I wondered which portrait she would hang up in the den.

After that, I made the definitive decision that I would never belong. It was time for me to get back to Atlanta, the big city where my mother was still looking for her possibilities. There was no way she could do as well without my cute cherub face beside her, right? It was a better image, a better story. We could hustle up a fairy tale of our own. But when you are poor, and no matter how mature you seem for an underage person, **14. Other people will decide what is best for you.**

Auntie decided it was best for me to stay with her. It was no secret that she lost a baby a year before I was born. She had wanted three. I'd be safer with her.

But Mama came to get me. We all sat and had a cordial dinner. I don't remember the conversation or if they asked her about jail. But I remember it was spaghetti night. And something about that made my stomach hurt. I didn't want her to see me like this. Like a domesticated cat. I wanted to be in allegiance with her. And yet.

I felt embarrassed by the clothes she wore. I could tell they were Kmart basics. I felt embarrassed by a couple of casual lies I could catch in her speech. She said she stayed with Sister Cherry when she got out, but I knew Sister Cherry didn't mess with us like that no more after we ran her light and water bill up the full three months we stayed with her. There was no way she would take Mama in after being in jail for a bounced check.

My mama spoke like she was stable, though, which made me feel queasy. I didn't believe it and I doubted my aunt believed it either. Would she let me leave with Mama? Was it her place to say?

The sisters got into a fight that night. I had fallen asleep to my mother praying at the foot of the guest bed. When my eyes opened again, there were blurry figures scuffling over the bed. My mother's fists flew into my aunt's nightgown, and she shoved her back into the bed. They wrestled right atop my body, over what I assumed was who could claim me. My uncle burst into the room and ripped them apart. I lay wide eyed in the dark all night, my mother praying herself to sleep beside me.

We were on our way back to Atlanta the next day. Mama had two Greyhound tickets for us tucked into her Bible. I felt sick the whole bus ride, and even more so on the city bus to our new home. Mama told my aunt she worked it all out, but she hadn't told me anything yet. I wondered if my *Hercules on Ice* T-shirt made me look too much like a normal kid to tell the truth. She was speaking to me like a child for the first time ever, muttering that it was all right every few minutes.

We got off the bus in front of a hotel. Mama squeezed my hand tight as we walked up. After she had swiped her card into the room, we lay on the king-sized bed and split a bag of cheese puffs. She told me the manager here was an asshole but she had paid up for two weeks so we had time to figure something out.

Here was the truth. She said what she needed to say to get me back, but nothing had changed. The knot in my stomach loosened. Maybe because **15. home still feels like home, when you're surviving together.** I felt happier than I had in a year, just being in the know with Mama. Christmas had been a highlight. My aunt kept her tree up year-round, and I was excited to open gifts instead of grieve over toys Mama already warned me she couldn't afford. But after all the goodies were opened, I longed for Christmas with Mama: hanging green construction paper shaped like a tree on the wall, decorating with pine cones and leaves from around the neighborhood. Finding whimsy in nature, in each other.

Mama would tell me another truth that day too: she'd been diagnosed with breast cancer. She'd have to start chemo right away.

The final rule to remember, and the one that keeps you safest, is this: **16. There are no neat, happy endings. Just the next step in the journey.** Remember not to tell your story to just anyone. They'll listen to your unfathomable life with pity in their eyes before asking how it all worked out. Half the time it's still working out. There's been no cash settlements, no miracles. You are trying your best. You are learning from your experiences. You can survive for years once you understand the rules.

RYAN BRADLEY

The Lost List

FROM *The Sewanee Review*

MY GRANDFATHER ONCE taught me how to use a sextant. We were at sea, motoring toward Baja California's Isla San Martín, many miles off Punta Colonet, out of sight of land. The time was important, as I recall. We took turns squinting into the sextant's sight, lining up the angle of the noonday sun so that the mirrors reflected its image onto the horizon line, which kept bouncing up and down with us and the boat and the ocean's swell. It was hot, and awkward, and I remember wanting to give up on the task several times. Someone on board—my uncle, most likely—snapped a photo of us. I must have been aware of his taking it, because I'm hamming it up, brow furrowed and squinting hard into the sight, like I know what the hell I am doing. It's not a good photo of me, but my grandfather looks perfectly at ease. He'd navigated this way during World War II, up to and even after his ship, a combat cutter, was torpedoed by a German sub and partially sank in the North Atlantic. He would have died were it not for some Icelandic fisherman who happened to be trawling nearby, and to whom I owe my existence. After making note of the angle, I remember retreating into the shade and staring at a nautical chart, then drawing a line from where we had been to where we now, with the help of the sextant, supposed we were. It seemed both very precise—the instrument, the charts, the various calculations—and something approximating a tremendous guess. The great blue sky and deep blue sea and us, on a little white boat, out in the vastness, trying to find our way.

*

About a year ago I began keeping a list of lost things: objects and areas that acted as engines of disappearance or disorientation; individuals who had vanished suddenly and mysteriously, then returned, or not; animals that had taken strange and extraordinary rambles trying to find—something, whatever it was wasn't always clear. I suppose my intent was something like the sun lines I'd learned from my grandfather, the plotted points on a nautical chart. If I could take all these entries and order them just so, perhaps they would lead somewhere. When I began the list, the world was shutting down, the future felt terribly uncertain, and I felt lost. My lost list was a way to calm my mind, order chaos, plot a course through the unknown. I began with places.

The first entry is the Box-Death Hollow Wilderness, in southern Utah—a mess of slot canyons, dry washes, and a few trails. People often get lost there. In 2012, a fifty-nine-year-old woman hiking the Box-Death Hollow jumped down a small ledge and broke her leg. Lying there, she realized she hadn't told anyone where she was. She was also a diabetic and had failed to pack food. Forty years earlier, however, she'd taken a survival course; she had on her person a scarf and a walking stick, which she used to fashion a brace for her leg. During the day, she slept, so that she could stay up all night, huddled beneath her poncho in order to stave off hypothermia. She did not wander, for she knew that she wouldn't get far with her leg. More importantly, she recalled from her course that once someone began looking for her, she had a much better chance of being found if she stayed put. On the fourth day, a local search and rescue team spotted her.

Beneath PLACES there are entries for the Black Sea, the North Sea, the Orkney Islands, the Bermuda Triangle, and Mocha Island, off the coast of Chile, where shipwrecks are so common that many of its houses are cobbled together from the scavenged parts of boats run aground. The Lost Sea in Tennessee is an underground lake, the largest in the United States, and where some twenty thousand years ago, a giant jaguar, presumably lost in the darkness, plunged into a crevasse. The aforementioned Box-Death Hollow is alongside Cucamonga Canyon, in the San Gabriel range, near where I live in Los Angeles. The San Gabriels are young, still-growing mountains, crumbly and steep—difficult terrain and, on a clear day, visible to some twelve million Californians. People approach these mountains casually and spend a dangerous amount of energy ascending them, unaware that the descent is the more difficult journey. A few years ago, Eric DeSplinter and Gabrielle Wallace went on a hike near Cucamonga Peak. Wallace slipped on the ice near the summit and slid several hundred feet off the trail while DeSplinter scrambled after. They saw a canyon below: Cucamonga. Maybe it would be a faster way back down? Night was falling. They descended. Four days later, they were found on a cliff's edge between waterfalls, and had to be airlifted to safety by helicopter.

What was it about these places that drew people to them? That drew *me* to them? Armchair travel, sure. But, also, something more. These places swallowed people up. I wanted to visit them all. Instead, I did the next best thing: I added and added to the list. I added an entry on Lop Nur, a dry salt lake in northwest China where an explorer named Peng Jiamu disappeared in 1980. His body has never been found. The hills surrounding the lake are prone to collapse, and perhaps that's what took him. Under the entry for the Vortex Spring, north of Ponce de Leon, Florida, I have written "—where, on August 20, 2010, employees in the dive shop noticed Ben McDaniel's pickup hadn't moved for two days. McDaniel was a regular at Vortex Spring and was last seen leaving for a dive that would take him into a cave fifty-eight feet below the water's surface. No trace of him has ever been found, and the cave systems extending out from the Spring are extensive, and not entirely mapped."

A lost place's power is inimical—these places draw people in and only sometimes spit them back out. Lost people are the inverse: not a place where people are regularly lost, necessarily, but individuals who became famously, sometimes bizarrely, lost. I'd had San Nicolas Island in the places section, for instance, but recently moved it to people and changed the entry to Juana Maria, who, circa 1833, was left on San Nicolas for nearly twenty years after most of her tribe, the Nicoleño, had been massacred, and the rest relocated to the California mainland. On October 13, 1853, soon after she was found and relocated, the *Daily Democratic State Journal* in Sacramento wrote this about her: "She existed on shell fish and the fat of the seal, and dressed in the skins and feathers of wild ducks, which she sewed together with the sinews of the seal. She cannot speak any known language—is good-looking, and about middle age. She seems to be contented in her new home among the good people of Santa Barbara." A few months later, she died of dysentery. I once visited her grave on a class trip to the Santa Barbara Mission.

Under PEOPLE is a Toronto firefighter named Constantinos "Danny" Filippidis, who vanished on a ski trip in Lake Placid, New York, and wasn't seen again until six days later, when he called his wife from the Sacramento airport on a number she didn't recognize. He was disoriented, still in his skiing gear when police found him. All he could remember was falling on the slopes and bumping his head. How, during those six days of his disappearance, he'd managed to travel more than three thousand miles from Canada to California, was a complete blank. And the story of Ada Blackjack, the sole survivor of a poorly planned 1921 Arctic expedition to claim Wrangel Island for Canada. Blackjack was hired as a seamstress and ended up living alone with a cat named Vic on Wrangel for the better part of two years after the four men on the expedition died of exposure and malnutrition. She was found, gaunt and smiling, in a reindeer parka she had sewn. Vic was still alive, too, and with her when she was found. And Karina Chikitova, a four-year-old from Sakha, Siberia, who was lost in the woods outside her village in the dead of winter for nearly two weeks before she was found, surviving on nothing but melted snow and berries she scavenged. There is Carlos Sánchez Ortiz de Salazar, a doctor from Seville, who disappeared in 1996 and was eventually declared dead. Twenty years later, he was discovered by two mushroom pickers in northern Tuscany. He was alive and well and had been living as a hermit, but by the time his family had flown in to see him, he'd disappeared again, deeper into the woods. I have the "castaway couple," Lucy Irvine and Gerald Kingsland. Kingsland was ex–British military, a professional adventurer type who, in 1980, put an advertisement in *Time Out*—the London-based entertainment listings magazine—that he was looking for a woman to live with him on a deserted island for a year. Irvine responded, and in 1982 they went to live on Tuin, in the Torres Strait, between Australia and Papua New Guinea. Kingsland was forty-nine, Irvine twenty-four. Kingsland got ulcers all over his legs. Irvine got so sick from a batch of bad beans she nearly died. After close to a year, a drought fell on Tuin, the water supply dried up, and the pair could not find the radio antenna they needed to call for help. They were saved just in time by Badu Islanders, who encountered the castaways and nursed them back to health. Kingsland and Irvine each wrote books about the experience, although Irvine's is better, more honest, more willing to interrogate her own ambivalences about the adventure, the island, and Kingsland. She was, and still is, a writer, and now lives a reclusive life in rural Bulgaria.

Next on the Lost List are THINGS. Those are tricky. Every second, so many things are lost, but how many of these lost objects take on a life of their own? The world's oldest recovered message in a bottle was part of an ongoing experiment, started in 1914, after one Captain Brown, of Aberdeen, Scotland, curious about the ocean currents, sent out on the slack tide 1,890 bottled messages. Ninety-eight years later, Marine Scotland Science in Aberdeen logged the 315th of these bottles, which was pulled out of the sea, caught in a fisherman's net off the Shetland Islands. Another seagoing Scottish object on my list: a toy ship, which two boys—Ollie and Harry Ferguson—launched from Peterhead, northeast of Aberdeen. It traveled across the North Sea to Denmark, then Sweden, then Norway, and eventually made passage aboard a full-size ship down to Cabo Verde, where it was relaunched, set free again to attempt an Atlantic Ocean crossing. This was in 2017. The little toy ship hasn't been seen since.

ANIMALS includes an Australian cattle dog named Sophie Tucker, who was tossed overboard in rough seas and swam five nautical miles to St. Bees Island, near the Great Barrier Reef, where she survived for four months by hunting feral goats and was eventually captured and returned home by park rangers. There's also a hippo named Huberta who, beginning in 1928, began traversing South Africa, covering thousands of miles and becoming relatively famous, as far as wandering hippos go. Eventually Huberta was shot and killed during her wanderings. A trial was held, four ranchers convicted, and her skull and skin were sent to London, to a taxidermist of some renown. More than twenty thousand people came to see her body the first month it was returned to South Africa, in 1932. I have just one entry under SPORTS, for orienteering. It's not a sport lost to time, but one that involves the process of navigating, of running through landscapes—sometimes dense forests, but also city streets and college campuses—while rapidly wayfinding.

A few entries don't fit in neatly with the rest. The MISFITS section is mostly made up of people, professional people, experts in what I have come to think of as the field of lostness. There's Joseph Kirschvink, a Caltech geoscientist, who studies what's known as magnetoreception, the ability many animals have to navigate using magnetic fields. Some animals—birds in particular, but also certain insects and reptiles—seem to be astonishingly good at finding their way in this manner. Consider, for instance, the Arctic tern, which travels forty thousand miles each year, from the Arctic to Antarctica and back. Or the leatherback turtle, which swims eight thousand miles from Indonesia to California. Or the monarch butterfly, whose North American migration spans more than a thousand miles and three generations. It's possible that humans navigate using magnetoreception as well. Or that we could. Or did. To test this hypothesis, Kirschvink built an isolated chamber, shielded from all external radio frequencies. Inside the chamber were large square coils, capable of generating low electrical currents along six directions: up and down, north and south, east and west. He put people in the chamber, in a comfortable chair, and had them sit in silence and close their eyes for seven minutes, while he subtly shifted instruments around, moving the electrical currents to mimic changes in the Earth's magnetic fields. He does this all while measuring participants' brain waves via electrodes attached to their heads. What he's found is that the human brain can indeed pick up on these changes, that our sensory system is capable of processing the geomagnetic field all around us, and that it's possible our nomadic hunter-gatherer ancestors used this hidden sense to navigate and survive. We haven't so much lost the ability—it's still there, our brain still picks up this information, but we haven't trained ourselves to notice it because we don't need to navigate the world like we used to.

The other day I went looking for the photo of me and my grandfather and the sextant, but I couldn't find it anywhere. I dug out some old hard drives from the garage, even. Had I imagined the moment? I emailed my uncle, whose boat we were on, and who is a meticulous archivist. He had it and sent it to me. But it wasn't quite as I remembered. There were two photos: one with me hunched and mugging, sextant in hand; the other with my grandfather holding the instrument, casually taking the sun line against the horizon. In my memory I'd merged the two images, which isn't so surprising. This is something we do—or that our minds are doing without us realizing—constantly. Our minds are monstrously efficient. My mind had merged the two photos into one memory. Maybe my mind was also picking up the Earth's magnetic field, then discarding it, replacing this forgotten navigational sense with some more modern and immediate concern like, I don't know, how many days were left on the free trial of a streaming service, how much I had in my bank account, where I'd left my phone.

There's a disorder, called topographical disorientation, that causes those suffering from it to get lost just about anywhere: on their commute, on their block, in their backyard, even inside their home. It was first described in 2008 by Giuseppe Iaria, an Italian psychologist at the University of Calgary. Iaria tells me that the act of wayfinding—of knowing where we are in the world as we move through it, and where we need to be to get where we want to go—is one of the most complex behaviors any animal—humans included—can perform. "Why is it so complex?" he asks. "It's not one single skill. It's a whole set of skills, all working together, or at odds." And just how much each skill is deployed varies by individual. Just as everyone sees the world slightly differently, they navigate it differently as well. "People have a bias in selecting certain information to pay attention to," Iaria says. Another complicating factor is the environment. There are certain places (deserts, forests, parking garages) that confuse us. We have trouble finding our way through them because we aren't sure what to pay attention to. There are too many repeating patterns (dunes, trees, cars) so we can't establish the bigger picture. Further complicating our navigational ability is that, for some of us, this external information is more important than for others. Some of us navigate by signpost and street name. Others pay a lot more attention to what our bodies are doing—the feeling of motion, the left turn, then the right. People who seem to have an innate sense of direction, or get it consistently wrong, move through the world this way.

"Then there is another skill that is completely independent of all the others," Iaria explains. "It's called path integration, or dead reckoning." It's an ancient function. "If you blindfold someone and put them in a room and ask them to perform what we call the triangle completion task—they start on one point, then we turn them slightly, on the path of the triangle's second side and walk

several steps. Then, we ask them to turn toward their starting position and walk there, completing the triangle." People do much,
much better at this than they think they will, Iaria says. They consistently get within a few feet of where they start. But as Iaria points
out: "There is yet another ability we have investigated, called cognitive maps."

Picture yourself as you read this. Where are you? Now, take
that zoomed-in view of yourself and expand it outward. Could
you point in the direction of the nearest grocery store? Could
you point in the direction of your water heater? Could you point
north? The picture each of us forms in our minds varies in fundamental ways. Some of us, when zoomed out, go straight up, and
see ourselves from above. Others stay in first person, but see the
world as if through glass walls, or no walls at all. The first group—
the one that sees themselves from above—more often does better at finding north. The second group, imagining the world with
glass walls, could more accurately point toward the water heater.
But for scientists, just exactly how we go about making these maps
is a little bit of a black hole. "It's very, very hard to have a snapshot
of the brain mechanisms involved in this," Iaria explains, "because
it involves so many different parts of the brain." Iaria observes that
children are only able to start forming effective cognitive maps by
the age of nine or ten; however, by the time an adult is forty-five,
they begin to lose this skill. "This basically tells you that the brain
needs to be in the perfect shape to support this specific behavior," Iaria says. Mapping, then, is such a heavy cognitive load that
we create efficient shortcuts for our most routine paths: our com-
mutes, or the midnight trips to the bathroom. Most of what we do
all day is like this—the unthinking background hum of existence,
like breathing, or turning a doorknob; the stuff we are told to focus on in meditation or end up focusing on during a drug trip.

It was while Iaria was researching how individuals form cognitive maps that he came across something astonishing: a group of
people who were unable to find their way around even the most
routine paths. It seemed as though they'd lost the ability to even
create cognitive maps. That's when he identified the disorder—
topographical disorientation—and, as he found more and more
people with it, the range of disordered experiences grew increasingly complex. At this point in his research, he has found several thousand individuals suffering from the impairment. About

30 percent of the group simply could not form maps in their mind. But for another 20 percent or so, the situation was stranger still. They could make the cognitive maps, but their maps were slightly to extremely inaccurate. For some, the maps were always rotated exactly ninety degrees, so when they felt certain they needed to go right, they could catch themselves, and make the necessary correction—they'd go left.

But within this group, there was a cohort—5 percent, to be exact—that most fascinated Iaria. The manifestations of the disorder within this cohort seemed to point toward a deeper truth about the very tenuous perceptions of our existence. For this 5 percent, mental maps are in perpetual flux. They shift anywhere from 45 to 180 degrees, oscillating so wildly that no point in their reality is fixed. And yet, they do not suffer vertigo. They have nothing wrong with their inner ear. Their balance is fine. Even stranger was the solution many of those afflicted by this particularity had come up with: they find a tight space, a closet or a bathroom stall, and close their eyes; then, they quickly spin around. The spin seems to steady their mental map, causing it to reset. Iaria told me about a woman, now in her seventies, who had lived all her life with this disorder and had grown so adept at the reset trick she could close her eyes and simply imagine herself spinning—once, quickly—and that was enough.

I like imagining that this offers a lesson for the rest of us. Before chatting with Iaria, I'd spoken to another psychologist who also studied cognitive navigation. He told me a story of a Canadian park ranger who was so certain that the trail was in the direction he was headed that he ignored his compass, which he had convinced himself was broken (it wasn't), until, at last, he finally submitted to the truth: he had no idea where he was. People have a very hard time accepting that they are lost—taking a beat, resetting, processing new information, and then forging a new path. Iaria's patient had forced herself to take these beats, these hard resets, simply to move through the world. Why was it so hard for the rest of us? Even when we put ourselves into very specially designed places that promised to get us lost, we often barrel ahead without thought or pause. I know this because Adrian Fisher, the world's foremost designer and builder of mazes, told me that's what we do. This bullheadedness of ours is precisely what he exploits in his creations.

*

"Don't assume anything, that's the first rule," Fisher says. He's telling me about some of the ways he designs his mazes to trick people. In one of his more recent and monumental mazes, he placed several water fountains at a crucial junction to block the path to the solution. The fountains are those modern, in-ground fountains popular in malls and amusement parks, where there's no barrier to the streams of water, no pool around them; just jets, jetting out of the ground. The farther you are from the jets, the lower their height; the closer you get, the higher their jets shoot, hiding the way out. The solution only comes when you get so fed up that you walk away, backtracking through the maze until you hit another sensor that triggers the fountains to drop one final time, releasing you from the maze's, and the maker's, grip. "I want to humiliate you. I want you to give up," Fisher says. He sounds delighted.

Fisher is speaking to me from his office in the attic of his home at the edge of the village of Durweston, in the English countryside, where he is hard at work on some maze-based paintings. Fisher designs mazes for books, malls, even the sides of buildings. He co-created the world's very first corn maze in 1993. He has been the world's leading supplier of mirror mazes since 1991. He has built forty-seven hedge mazes in forty-two countries. "No one in the history of mankind has ever built more," Fisher says. And: "Would you expect that now I have a lot of business from cruises? Petri dishes on water, if you ask me. But that's all postponed indefinitely, so what am I doing? Little puzzles. More art. Something, always." Talking to Fisher is like being in one of his mazes. Suddenly we round a corner and he is describing the plot from *The Dream of Poliphilus.*

Hypnerotomachia Poliphili—or *The Dream of Poliphilus*—is an incunabulum, published at the end of the fifteenth century, set in 1467, printed by Aldus Manutius in Venice, its author unknown. It's an extremely weird text, with words in Latin, Greek, Italian, a combo of the three, plus a bunch of made-up words and even some made-up Egyptian hieroglyphs. We follow our hero, Poliphili, or Poliphilus, as he wanders through a dreamland in search of his love, Polia. Poliphili, from its Greek roots, means "friend of many things." Polia is simply "many things." It's an allegory, and not a very complicated one, though the plot is as strange as the made-up words: Poliphilus gets lost in a wild forest; encounters dragons, wolves, and fantastic buildings; and he escapes by falling asleep in his dream, awakening in another dream. We're deep in dream within a dream territory, and a pack of nymphs now take Poliphilus to meet their queen, then present him with three doors, or gateways. "The left gate, it's all about science and rationality," Fisher says, excitedly. "Then, the right, it's all art and beauty and aesthetics, where colors are exquisitely true. Then, the central door: the door of true love." When he opens the third door, "there's Polia, who opens an extra dimension of passion, of love. It's like what I'm trying to do with a maze. Take you on a journey. Get you through that third door." I am honestly not sure what Fisher is getting at. Does he really believe a maze can take people on a journey that ends in love? When I ask, the conversation doubles back. "Once someone gives up on what they thought they were supposed to do in the maze, that's when you start to see the really interesting open-mindedness, the willingness to throw out what they assumed, and try something new. So—open their minds? Their hearts? Yes." I ask him how he does this in ways that don't involve, for instance, complex, motion-triggered fountains. "The easiest trick," Fisher says, "is to simply build a tower in the center of a maze. You believe that is the goal, so you think, ah, here's the entrance, the point is to get to the center! But of course, that's a red herring." He likes tunnels, too, since they can be disorienting. He might build a tunnel that slopes a little, to slip people under a pathway—a "subversive passage," he calls it—or a tunnel that curves slightly, so people think they are going in a straight line when they aren't. The point is to get them into the tunnel and spit them out into a place that will force them to shake their assumed notions, to give up on the map of the maze in their mind and give in to that hard reset, so that they can accept things as they come. Maze-building, then, is the art of instilling mindfulness, and it isn't easy.

Over the years, Fisher has found that the most efficient maze solvers he encounters are generally young children. Their iterative approach—taking what comes, learning from their mistakes, unafraid to double back and try a new route—more often than not leads them to the solution far faster than adults. The latter tend to cling to what they think will eventually lead them to the solution, when often the opposite is the case. When I observe that this truth tends to extend to our lives beyond maze solving, Fisher laughs and says, "Yes. We've forgotten how to be lost, or accept that we are lost." When I ask if this is what he meant when he said that mazes could be a path to love—that getting lost, accepting one was lost, was accepting a kind of vulnerability, Fisher responds, "See? Now you're getting there."

I pulled up a video tutorial about how to navigate by sextant, then another, and another. It was as complicated as I remembered: the slow work of lining up an eyepiece with the sun, moving the sextant's arm so that its mirrors then move the sun's mirrored reflection down along the horizon line, then tilting the sextant this way and that, turning the finer knob, noting the degrees, checking again and again to make sure that the reflected image of the sun was perched just so, a golf ball balanced on the tee of the horizon. And the timing *was* important: at noon the sun reaches its highest point in the sky, but just how high it reaches can tell you quite a lot about where you are, depending on the day of the year. If, say, the noonday sun is directly overhead, and it's December 21, you consult a table and find out that you are along the Tropic of Capricorn, 23.5 degrees south of the equator. But that's just latitude. For longitude you need another reading, and an accurate clock, and the knowledge that the Earth spins at a steady pace, 15 degrees every hour. I looked into buying a sextant but then considered where I was, in a place with no flat straight sealike horizons. If my house were a boat, it'd be hemmed in by several hills, a small range of mountains in the distance, then a bigger one, the San Gabriels, and, out toward the sea, many miles of dense urban Los Angeles. I wondered, instead, what it might be to wayfind in a city: blindfolded, put in a car, and driven around for miles. The vehicle stops, you're helped outside, and then the blindfold comes off.

But as the car screeches off, you realize it's irrelevant, because *you're* blind. Now you must get back to where you started. What do you do? This exact scenario is a standard form of testing in many blindness training centers. When Bryan Bashin—who had been legally blind since his sophomore year of college—first heard about it, he thought it sounded impossible. And then, after a few months of training, he was subjected to this very scenario. His first move was to strike out at random. It was, as he recalls, a suburban, low-density neighborhood. Nobody seemed to be home. He walked several blocks, listening for signs of life. He heard running water—a hose. Someone was there, watering. A garden? He threw up his hand in greeting and called in that direction. The person came over to greet him. He asked the person some questions about where he was. "The whole key," Bashin tells me, "is to say you're lost, to ask for directions, to out yourself as a blind person." Part of his training required that he walk around with a non-collapsible cane. There is no hiding his condition. The cane, he says, "is your path to authenticity. Instead of wishing you were somebody you no longer are, someone who had sight, you accept the person you are becoming. Blindness training is really not about eyesight at all," he says. "What it's really about is your relationship to change. We live in an unprecedented time of control and knowing," Bashin continues. "I think, for most of human history, this bewilderment with our surroundings was something we all experienced. And now, those muscles have completely gotten flabby. Everything is known and secure, every street has a name. I think it's really healthy and deeply human to be lost, to deepen our sense of place and significance."

Bashin is now CEO of the LightHouse, a San Francisco–based organization that specializes in navigational tools for the blind, including tactile maps. Years ago, I had received one of these maps as a gift. It was a beautiful object: a slice of the Eastern Seaboard with different raised patterns for state lines, coast lines, major interstates, mountain ranges. But most of LightHouse's maps are much smaller scale—which is to say, for walking. Through LightHouse I was put in touch with Jerry Kuns, who showed me how a blind person uses a map to get around. Kuns, who is in his late seventies and mostly retired, has had several impressive careers working for the state of California and for technology companies like Apple as a mobility consultant. Now, he's a tour guide. He gives walking tours of San Francisco, to sighted or unsighted people, simply because he likes to walk around in his town.

The first time he visited San Francisco, he was fourteen years old, and got lost. He missed the last train back to Berkeley and was out wandering through the Tenderloin and Chinatown late into the night. "I'm a country boy," he tells me. "I thought I was going to end up on somebody's plate." He'd grown up in rural Ohio, Yosemite, and the Berkeley Hills; he was attuned to the wind in the trees, the water in the creeks, the cows in the fields. Now, he had to take cues from pedestrians, from oncoming cars as he stepped off the curb. He didn't panic that night in San Francisco, alone, lost, and out well past his curfew. He could hear, for the first time, live jazz coming from nightclubs. He heard bustling bars and the chatter from a café. He went toward the chatter, entered, and ordered a cup of hot chocolate. "There I was, this very-low-vision kid, nearly blind, hovering over my cup, figuring I'll just wait until morning, and this delightful young lady was there next to me with her fellow, and they noticed me. They said, 'Hey kid. What are you doing out here?'" They let him sleep on their couch for the night and drove him back home to Berkeley the next morning.

When Kuns was traveling more for work, he was on business in downtown Minneapolis when a bus dropped him off a few blocks sooner than he'd planned. There were several inches of snow on the streets, making it hard to feel the sidewalk and read the corners. He was trying to figure out how far he might be from his destination, but he struggled to piece it together, to form the map of where he was in his mind. Finally, he just went out in the street and yelled, "Where the fuck am I?" to anyone who might be within earshot, and someone driving by in a car yelled back. He realized, ah, it's just the next block over, on the right. "Finding yourself, it's important not to lose yourself," Kuns says. "You need to know when you need to find somebody. Still," he adds, "it's good to know how to read a map." He hangs his phone on a light so his hands can be free, then turns to his desk to pull out some of his tactile maps. "I've taught lots of sighted people how to read maps," he says. Next, he tells me a few stories of long road trips he's taken. He is always the navigator while his friends drive. Once, one of his friends insisted he was wrong, and chose the GPS over his directions. "That was the last time she made that mistake," Kuns says.

"Now, look at this one—" Kuns runs his hands over a large, ridged object. It is pink and white, outlined in blue. It looks, to me, a little fleshy—like a shiny, wrinkly, skinned blob of a creature. It is a topographical map of the city of San Francisco. There are no streets or buildings or anything other than the many hills and valleys and miles of coastline. Kuns's hands make quick and careful work of the landscape. I realize he is giving me his own sort of tour. "I can feel Fisherman's Wharf, right here, and this is Nob Hill. And downtown is right in here, and right here the wharves bend to the right and then to the left and that's where the Ferry Building is." He tells me about taking blind kids on his walking tours and first letting them feel through where they'd be going on this map, getting them to connect the hills to the landscape, another way of helping them know where they are. "Then, jump between the topo map and"—he pulls out another paper map, smaller and ridged, similar to what I'd been given many years ago—"the grid map, here, that's a huge transition. Here's a simple intersection . . ." He takes us across Twenty-first Street, his hand carefully gliding across the street lines, then over to the key in the corner, measuring distance, gauging the length of the block. It reminded me of my grandfather at his charts, plotting our course with his protractor and parallel ruler, connecting the dots of where we were with where we intended to go. It feels good to be traveling like this, across a bumpy piece of paper, led by a blind man. For a moment, I wonder about my Lost List, and where this might fall within it. But then I return to the walk we are on, Kuns and I. How glad I am to be on it, how I have no idea where it will lead.

Contributors' Notes

*Notable Essays and Literary
Nonfiction of 2021*

Notable Special Issues of 2021

Contributors' Notes

BRIAN BLANCHFIELD is the author of three books of poetry and prose, most recently *Proxies: Essays Near Knowing*. Recipient of the Academy of American Poets' James Laughlin Award and a Whiting Award in Nonfiction, he lives now in Missoula, where he is a professor of creative writing at the University of Montana. He is also a member of the core faculty at Bennington Writing Seminars.

RYAN BRADLEY is a journalist, editor, and essayist who frequently contributes to the *Virginia Quarterly Review* and *The New York Times Magazine*. He has won a Los Angeles Press Club award for feature writing and been nominated for a National Magazine Award. He lives in Los Angeles.

JASON BROWN is the author of three collections of short stories, including *A Faithful but Melancholy Account of Several Barbarities Lately Committed*. He is writing a memoir called *Character Witness*.

JUNG HAE CHAE is a Korean American writer. Her work has appeared in *Agni, Crazyhorse, Guernica, Ploughshares*, and elsewhere, and has been anthologized in the 2019 Pushcart Prize Collection. Most recently, she won the 2021 Crazyhorse Prize in Nonfiction and the 2019 Emerging Writers Contest in Nonfiction from *Ploughshares*. Her work has been supported by scholarships and fellowships from New Jersey State Council on the Arts, Idyllwild Arts Foundation, Monson Arts, Sewanee Writers Conference, Squaw Valley Writers Conference, and others. Currently, she is at work on a memoir that explores the matrilineal *han* in the Korean diaspora.

ANDREA LONG CHU is the book critic at *New York* magazine. Her nonfiction book *Females* was a finalist for the 2019 Lambda Literary Award in

Transgender Nonfiction. Her writing has appeared in *n+1, New York, The New York Times Magazine, The New Yorker, Artforum, Bookforum, Boston Review, Chronicle of Higher Education, 4Columns, The Drift,* and *Jewish Currents.* She lives in Brooklyn.

MELISSA FEBOS is the bestselling author of four books, most recently, *Girlhood,* winner of the National Book Critics Circle Award in criticism, and *Body Work: The Radical Power of Personal Narrative.* She is the recipient of awards and fellowships from the Guggenheim Foundation, the National Endowment for the Arts, MacDowell, Lambda Literary, the Barbara Deming Foundation, the Black Mountain Institute, and others. She is an associate professor at the University of Iowa.

CALVIN GIMPELEVICH is the author of the short story collection *Invasions.* His essays and stories have appeared in *Ploughshares, Kenyon Review, Electric Literature,* and *Them.* He is the winner of a 2022 NEA Fellowship in prose and a recipient of Lambda Literary's Judith A. Markowitz award, in addition to grants and fellowships from Artist Trust, Jack Straw Cultural Center, 4Culture, and Seattle's Office of Arts & Culture. He was born in San Francisco.

KAITLYN GREENIDGE's debut novel, *We Love You, Charlie Freeman,* was one of the *New York Times* critics' Top Ten Books of 2016 and a finalist for the Center for Fiction First Novel Prize. She is the features director at *Harper's Bazaar* and a contributing writer for the *New York Times,* and her writing has also appeared in *Vogue, Glamour,* the *Wall Street Journal,* and elsewhere. She is the recipient of fellowships from the Whiting Foundation, the National Endowment for the Arts, and the Radcliffe Institute for Advanced Study. *Libertie* is her second novel.

DEBRA GWARTNEY is the author of two memoirs, *Live Through This,* finalist for the National Book Critics Circle Award, and *I Am a Stranger Here Myself,* winner of the River Teeth Nonfiction Prize. She is coeditor with her husband, Barry Lopez, of *Home Ground: Language for an American Landscape.* Her essay "Suffer Me to Pass," from *VQR,* was selected for a 2020 Pushcart Prize. Debra lives in western Oregon.

NAOMI JACKSON is the author of a novel, *The Star Side of Bird Hill.* Jackson studied fiction at the Iowa Writers' Workshop. She traveled to South Africa on a Fulbright scholarship, where she received an MA in creative writing from the University of Cape Town. She is a graduate of Williams College. Jackson's writings have appeared in *Harper's Magazine,* the *Washington Post, Virginia Quarterly Review, Poets & Writers,* and *The Caribbean Writer.* She is the recipient of residencies and fellowships from MacDowell Colony, Hedge-brook, Camargo Foundation, Bronx Council on the Arts, and the Schomburg Center for Research in Black Culture. Jackson is an assistant professor of English at Rutgers University–Newark. She lives in New York City with her family.

TANNER AKONI LAGUATAN is a surfer living with his little black dog in Laguna Beach, California. His piece in *The Best American Essays 2022* is his first published essay. He is at work on a memoir about Hollywood, weed, and two hundred years of Filipino American family history.

AUBE REY LESCURE is a French-Chinese-American writer and deputy editor at *Off Assignment*. She is the coauthor of *Creating a Stable Asia* and the translator of the essay anthology *Le Système Économique Chinois Face à ses Défis* (制度改变中国). Her fiction and creative nonfiction have appeared in *Guernica*, *The Florida Review* online, *WBUR*, *Jellyfish Review*, *Entropy*, and elsewhere. Her debut novel, about coming of age in Shanghai, will be published by HarperCollins in 2023.

ALEX MARZANO-LESNEVICH is the author of *The Fact of a Body: A Murder and a Memoir*, which received a Lambda Literary Award, the Chautauqua Prize, and awards in France and Canada. It was translated into eleven languages and is in development with HBO. The recipient of fellowships from the National Endowment for the Arts, MacDowell, Civitella Ranieri, and the Bread Loaf Writers Conference, Marzano-Lesnevich has written for the *New York Times*, *Harper's Magazine*, *AGNI*, *Elle France*, and many other publications. They live in Portland, Maine, and are an assistant professor at Bowdoin College. Their next book, *Both and Neither*, about living beyond the binary, is forthcoming and was excerpted in *The Best American Essays 2020*.

LINA MOUNZER is a Lebanese writer and translator. She contributes regularly to the *New York Times* and her work has appeared in *The Paris Review*, *The Economist*, and *The Baffler*, as well as in the anthologies *Hikayat: Short Stories by Lebanese Women* and *Tales of Two Planets*. During 2021, she wrote a monthly column for the Lebanese daily *L'Orient Today*, chronicling social changes in the wake of the country's economic collapse.

JESUS QUINTERO read his first work of fiction at the age of twenty-one (Michael Chabon's *Wonder Boys*, because of the cover's jumping, candy-apple-green '64 Impala and the possibility that it might be about gangs). He received his MFA in creative writing from the University of San Francisco. He is working on a memoir and teaches English and creative writing at De Anza College in the San Francisco Bay Area.

ELIAS RODRIQUES is a Jamaican writer currently based in New York. His first novel is *All the Water I've Seen Is Running*.

GARY SHTEYNGART is the author of numerous books, including the memoir *Little Failure* and the novels *Lake Success, Super Sad True Love Story,* and *Our Country Friends*.

ERIKA J. SIMPSON is a Southern girl living in Denver, Colorado, with her partner and cat. She holds an MFA in creative writing from the University of Kentucky and is the recipient of the 2021 MFA Award in Nonfiction. Her greatest joy comes from birthday visits with her sister and loving on her niece. She is currently working on a memoir, as well as a black speculative fiction collection.

ANTHONY VEASNA SO (1992–2020) was a graduate of Stanford University and earned his MFA in fiction at Syracuse University. His writing has appeared in *The New Yorker, The Paris Review, n+1, Granta,* and *ZYZZYVA.* A native of Stockton, California, he taught at Colgate University, Syracuse University, and the Center for Empowering Refugees and Immigrants in Oakland, California.

ANGELIQUE STEVENS teaches creative writing, literature of genocide, and race literatures. Her nonfiction can be found in *Literary Hub, New England Review,* and *The Chattahoochee Review.* She holds an MFA in creative nonfiction from Bennington College and an MA from SUNY Brockport in literature. Her honors include an alumni fellowship from Bennington College's MFA program; fellowships from the Bread Loaf, Tin House, Sewanee, and Kenyon Review writers workshops; a fellowship to the inaugural cohort of the Periplus Collective; and a fellowship to the Lighthouse Writers Workshop Book Project. She is a founding member of the Straw Mat Writers Group and a member of the board of directors of Water for South Sudan. She finds inspiration in wandering—being in places that push the boundaries of comfort, experience, knowledge, and hunger.

JUSTIN TORRES is the author of the novel *We the Animals,* a national bestseller, which was adapted into a feature film. His stories and essays have appeared in *The New Yorker,* the *Washington Post,* the *Los Angeles Times Image* magazine, and several other publications. He lives in Los Angeles, where he is an assistant professor of English at UCLA.

VAUHINI VARA is the author of *The Immortal King Rao,* a novel, and the forthcoming story collection *This Is Salvaged.* She has written and edited for *The New Yorker, The New York Times Magazine, The Atlantic,* and elsewhere and, for her nonfiction, has won honors from the International Center for Journalists, the McGraw Center for Business Journalism, the Asian American Journalists Association, and the South Asian Journalists Association. Her fiction has been honored by the O. Henry Prize, the Rona Jaffe Foundation, and the Canada Council for the Arts. She is a mentor at the Lighthouse Writers Workshop Book Project and the secretary at Periplus, a mentorship collective serving writers of color.

ELISSA WASHUTA is a member of the Cowlitz Indian tribe and the author of *White Magic, Starvation Mode,* and *My Body Is a Book of Rules.* With Theresa Warburton, she coedited the anthology *Shapes of Native Nonfiction: Collected Essays by Contemporary Writers.* Elissa is an associate professor at Ohio State University, where she teaches in the MFA Program in Creative Writing.

Notable Essays and Literary Nonfiction of 2021

SELECTED BY ROBERT ATWAN

Notable Special Issues of 2021

Michigan Quarterly Review, Sixtieth
Anniversary Issue, ed. Khaled
Mattawa, 60/1

The Missouri Review, How Did I Get
Here? ed. Speer Morgan, 44/3

n+1, Take Care, eds. Mark Krotov et
al, #39

The New Atlantis, Projects for Renewal,
ed. Ari Schulman, #63

North Dakota Quarterly, Malicious
Compliance, ed. William Caraher,
88/3&4

Northern Appalachia Review,
Transformation, ed. P. J. Piccirillo, 2/1

Notre Dame Magazine, Doing Good, ed.
Kerry Temple, 50/1

Orion, Bodies of Nature: Survival
Lessons from Disabled Communities,
ed. Sumanth Prabhaker, 40/4

Oxford American, The Food Issue, guest
ed. Alice Randall, Spring

PANK, Environmental Futures Folio,
guest ed. Aram Mrjoian, April

Plough Quarterly, Beyond Borders, ed.
Peter Mommsen, #29

Potomac Review, The Diversity Issue, ed.
John Wei Han Wang, #68

Prism, Scab, eds. Tanvi Bhatia and
Emily Chou, 59/3

Room, City Rhythms, ed. Isabella Wang,
44/2

Root Quarterly, Fearful Symmetry,
ed. Heather Shayne Blakeslee,
III/3

Ruminate, Forged, ed. Jen Stewart
Fueston, #59

Salmagundi, Revisiting the Culture
Wars, ed. Robert Boyers and Peg
Boyers, #210/211

Slag Glass City, The Blissful City, ed.
Barrie Jean Borich, June

Smithsonian, Twenty Years After 9/11,
Ed. staff, September

Stranger's Guide, Dreams of California,
ed. Kira Brunner Don, #13

Under the Gum Tree, Celebrating
10 Years, ed. Janna Marlies Maron,
#41

Virginia Quarterly Review, Fresh Kills
Sublime, ed. Paul Reyes, 97/4

Ed. staff, *Water~Stone Review,* Ghost(s)
Still Living, ed. Meghan Maloney-
Vinz, #24

World Literature Today, Reflections on
the Tulsa Race Massacre Centennial,
ed. Daniel Simon, Spring

ZYZZYVA, The Family Issue, ed. Laura
Cogan, #121

Note: The following essays should have appeared in Notable Essays and
Literary Nonfiction of 2020. It's a longer list than usual due largely to the
delays and disruptions caused by the pandemic.

Blanche McCrary Boyd, It's Always
Now, *Journal of the Plague Years,*
July 12

Brooke Champagne, Kingdom of
Babes, *Hoxie Gorge Review,* Spring/
Summer

Clara Collier, Plagues, *Libertie,* 1/1

Christine Shields Corrigan, Relics
to Reliquary, *Horn Pond Review,*
November 21

Dana Delibovi, Heavy Is the Root of
Light, *After the Art,* June

Peter Filkins, Words Preserved Against
a Day of Fear: Remembering Joseph
Brodsky, *The American Scholar,* Summer

Allyn Gaestel, All In and Out of Time,
The Common, August 19

Emma Gomis, KArEN, *Denver Quarterly,*
54/3

Charles Hood, Audubon's Tiny Houses,
Catamaran, 8/3

Amaud Jamaul Johnson, The Fault
Lines of Midwestern Racism Run
Deep, *Literary Hub,* September 22

Robin D. G. Kelley, Getting to Freedom City, *Boston Review,* 45/3

Richard Scott Larson, Home Video, *Hobart,* October 19

Dinah Lenney, Altered States, *Los Angeles Review of Books,* April 12

Muriel Leung, Obsessed, Unbound, *The Texas Review,* 40/3&4

Monica Macansantos, Returning to My Father's Kitchen, *Lunch Ticket,* #17

Marianne Manzler, On the Making of a Mumu, *Fourth Genre,* 22/2

Amanda Montei, Losing the World, *The Rumpus,* June 16

Dinty W. Moore, But I Digress: An Essay on the Essay Featuring Assy McGee, *The Texas Review,* 40/3&4

Courtney Lund O'Neil, Angel Town, *Columbia Journal,* #58

Mark Polizzotti, Breton's Smartphone, *Catamaran,* 8/1

Rosette Royale, Home and Free, *Portland,* Winter

Iris Smyles, In the Merdre with Alfred Jarry, *Splice Today,* April 3

Emma Stough, How Much of This Is Mine, *Foglifter,* #5/2

Jill Talbot, Toward a Country and Western Song, *Gulf Coast,* 32/2

Sydney Tammarine, Blue Hour, *Ploughshares,* 46/1

Ashley P. Taylor, Dinner Theater, *Black Rabbit Review,* #2

Jennifer Tseng, Most of My Dream Fathers Are Women, *Ecotone,* #28

An Uong, The Making of American Money, *Hyphen,* May 20

Notable Special Issues of 2020

The Texas Review, All-Essay Issue, guest ed. Katie Jean Shinkle; ed. Nick Lantz, 40/3&4

Yellow Medicine Review, Women's Wisdom, Women's Strength, guest ed. CMarie Fuhrman, Fall

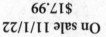